Social Culture and High-Tech
Economic Development

Social Culture and High-Tech Economic Development

The Technopolis Columns

Fred Phillips

First published in 2006 by
PALGRAVE MACMILLAN
Houndmills, Basingstoke, Hampshire RG21 6XS and
175 Fifth Avenue, New York, N.Y. 10010
Companies and representatives throughout the world.

PALGRAVE MACMILLAN is the global academic imprint of the Palgrave
Macmillan division of St. Martin's Press, LLC and of Palgrave Macmillan Ltd.
Macmillan® is a registered trademark in the United States, United Kingdom
and other countries. Palgrave is a registered trademark in the European
Union and other countries.

ISBN 978-1-349-54794-4   ISBN 978-0-230-59724-2 (eBook)
DOI 10.1007/978-0-230-59724-2

A catalogue record for this book is available from the British Library.

Library of Congress Cataloging-in-Publication Data

Phillips, Fred, 1952–
    Social culture and high-tech economic development : the technopolis
columns / Fred Phillips.
        p. cm.
    Includes bibliographical references and index.

    1. High technology industries—Social aspects. 2. Industrial
location—Social aspects. 3. Economic development. 4. Regional planning.
I. Title.
HC79.H53P55 2006
306.3—dc22   2005056584

10 9 8 7 6 5 4 3 2 1
15 14 13 12 11 10 09 08 07 06

Transferred to Digital Printing 2011

For Hyonsook

Contents

List of Tables	x
List of Figures	xi
List of Abbreviations	xii
Acknowledgements	xv
Preface	xviii
List of Contributors	xx
Introduction: Technology-Based Economic Development and the Initiatives that Advance it *Fred Phillips*	1

Part I Austin

1	Toward a Modern Economics *Fred Phillips*	15
2	Memoir on the History of the Austin Software Council *Fred Phillips*	18
3	The Austin Experience: Behind the Success Factors *Fred Phillips*	22
4	Toward an Intellectual Foundation for "Shared Prosperity" *Fred Phillips*	28
5	The Business School in a Time of Transition *Fred Phillips*	49
6	Anointing "a City of Light and Wisdom" *David Gibson*	61
7	Advantage Austin II *George Kozmetsky and Patricia A. Hayes*	64

Part II   Portland

8	Portland Looks at International Benchmarks *Fred Phillips*	69
9	The Power of Combination: Three Unpopular Truths about Civic Entrepreneurship *Fred Phillips*	75
10	Gaining on Us and Closing Fast *Fred Phillips*	80
11	Sometimes, Montana *Fred Phillips*	84
12	Lack of Investment Puts Portland Behind *Fred Phillips*	87
13	Twelve Hurdles to Starting an Executive MOT Program: How and Why to Overcome Them *Fred Phillips*	91
14	Do We Know How to Play This Game? Some Thoughts on Regional Leadership *Ralph R. Shaw*	105
15	Bring Back Oregon's Common Sense of Purpose *Chet Orloff*	118
16	Please, Portland, Don't Pearlize Joe's Garage *Pierre Ouellette*	120

Part III   And Beyond

17	Sustaining a Technopolis Initiative *Fred Phillips*	125
18	WTO vs. WTA? Exploring the World Trade Organization's Impact on Technopolis *Fred Phillips*	152
19	Why Do Universities Transfer Technology? *Fred Phillips*	157
20	Universities and Incubators *Fred Phillips*	163
21	Does Place Matter? Quality of Life and Wandering Alumni *Fred Phillips*	186

22 Short Takes   190
    Fred Phillips

23 Technology Is the Engine of a New Russian Revolution   203
    David Gibson

24 Conclusion   205
    Fred Phillips

Appendix   218

Works Cited   247

Bibliography   258

Index   265

List of Tables

3.1	Timeline of the Austin technopolis: broad scale	23
3.2	Austin technopolis critical success factors	24
3.3	Technology-oriented civic, trade, and professional organizations and event hosts in Austin, 1990s	24
3.4	Austin's success factors and disadvantages	25
4.1	Common elements of shared prosperity concepts from diverse sources	34
4.2	Influencers for regional/community cooperation	42
4.3	Shared prosperity initiatives compared with conventional aid efforts	43
4.4	Some IC² Fellows: Their expertise and affiliations	46
17.1	Technopolis success factors	126
17.2	Timeline of the Austin technopolis	129
17.3	Bangalore timeline	131
17.4	Success factors for regional technology entrepreneurship initiatives	147
20.1	Leading private incubators in 2000 and their status in 2005	170
20.2	UNM's cooperative arrangement with DoD requires community outreach.	177
22.1	2003 GDP growth in selected OECD nations	192
17.1	Technopolis success factors	211
24.1	Themes for technology-based economic development	214
A.1	Levels of tech-based ED initiatives	221
A.2	The three elements of economic development	222
A.3	Technology-based economic development	226
A.4	Strategies for increasing technology-based employment	229
A.5	Types of technology development initiatives	229
A.6	Technology-based ED initiatives: Key features compared	244

List of Figures

I.1 The innovation arrow   7
I.2 Globally networked entrepreneurship partners
     linked by talent, technology, capital and
     know-how   8
3.1 Early growth of technology companies in Austin   25
4.1 Networking for inter-regional skills transfer   40
4.2 Fuzzy objectives for diverse participation in the
     early Austin Software Council   45
17.1 Launch year of cluster initiatives surveyed by
     Sölvell   143
17.2 The IC^2 model of value-added economic
     development   146
20.1 Incubation and technology transfer organization
     at Rensselaer Polytechnic Institute   175

List of Abbreviations

AACSB	The Association to Advance Collegiate Schools of Business
AIDS	Acquired immune deficiency syndrome
AMD	Advanced Micro Devices Corporation
AOL	America OnLine
APEC	Asia-Pacific Economic Conference
ASC	Austin Software Council (forerunner of Austin Technology Council)
ASEAN	Association of Southeast Asian Nations
ATC	Austin Technology Council
ATI	Austin Technology Incubator
BBA	Bachelor of Business Administration
BC	British Columbia, Canada
CASE	Computer-Assisted Software Engineering
CBIRD	Cross Border Institute for Regional Development
CD-ROM	Compact Disk, Read-Only Memory
CEO	Chief executive officer
CI	Cluster initiative
COMDEX	Computer dealers' exposition run by MediaLive International, Inc.
CRM	Customer relationship management
CSF	Critical success factor
DNA	Deoxyribonucleic acid
DoD	Department of Defense (USA)
DRAM	Dynamic random-access memory
DVD	Digital video disk
ED	Economic development
EDA	Electronic design automation
ERP	Enterprise Resource Planning
EU	European Union
EZ	Enterprise zone
EZ	Export zone
FBI	Federal Bureau of Investigation (USA)
FDI	Foreign direct investment
FOI	Freedom of Information Act, and activities taking place under the banner of such open-records laws
FTA	Free trade agreement

FTE	Full-time equivalent
FTF	Face-to-face
GATT	General Agreement on Tariffs and Trade
GDP	Gross domestic product
GMU	George Mason University
HIV	Human immunodeficiency virus
HP	Hewlett-Packard Corporation
IC²	Innovation, Creativity and Capital (name of Institute at University of Texas at Austin)
ICT	Information and communication technology
IMF	International Monetary Fund
INS	Immigration and Naturalization Service (USA)
IP	Intellectual property
IPA	Investment promotion agency
IRS	Internal Revenue Service (USA)
ISO	International Standards Organization
K-12	Kindergarten through 12th-grade (high school) education, in the USA system
KTEC	Kansas Technology Enterprise Corporation
MAI	Multilateral Agreement on Investments
MBA	Master of Business Administration
MCC	Microelectronics and Computing Consortium (Later, Microelectronics and Computing Corporation)
MEC	Mason Enterprise Center, at George Mason University
MEDB	Maui Economic Development Board
MHPCC	Maui High-Performance Computing Center
MIT	Massachusetts Institute of Technology
MITI	Ministry of International Trade and Industry (Japan)
MOT	Management of technology
MRP	Material Resource Planning, or Materials Requirements Planning
MRTC	Maui Research and Technology Center
MS	Master of Science (alt. form of M.Sc.)
MSM	Maastricht School of Management
MSSTC	Master of Science in Science and Technology Commercialization
MST	Management in Science and Technology
NAFTA	North American Free Trade Agreement
NASA	National Aeronautics and Space Administration (USA)
NASVF	National Association of Seed and Venture Funds
NBIA	National Business Incubator Association

NGO	Non-governmental organization
NPO	Non-profit organization
NSF	National Science Foundation (USA)
NSI	National systems of innovation
OAS	Organization of American States
OEA	State of Oregon's Department of Administrative Services' Office of Economic Analysis
OECD	Organization for Economic Cooperation and Development
OGI	Oregon Graduate Institute of Science & Technology
PBS	Public Broadcasting System
PCR	Polymerase Chain Reaction
PDC	Portland Development Commission
PSU	Portland State University
R&D	Research and development
RITE	Regional initiative for technology entrepreneurship
RPI	Rensselaer Polytechnic Institute
RTB	Regional trading bloc
SAO	Software Association of Oregon
SBDC	Small Business Development Corporation
SBIC	Small Business Investment Corporation
SBIP	Science-Based Industrial Park (Taiwan)
SI	Systems of innovation
SME	Semiconductor manufacturing equipment
SME	Small and medium enterprises
TED	Technology-based economic development
TIF	Tax increment financing
UBC	University of British Columbia
UN	United Nations
UNCTAD	United Nations Conference on Trade and Development
UNM	University of New Mexico
UNU	United Nations University
URD	Urban renewal district
USFS	United States Forest Service
UT	University of Texas
VC	Venture capital, or a venture capital investor
WTA	World Technopolis Association
WTO	World Trade Organization
WWW	World-wide web
Y2K	Year 2000

Acknowledgements

Most of the chapters herein are appearing in print for the first time. The provenance of the remaining chapters are as follows. My thanks to the original publishers for allowing the material to be brought together in book form.

"Memoir on the History of the Austin Software Council" (Chapter 2) was published in the newsletter of the Austin Software Council (now the Austin Technology Council) in the mid-1990s. Ironically, the date of publication is lost to history.

Parts of Chapter 3, "The Austin Experience," were delivered as a plenary talk at the 1999 convention of the National Association of State Seed & Venture Funds.

A version of Chapter 4, "Toward an Intellectual Foundation for 'Shared Prosperity,' " will appear in 2006 in the journal *Systemic Practice and Action Research* as "Toward an Intellectual and Theoretical Foundation for 'Shared Prosperity.' "

Chapter 6, David Gibson's "Anointing a 'City of Light and Wisdom' " was first published in the *Austin American-Statesman*, October 19, 1999. Reprinted by permission.

Chapter 7, George Kozmetsky and Patricia A. Hayes' "Advantage Austin II," first appeared in the *Austin American-Statesman*, September 4, 1991, p. A15. Reprinted by permission.

Chapter 8, "Portland Looks at International Benchmarks," was the record of the *Symposium and Workshop on Entrepreneurship and Intrapreneurship for Economic Growth and Quality of Life in Oregon and Southern Washington: International Benchmarks* conference held in Portland in October, 1999, with sponsorship from The Center for Entrepreneurial Growth at Oregon Graduate Institute, Multnomah/ Washington Counties Regional Strategies Board, Battelle-Pacific Northwest National Laboratories, Portland State University, the University of Washington, and the Oregon Emerging Business Initiative (OEBI). This summary was presented at the Western Regional Science Association's 2000 conference on Kauai.

Chapter 12, "Lack of Investment Puts Portland Behind," first appeared in the *Portland Business Journal*, September 27, 2002, p. 39.

Chapter 13, "Twelve Hurdles to Starting an Executive MOT Program: How and Why to Overcome Them," was presented at the 2nd

International Conference on Technology Policy and Innovation, Lisbon, 1998.

Chapter 14, Ralph R. Shaw's "Do We Know How to Play this Game? Some Thoughts on Regional Leadership" was a speech delivered to The Association of Commercial Realtors, March 7, 2002. Reproduced with permission.

Chapter 15, Chet Orloff's "Bring back Oregon's Common Sense of Purpose," first appeared in *The Oregonian*, May 22, 2002. Reprinted by permission.

Chapter 16, Pierre Ouellette's "Please, Portland, Don't Pearlize Joe's Garage," first appeared in *The Oregonian*, December 19, 2002. Reprinted by permission.

Chapter 17, "Sustaining a Technopolis Initiative," was presented as "Sustainability of Regional Initiatives for Technology Entrepreneurship" at the European Foundation for Management Development's 35th Entrepreneurship, Innovation & Small Business (EISB) Conference, Barcelona, September 12–14, 2005, where it won a "Best Abstract" mention from the Gate2Growth Academic Network, Directorate General Enterprise of the European Commission under its 5th framework program.

Chapter 18, "WTO vs. WTA? The World Trade Organization's Impact on Technopolis," is an expansion of a poster presentation by F. Phillips and M. Burningham, "WTO vs. WTA? Exploring the World Trade Organization's Impact on Technopolis," 4th International Conference on Technology Policy & Innovation, Curitiba, Brazil, August, 2000. The research was supported in part by the Northwest International Business Educators' Network, through the Center for International Business Education and Research (CIBER) at the University of Washington. A later expansion of these ideas, titled "Trading Down: The Intellectual Poverty of the New FTAs" (*Technological Forecasting & Social Change*, Volume 71, Issue 8, October 2004, pp. 865–76), was named to the Ambar/Emerald Hall of Fame as one of the best fifty papers of 20,000 papers reviewed in the top 400 management journals in 2004.

Chapter 20, "Universities and Incubators," had its origins in a consulting report "University-Connected Incubators" for the Chancellor's Office of the Oregon University System in November, 2002.

Chapter 22's "Short Takes" were originally editorials in *Review of Technology & Economic Development* (http://www.generalinformatics. com/technopolistimes.html). Parts of "This Law, That Law, and the 5K Nasdaq" appeared in *Technological Forecasting & Social Change* (60:1, January, 1999). They are used here with permission of General Informatics and Elsevier Science, respectively.

Chapter 23, David Gibson's "Technology is the Engine of a New Russian Revolution," was originally published on November 26, 1999, by the *Austin American-Statesman*, p. H6. Reprinted by permission.

Part IV of the Appendix was originally a working paper, "A Taxonomy of Technology-Based Economic Development Initiatives," by Fred Phillips, Bertha Vallejo, and Patricia Mhondo. Maastricht School of Management, August, 2005.

Preface

Publications on technology based economic development ("TED") started as a trickle and have grown to flood proportions. Recent years have also seen a proliferation of tech-based development initiatives in communities worldwide. Unfortunately, solid understanding of technology's modern role in economic development is not equally widespread. One aim of this book is to help develop such understanding.

The book is also motivated by the fact that earlier publications have been, variously, shallow consultant-speak, narrowly discipline-bound, or trying to answer the wrong questions. *The Technopolis Columns*, in contrast, is based dually on my academic studies and those of colleagues, and on my (and sometimes their) experience instigating and consulting for TED initiatives around the world. I have aimed for rigor and readability, for a comprehensive treatment that examines all aspects of TED regardless of disciplinary or professional boundaries, and for practical relevance and applicability.

The concentration of the TED phenomenon in metropolitan regions leads to this book's use of the term technopolis. Discussion also ranges, however, over several other flavors of TED initiatives (cluster building, shared prosperity initiatives, and so on), again aiming to clarify terms and help economic development professionals make wise choices.

The chapters are varied in their tone and format, ranging from formal to casual. In all of them, I've tried to avoid jargon without sacrificing depth, and in this way make the book useful, also, for scholars in a number of disciplines who hear colleagues in other TED-related disciplines using incomprehensible terminology.

Those who are new to the profession will benefit from the Appendix, titled "A Primer on Technology-Based Economic Development." Even experienced professionals, however, will find something of interest in the Appendix, perhaps especially in Part III.

Some of the book's material first appeared as op-eds in Austin and Portland newspapers. Thus the "Technopolis Columns," the subtitle also meant to imply that the book examines the critical factors that uphold the superstructure of the successful techno-region. Contributors' chapters are identified by the contributors' names. I thank the contributors for their incisive thoughts, their articulate expression, their friendship, and their permission to use their material here.

Some of their contributions are eloquent, bordering on poetic. Rightly so! Cities are objects of passion, people write songs about cities, and places affect our psyches in deep ways. (I recall expressing, to an executive who prided himself on his rationalism, how every square inch of ground in Austin seems to sing to me. He admitted he felt the same about coastal Connecticut.) Passion must be personal, so I have used the pronoun "I" in the text, for which I beg the indulgence of academics. My messages herein, and those of the contributors, show a mix of advocacy, scholarship, practical advice, passion, and a sense of urgency.

The book could well have been sub-subtitled "Austin, Portland, and Beyond." The "beyond" material, drawn from far-flung consulting engagements and from my experience as Associate Dean of Maastricht School of Management in the Netherlands, balances the emphasis on the Austin–Portland axis. The consistent choice of Austin and Portland examples keeps the discussion cohesive, and reflects a research technique similar to depth-interviews and ethnography. It is amplified by extensive reference to scholarly, trade, and current-events literature.

Though a very few of the allusions within will be especially meaningful for Austinites and Portlanders, the book is by no means written especially for them. *The Technopolis Columns* is for everyone, in every locality, who sincerely wants to grow a local technology economy. Alert readers will draw useful nuggets – what to do, what not to do, whom to do it with, and so on – from a careful reading even of those few passages which may seem to be (but are not) inside jokes.

Readers are invited to make use of the database of technopolis regions, related articles, and other updates at http://www.generalinformatics.com/technopolistimes.html, and to email me at fp@generalinformatics.com.

List of Contributors

David V. Gibson is Associate Director and The Nadya Kozmetsky Scott Centennial Fellow at the IC^2 Institute, The University of Texas at Austin. In 1983, he earned his Ph.D. from Stanford University in organizational behavior and communication theory. He teaches Knowledge/ Technology Transfer and Adoption in IC^2's Master of Science in Science & Technology Commercialization degree program. His papers on the management of technology/knowledge and the growth and impact of technopoleis or regional technology centers have been translated into Mandarin, Japanese, Korean, Russian, Spanish, Italian, French, German, Finnish, and Portuguese.

Dr Gibson is Co-Chair of the *International Conference on Technology Policy and Innovation*. He is co-editor of *Creating the Technopolis: Linking Technology Commercialization and Economic Development* (Ballinger 1988), *The Technopolis Phenomenon: Smart Cities, Fast Systems, and Global Networks* (Rowman and Littlefield 1992), and *Knowledge for Inclusive Development* (Quorum 2002). He is co-author of *R&D Collaboration on Trial: The Microelectronics and Computer Technology Corporation* (Harvard Business School Press 1994).

Patricia A. Hayes was president of St Edwards University. Dr. Hayes is now President and CEO of the Seton Healthcare Network.

George Kozmetsky (1917–2003) led a life that successfully combined academia, industry, government and family. After his decorated service in the Army Medical Corp during World War II, he earned the MBA and DBA degrees from Harvard University. He was a founding faculty member of the Graduate School of Industrial Administration at Carnegie Tech (now Carnegie-Mellon University), and co-founder and Executive Vice President of Teledyne, Inc. He served on numerous boards including Gulf Oil, La Quinta, and Dell.

Dr. Kozmetsky served as Dean of the College and Graduate School of Business of the University of Texas at Austin (1965–1981), and in 1977 founded the IC^2 Institute.

Dr. Kozmetsky was awarded the National Medal of Technology by President Bill Clinton in 1993. Among his other earned awards were the Dow Jones Award of the American Assembly of Collegiate Schools of Business for outstanding contributions to management education (1987–88), the Thomas Jefferson Award from the Technology Transfer Society for advancing technology transfer (1988), and induction into the

Texas Business Hall of Fame in recognition of his business contributions to the State of Texas. In 1989, he received the University of Washington Alumnus Summa Dignatus Award. He was the first recipient of the Entrepreneurial Leadership Award from the MIT Enterprise Forum of Cambridge, Inc., and won a YMCA award for advancing gender equity in business.

Dr. Kozmetsky served state and federal governments as an advisor, commissioner, and panel member. He and his wife Ronya donated generously to civic and medical causes.

Patricia Mhondo is a recent MBA graduate of Maastricht School of Management in the Netherlands.

Chet Orloff is director of the Pamplin Institute and Museum, an adjunct professor of Urban Studies and Planning at Portland State University, director-emeritus of the Oregon Historical Society, and founding president of the Museum of the City. He practices history with numerous public and private agencies and firms throughout the Pacific Northwest and helped initiate the nation's Lewis and Clark Bicentennial efforts. In addition to his professional work, Mr Orloff serves on numerous local, state, and national committees and commissions relating to history, planning, and urban design.

Pierre Ouellette has played guitar professionally since age 13. After performing with numerous musicians of note, including Paul Revere and the Raiders (in 1963), and the internationally acclaimed jazz bassist David Friesen, he was inducted into the Pacific Northwest Rock Hall of Fame. As a free-lance producer/copywriter, Mr Ouellette turned out radio, TV, and print material for various advertising agencies. Eventually, he co-founded a full-service agency that specialized in the emerging high technology field and eventually became the second largest agency in Oregon.

Mr Ouellette's novel *The Deus Machine* leveraged his experience in high technology. It was published in 1993 in hard cover, immediately optioned by New Line Cinema, and followed in 1996 by the publication of *The Third Pandemic*, a second successful high-tech novel.

In recent years, Mr Ouellette has been writing and directing video pieces. He drew on his roots in the world of professional music to develop and produce *The Losers Club*. The film premiered in January, 2004 to critical acclaim and was later aired on public television.

Fred Phillips is Associate Dean and Professor of Marketing, Entrepreneurship, and Research Methods at Maastricht School of Management. He is also a Research Professor at Oregon Health & Science University, and a Senior Fellow of the IC^2 Institute at University of Texas at Austin, which originated the academic study of the technopolis phenomenon. Dr Phillips is author of *Market-Oriented Technology Management: Innovating for Profit in Entrepreneurial Times* (Springer Verlag, 2001) and *The Conscious Manager: Zen for Decision Makers* (General Informatics 2003), and has edited several books in management science and technology management. He lived in Austin for twenty-six years and in Portland for nine years, playing leading roles in the development of both technopoleis. He has consulted worldwide on the technopolis formation process and on new business incubation. He can be reached at fp@generalinformatics.com or phillips@msm.nl.

Ralph R. Shaw's experience in investment and corporate management extends over forty years, encompassing securities analysis, institutional securities marketing, mutual fund portfolio management and the management and direction of corporations both private and public. In January, 1983, Ralph Shaw and US Bancorp formed Shaw Venture Partners with Mr Shaw acting as General Partner, and in 1994 the firm's third fund, Shaw Venture Partners III, was approved as a Small Business Investment Company (SBIC). This brought total venture capital assets available for investment to $80 million.

Mr Shaw presently serves on the boards of directors of Schnitzer Steel, Inc., Magni Systems, Inc., Integra Telecom, Inc., Rentrak Corporation, Telestream, Inc., and BMG Controls, Inc. He is a Trustee of St Vincent's Medical Foundation Council of Trustees, Chairman of the Council of Economic Advisors for the State of Oregon, a member of the Board of Advisors for the World Affairs Council and a Trustee of the Tax-Free Trust of Oregon. Mr Shaw previously served on the boards of Costco Wholesale Corporation, Will Vinton Studios, Inc., WebCriteria, Inc., and other companies.

Mr Shaw is a graduate of Hofstra University, having earned a degree in Public Accounting, and of New York University's School of Law where he received a Juris Doctor degree.

Bertha Vallejo Carlos is a Ph.D. candidate at the MERIT/UNU-INTECH Programme in Economics and Policy Studies of Technical Change. She completed her Master's in International Political Economy at the University of Tsukuba, Japan in 2001. Earlier she took courses on Latin American Economy at the University of Santiago de Chile, as part of her Bachelor in Economics from the Instituto Tecnológico y de Estudios Superiores de Monterrey (ITESM) in Monterrey, Mexico. Her research specialization is in capability building and technology transfer/acquisition in developing countries, with a particular emphasis on the automotive industry and issues related to SMEs' integration with the production chain in developing countries.

Introduction: Technology-Based Economic Development and the Initiatives that Advance it

Fred Phillips

In today's usage, a technopolis is a region trying to build and maintain a healthy, technology-driven economy. Regions that succeed are likely to have:

- A robust local value chain including strong R&D, manufacturing, marketing and distribution, and intensive international connections.
- A critical mass of companies in one or more well-defined "clusters."
- A relatively compact geography. This allows a successful specialized economy, impossible in more sprawling, diverse places (which may well have a greater total high-technology employment – see Markusen *et al.* 2001).

Technopolis regions grow by:

- Attracting new companies
- Nurturing existing indigenous firms
- Encouraging entrepreneurial start-ups
- Providing a supportive and innovative educational, social, tax, quality-of-life, cultural, institutional and hard-infrastructural context for research, technology entrepreneurship, and business, and
- Reaching out to other technopoleis for networking purposes.

The technopolis concept predated the notion of cluster. Early definitions of technopolis included the artificial science cities, such as Tsukuba, Japan, that had much R&D but little product development or distribution capability. Sheridan Tatsuno, author of *The Technopolis*

1

Strategy, explains the origin of the term:

> Japan's Ministry of International Trade and Industry coined the term 'Technopolis' back in 1982. I believe they got the idea from [France's] Sophia Antipolis. MITI's Technopolis concept envisioned building a nationwide network of idyllic research towns near cities of 500,000 (like Sophia). I visited 18 of the 26 Japanese technopoleis and popularized the term with my book. The IC^2 Institute further popularized it at its 1987 Technopolis conference.[1] Later, the International Association of Science Parks used the term Technopark or Techpark.
>
> [IC^2 Fellow and Bechtel executive] Mike Wakelin said he changed the name of the Bechtel division where I worked in 1979–1980 to the Technopolis division in the mid-1980s. He sponsored a Technopolis conference in San Francisco, where I spoke in 1990.

Today, successful technopoleis drive toward a more complete, robust value chain. As defined by Porter (1998), "cluster" is an idea both broader and narrower than technopolis. As a generalization of technopolis to non-tech industries, the broader concept of cluster allows us to speak of the Louisiana entertainment cluster, or the furniture clusters in North Carolina and northern Italy. However, cluster theory and cluster initiatives do not encompass the inter-sectoral cooperation and total regional futures orientation of technopolis. Both technopoleis and other clusters require concentrations of customers, suppliers, and infrastructure. Technopoleis have special needs in this regard, with more emphasis on higher education, research, and formal knowledge.

Clusters may grow because of the sheer scale of locally available resources from all industries ("urbanization economies") or because of knowledge transfer stemming from proximity of other companies in the same industry ("localization economies"). Most evidence (Malmberg, Sölvell *et al.* 1996; Maskell and Malmberg 1999) shows that high tech industries benefit much more from localization economies.

Howard Stevenson of Harvard Business School studies entrepreneurship and regional development. Stevenson (Oregonian 2002) says social culture is an important success factor for regional growth, and that an educated workforce is much more important than tax rates. Social culture, says Stevenson, determines:

- Propensity to reinvest the rewards of business success in still more local businesses – rather than in real estate or offshore bank accounts – and in the social welfare of locals.

- Attitudes toward the success of others. Do we ostracize entrepreneurs, or celebrate their successes?
- Willingness to embrace change.

"I've never met an entrepreneur," says Stevenson, "who said 'I'm not going to start my business here because the tax rate is five points higher.' " Finding the right workforce is the real issue. Stevenson also mentions supporting education and the importance of forgiving bankruptcy laws.

Society? Culture? Local character? All are important. To fully use the lessons of technopolis development, however, we must consider *history*. We must presume that locales that were not ready in the past to make themselves technopoleis can become ready. If this presumption were false, the many regional efforts to imitate Silicon Valley would be for naught. Thus, *change* is involved in technopolis development. Change doesn't happen all at once, but rather is a matter of contagion of ideas, attitudes and actions. So, part of the technopolis phenomenon is the "tipping point" effect in complex systems, popularized by Gladwell (2002). Other parts of the technopolis phenomenon, clearly, involve other effects – altruism, cooperation, and so on – studied by social psychologists and social anthropologists.

Yet the world is not full of Silicon Valleys. *The contagion is not as likely to start in one place as in another.* To find out why, we must look beyond the socio-cultural, and examine the history of a locale.

Austin, for example, built on the traditions of the oil wildcatter and "Texas pride." A "Japanese manufacturing miracle" led to an American backlash in the form (among others) of the microelectronics consortium MCC locating in Austin, which in turn beefed up the electrical engineering research and teaching capability of the University of Texas. Prior to the 1960s, graduates of the university in this sleepy state government town had followed the money to conventional careers in other cities. The nationwide counter-culture movement of the 60s led that decade's grads to stay in Austin, enjoying its quality of life, regardless of job prospects. A highly educated, under-employed workforce was a powerful magnet for company relocations and venture capital in later years. The music scene had spread Austin's fame. (I hitchhiked Europe as a college sophomore, meeting French and Swiss kids who exclaimed, "Austin! Armadillo World Headquarters! Janis! Johnny Winter!") When high tech started to grow in Austin and the prospect of making a living there became realistic, educated people all over the world thought Willie Nelson and Jerry Jeff Walker might have the right idea. They followed the stars in their eyes until they reached Congress Avenue – adding to the local talent pool. They drank at the Broken Spoke, talking with ranchers, hippies, and Latinos, advancing the cultural cross-fertilization that bred entrepreneurial creativity.

You can't buy that kind of history. It's mostly accidental. And this is discouraging to other metropolitan areas that need the job growth high tech brings. Here the historical and sociological views converge, as both emphasize the role of outstanding individuals. These individuals – change agents, visionaries, godfathers, godmothers, opinion leaders, connectors, mavens – shape attitudes and events, communicate across the right networks, and think outside the box. They do much, much more than the typical individual in the community, and they are essential for technopolis development. They show the community how to build on its strengths in new ways, ways that change the community's views of its own history, and ways that overcome the deadly recipe of "We don't have much wealth or infrastructure, but we'll invest what we can and hope for the best."

When I traveled in the mid-1990s, I encountered foreigners who enthused, "Austin! Yes, the Austin Technology Incubator!"[2] In Austin, I hosted dozens of delegations from several countries, showing them the city, the IC² Institute, and the incubator. They carefully recorded the details of intellectual property management, transportation infrastructure, incubator financing, and even some of the history. But though they may have felt the attitude, they did not stay long enough to be able to articulate in their trip reports the way history and community leaders *create* attitude, nor the way attitude supports technopolis. Attitude is an essential part of the infrastructure!

Later, the IC² Institute began to emphasize the long-term visiting scholar opportunity (rather than the one-day visit by a delegation) as a better way of getting the feel of the community worldview. This practice was notably successful. It continues at the Institute to this day, and I later replicated it at Oregon Graduate Institute of Science & Technology in Portland and at Maastricht School of Management in the Netherlands.

Junkets to other technopoleis can build valuable, lasting networks. When they are just a way to find out what other people are doing, the trips are of limited value. A region with historical disadvantages will have to do something original and different from what has gone before. Regions with the right history and resources may know – or find out – what to do, but as Peter Drucker said in the context of the 1980s manufacturing crisis, "What we have to learn from the Japanese is not what to do, but *to do it*." All the knowledge, money and infrastructure in the world, Drucker implied, cannot substitute for will, attitude and follow-through.

Technopolis development does involve some modern analysis and new principles, especially as knowledge-intensive industries change the old rules. But much of it is simple civic boosterism, and people have instinctively known how to market their community pride in every era of fast socio-technical change and new frontiers. Sinclair Lewis' Babbitt will rise again and again as we settle cyberspace, nanospace, genospace and outer space.

Fukuyama (1995) believes "cultural differences will become the chief determinant of national success in the global struggle for economic predominance. ... Social capital will be as important as physical capital" or financial capital for regions in the future.

The term "social capital" is due to the sociologist James Coleman (1988), who defines it as "the ability of people to work together for common purposes in groups and organizations." (It is different from "human capital," a term used to describe the size and educational level of a region's workforce.) Where there is social capital, Fukuyama claims, there is wealth. His data are at the national level. His conclusions are more than plausible for metropolitan, sub-national, or cross-border regions, however, and they rest on the region's history: "The ability to cooperate socially is dependent on prior habits, traditions and norms, which themselves serve to structure the market." In other words, sociology and history trump pure economics in shaping the region's development. The "rational man" of economic theory is purely selfish, and social capital depends on "spontaneous sociability," that is, the ability to form viable new cooperative associations.

Culture is in fact (in Fukuyama's neologism) "arational." It all boils down to trust, "ethical habits and reciprocal moral obligations." These trust relationships take the form of civil and civic organizations, each of a scope that is wider than family-level yet not organized by state or national governments.

To understand high-tech prosperity, we might look at the historical diamond industry. Known for extreme collocation, this industry depended on handshake agreements, and few receipts were demanded. Knowledge workers (cutters, appraisers, buyers, retailers) worked in proximity, but the industry was international, indeed nearly global. Margins were high, and oversupply problems were addressed by market segmentation, value-added products (for instance, settings and arrangements), product differentiation, and (sometimes) cartels. The industry contributed to the wealth of design and distribution centers such as Antwerp, Tel Aviv, New York and Johannesburg.

Are high technology companies similarly based on trust? It would be a foolish entrepreneur who approached a venture capitalist without a mutual acquaintance as trusted intermediary. After that stage, however, technology industry is built on non-disclosure agreements, non-compete clauses, and (too often) stolen software code. High-tech economic development should be based on trusting alliances and partnerships. Everyone has his or her personal agenda, though, and the success of these partnerships depends on how overt and disruptive the personal agendas might be.

Much academic literature focuses on level of trust as a determinant of a nation's prospects for entrepreneurial growth. In the United States, however, where tech entrepreneurship has flourished, investors, entrepreneurs and employees have learned to trust each other "with eyes wide open." In the same way, despite erosion of customers' trust in companies offering maddening technical support, poorly secured personal information databases, and misleading advertising, e-commerce in the United States is growing robustly. As we study technopolis success factors we must look at the role of trust in a more sophisticated way. However, the contribution of social capital in the sense of "propensity to create new civic organizations" seems unarguable.

The innovation process shown in Figure I.1 illustrates the many stages between the laboratory and the store shelf, and also the many groups that have an interest in innovation and commercialization. If the entrepreneur is fortunate to live in a supportive society, then, except for a few organizations that sell competing products, or that espouse an ideology that excludes the entrepreneur's product, all these groups want the entrepreneur to succeed. If the entrepreneur builds a successful new technology company, all these interest groups will benefit due to the jobs and exports thus created, the fees and investment opportunities offered, and the greater efficiency and productivity the products make possible.

Much of what new entrepreneurs must learn is simply how to find these people and groups, how to ask for their help, and how to utilize the help in a time-efficient manner. These interest groups – which include angel networks, technology brokers, incubators, university-chamber of commerce partnerships and others – appreciate and admire technology knowledge and entrepreneurial acceptance of risk. They are not only helping entrepreneurs individually, but are combining in new kinds of organizations to more effectively build entrepreneurial

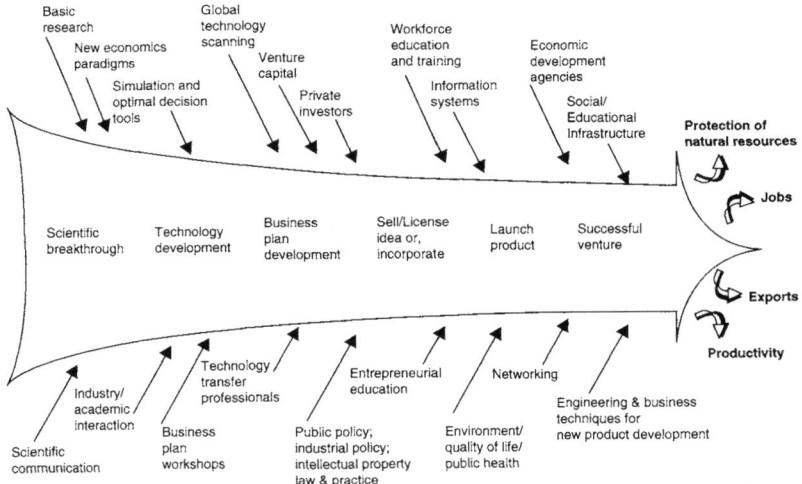

Figure I.1 The innovation arrow

communities, and to make enterprise formation less of a black art and more of a disciplined process.

One of the book's prominent themes is the accumulation of regional advantage by developing the kinds of knowledge that are not easily transferable to other regions. A second prominent theme is networking among regions, for the purpose of exchanging skills and contacts. At first glance, especially to readers of the recent economics literature on regional advantage, these themes may seem contradictory. Why cultivate distinctive advantages and then give them away? The answer, made clear by the following chapters, is that regions engage both in cultivation of comparative advantage and in external networking in order to:

- Barter for complementary skills and contacts.
- Consolidate relationships with contiguous regions in order to achieve critical mass in chosen clusters more quickly.
- Establish relationships in distant regions in order to find the best markets, technologies, suppliers, expansion locations, and so on.
- Advance political and humanitarian goals of development assistance.

Gibson and Stiles (1996) creatively elaborate the first one of these points, integrating it with the idea of Figure I.1 in order to rationalize the barter process along the innovation arrow. See Figure I.2. They call

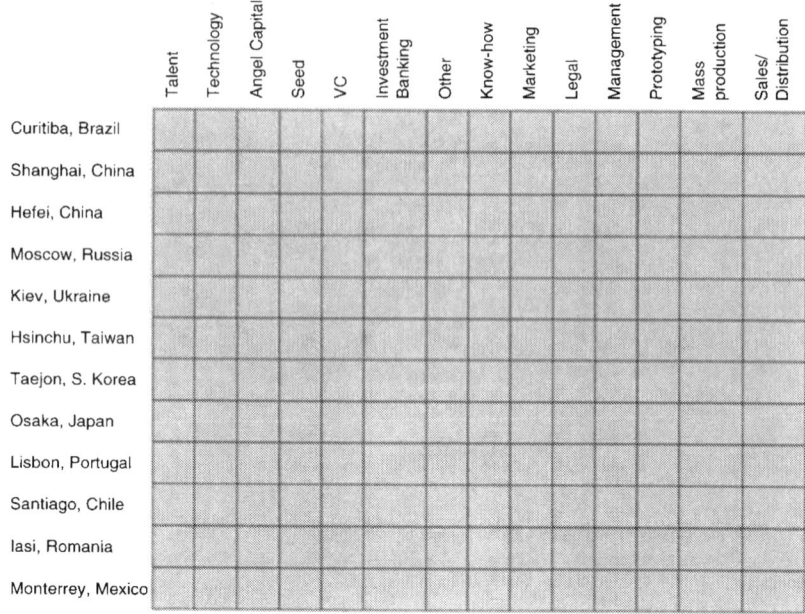

Figure I.2 Globally networked entrepreneurship partners linked by talent, technology, capital and know-how (Adapted with permission from Gibson and Stiles 1996)

this integration "Globally Networked Entrepreneurship." GNE is, of course, facilitated by the community groups and service providers described earlier.

This book brings the new technopolis principles home to today's aspiring techno-communities, and also rings the familiar notes of civic pride and export promotion. The case studies and opinion pieces that follow test the book's thesis that technopolis development can only flow from a smart combination of all or most of the following:

- Embracing change.
- Social capital.
- Cluster strategies that target specific company groups for collocation.
- Visionary and persistent leadership.
- Action.
- Constant selling.
- Self-investment in infrastructure.
- Outreach and networking.

Urban historian Peter Hall, interviewed in Zachary (2000), adds that industrial innovation has always bloomed in "edge cities," that is, locations at some distance from the entrenched interests of the dominant cultural centers, yet sufficiently sizeable and worldly to experiment ambitiously. We may conjecture that regions not blessed by "edge" location may hope to see innovation spring from social segments that are similarly far but not too far from the mainstream; they may try, that is, to substitute social distance for geographical distance in Hall's equation. (And we may perhaps conjecture further that America's land-grant universities, founded in the agricultural boondocks and now scurrying to establish campuses in their state's major cities, may soon again find advantage in being located on the margins.)

Hall notes exceptions in some remote areas, citing what I call, in Chapter 17, "cultural survival technologies." Examples include Scandinavia's lead in mobile telephony and Oregon's in radio and in signal processing; the two regions historical remoteness and sparse populations led to expertise in these technological domains that persists to this day. The challenge for today's regions is to identify not only their viable clusters, but their *distinctively* viable clusters.

Hall also remarks that the blossoming of creative cities lasts as little as 12–13 years and sometimes as long as a century and a half. A dozen years of creative prosperity is no mean feat, but regions hoping for sustainable advantage must aim for the upper limit of Hall's interval. Mature technopoleis cannot ride indefinitely on one technological pony, but rather need constant renewal. Silicon Valley has renewed itself repeatedly, moving from its start in microchips through successive strengths in PCs, Internet technologies, and mobile services. The chapters that follow elaborate on many aspects of these success factors.

Chapter 1 uses Austin's experience with "computational economics" to suggest each region's need to understand not only the technicalities of a chosen technological pony, but also its place in scientific history. This is useful not only for helping the region understand the trajectory and potential of the technology, but also for avoiding inefficient, distracting, and potentially fatal (to the cluster) activity on the part of people who "just don't get it."

The second chapter recounts the earliest days of the organization that is now Austin's largest trade association. Aspiring regions may take away some tips on organizational strategies, encouragement to persevere despite initial setbacks, and reassurance that great oaks from little acorns indeed do grow. The chapter names dozens of "technaissance heroes" who helped start the Austin Technology Council.[3] I ask readers not only to tolerate this recital, but to find ways to celebrate their own TED heroes.

Chapter 3 begins to look at what underlies the usual lists of regional success factors. It introduces the joint psychological–sociological view that continues through the subsequent chapters.

Chapter 4 gives an additional dimension to technopolis initiatives, that of sharing innovative potential through networks of regions. Readers worried about the seeming inequity of developing technology with public investment for the sole benefit of entrepreneurs and investors will find, in the shared prosperity notion, a positive social dimension of equity and development assistance. In Marshall's and Kozmetsky's view of shared prosperity, expanded upon here, planned interregional transfer of knowledge is not only more proactive than passive and random (e.g., trickle-down) mechanisms for wealth sharing, but it increases the payoff to the initiating region. Shared prosperity amounts to doing well by doing good, as this chapter's case studies show.

Engineer-entrepreneurs often under-value the potential contribution of the university's business school to the technopolis effort, and business schools share the blame when they react to, rather than lead, cluster initiatives. Chapter 5 suggests new roles for b-schools in technology-driven regional economies.

Following contributions by three Austin leaders, we move to Portland and look at that city's first international technopolis conference. Consensus conclusions and case studies from the conference (Chapter 8) indicate the complexities of transferring technopolis strategies across cultures. Fumio Kodama's idea of technology fusion implies that alliances are the wave of the future, and that companies will find profitable alliances in unlikely places. Chapter 9 explains why techno-regions must choose distant alliance partners proactively and wisely, and notes the unpleasant consequence of not doing so. In short, this consequence is economic colonization. The chapter makes it clear that the purpose of economic development is not just living wages, but control over the institutions that attract and create those well-paying jobs. In other words, ED is about political self-determination.

Chapter 10 continues the international view, noting in particular that many aspiring technopoleis don't have an international view. Leaders of these regions "really need to get out more" in order to understand the corollary of Chapter 9, that new competitors will also arise in unlikely places. (China, Brazil, Finland, and India were until recently, on the radar screens of few American communities.) Readers should heed the authorities quoted in Chapter 9: "Someone might be gaining on you," and "Never miss an opportunity."

Chapter 11, "Sometimes Montana," is a lighthearted comparison of Austin and Portland. It is a jumping-off point for further meditation on why, with so many cultural features in common, Austin seems so much more likely than Portland to rise to the challenges of the new economy. Chapter 12, an op-ed originally published in the Portland *Business Journal*, was a wake-up call and recipe for fixing Portland's predicament.

In Chapter 13 we return to the role of the university, looking at the opportunities and hurdles involved in teaching technology management to the students, managers, engineers and public officials who are the present and future of the technopolis.

Three Portland contributors follow. Ralph Shaw, dean of the city's venture capital community, offers Oregon a smack on the head with a two-by-four, a wake-up call even more blunt than mine. Prominent historian Chet Orloff shows how Oregon might apply some characteristics of its earlier golden age to a new future. Author, musician and P. R. executive Pierre Ouellette reminds us that ED efforts benefiting one segment of the population can devastate other groups that may be even more critically important to the technopolis effort.

Chapter 17 is the first to take us "beyond" Austin and Portland. It is devoted to the "persistent leadership" success factor. Many TED initiatives terminate themselves prematurely, either believing they have failed, or having made insufficient arrangements for continued funding. The chapter examines the factors that enable the initiatives to persist and thereby enjoy a chance of success.

ED programs – tax abatements, favorable lease terms, zoning waivers – are what economists call "distortions" of the free market. This is especially true for TED initiatives, which specially target strategically chosen industries. Today's international free-trade agreements aim to eliminate such distortions. The terms of various World Trade Organization measures specify that regions may be forced to cease offering discriminatory incentives. Globalization is the overwhelming economic fact of our time, and it may spell the end of economic development as we know it. Too little has been said about the obvious threat to the ED community; Chapter 18 takes up this theme.

Chapters 19 and 20 go back to college to look at the academy's role in transferring technology and (through more case studies) incubating new companies. Chapter 21 examines cities' role in attracting bright young graduates who will drive the communities' new and creative directions.

Chapter 22's collection of short editorials reinforces the topics of the earlier chapters, and introduces a few new considerations. David Gibson's contribution in Chapter 23 shows how these considerations are playing out in post-Soviet Russia. A concluding chapter recaps the themes of the book, in the light of the earlier chapters' discussion.

The Appendix goes back to basics, explaining economic development and TED from elementary principles and building up to a detailed classification of several varieties of TED initiatives. A helpful bibliography follows.

I hope scholars, government officials and economic development agencies will find useful tools herein, and succeed in building distinctive and prosperous regional economies.

Notes

1. Organized by Stephen Gomes, then at Bechtel.
2. Austin's overseas image continues to evolve. In 2004, while helping me with a train reservation, a Deutschbahn operator asked, "Austin? You're not Mr Armstrong, are you?" Though I first thought she meant astronaut Neil Armstrong, who lives in Austin, she was referring to Tour de France champion and Austin resident Lance Armstrong.
3. A previous director of the IC^2 Institute trademarked the term "technaissance" for use in Institute promotional material.

Part I
Austin

1
Toward a Modern Economics

Fred Phillips

In 1992 the IC^2 Institute at the University of Texas at Austin commenced a series of conferences on "Computational Economics," with support from the US National Science Foundation (NSF) and the engineering society IEEE. The programs covered a variety of topics on the mutual impact of advances in computation and economics. They are one aspect of the growing interest in computation on the part of scientists of all stripes and disciplines.

Dozens of research areas can fall under the computational economics rubric. They range from the purely scientific to others that are oriented to the practicalities of economic development. Thus, the name Computational Economics may not be the right one; these topics suggest something closer to what the Japanese in the 1970s called "Information Society."

The areas include experimental economics; computational experiments in other sciences, for example chemistry; manufacturing systems; regional software center strategies; economic development via software (e.g., a Baltic States software incubator was discussed); organizational and collaborative computing; data visualization; simulation; telecommunications; optimization-based microeconomics (Thompson and Thore 1992); robotics; artificial intelligence; multimedia; databases; archiving of documents and scientific knowledge; algorithms and architectures; retailing systems; networking; supercomputing; parallel computing; software engineering; global management information systems/decision support systems; and research on the information aspects of modern capitalism.

Computation is a common interest for scientists in widely diverging disciplinary areas. The Computational Economics conferences, for example, draw people interested in geology, chemistry, economics, and artificial intelligence. There is also a technology marketing component to Computational Economics, that is, integrating computers into our lifestyles and workstyles.

In his treatise on trends in art and technology, Hardison (1989) distinguishes "modernist" from "modern." The modernist uses new media and new social directions to reaffirm traditional or nostalgic values. In this sense, Ernest Hemingway and Ezra Pound were modernist writers. Modern works, in contrast, use innovations in language, media, and society to say new and different things. Hardison says, "Modern art recognizes a radical discontinuity between past and present, and affirms the present." Modern art – but not modernist art – celebrates technology. Hardison cites "Hart Crane's decision ... to make the Brooklyn Bridge the central symbol of his poem about America."

What does this have to do with computational economics? Just that the overwhelming concern of the 1992 conference attendees was securing access to fast computers in order to run bigger econometric models of the traditional type. One maverick in the audience remarked to me that there wasn't a computer to be seen at the conference. What about (this maverick continued) the power of computers for presentation? For data visualization, visual modeling, groupware, rapid simulation modeling, databases? These developments mean we can change (in new and better directions) the substance and practice of economic research – not just do the same kind of research faster.[1] The computer offers the opportunity to do modern, as opposed to modernist, economics.

Examples of modern economics include Data Envelopment Analysis (which requires solving a large constrained minimization for every point of a large data set, a task undreamed of when computers were slower), expert systems for trading financial instruments, and computerized visual exploratory data analysis.

The IC^2 Institute's interdisciplinary character in that era made it a natural incubator for modern economics. Hardison considers it significant that the modern writer Gertrude Stein studied psychology under William James, attended Johns Hopkins medical school, and befriended Matisse, Picasso and Hemingway. Her literary corpus was, he says, "so radical that many serious readers have still not caught up with it." I don't want to stretch a comparison between the IC^2 Institute of 1992 and Stein's Paris salon of the 1930s, but both may be called a support structure for radical modern developments.

The modern does not necessarily reject traditional values, nor are modernists by definition reactionaries. Modernism, Hardison says, regards tradition as a protection against excess, while modern art "is always on the point of declaring history to be a burden." Balance and moderation are important. Yet, fifty years after the introduction of the automobile, cars were still styled like horseless carriages. Their design did not acknowledge that cars had changed society so radically that a car could be seen as a car. I hope we can develop the full potential of computational economics in a more speedy and straightforward way.

Note

1. With reference to parallel computers, Zenios (1992) says, "Indeed, it is a mis-use of the technology to try to solve faster existing applications ... The major thrust of parallelism is to solve applications that were not considered within reach with serial computers."

2
Memoir on the History of the Austin Software Council

Fred Phillips

The Austin Software Council is Austin's largest trade association, with two hundred corporate members and six thousand individual subscribers in 2005, and influential even beyond what its size would suggest.

In 1991, when I was Research Director at the IC^2 Institute, George Kozmetsky asked me to organize a conference on the Austin area's software industry and its competitive readiness. This was to be one of a series of IC^2 "Tiger Workshops" in which leading thinkers and doers looked at the future of an industry, assessed our region's strengths, and mapped out needed community actions. The software tiger workshop idea stemmed from talks George had been having with Dr Jim Browne of the University of Texas and Scientific and Engineering Software, Inc. (SES).

Rick Goldgar, then with SES, and I organized the conference, and Rick was conference chair. Attendees remember Laszlo Belady, in his keynote talk, urging the Austin community to organize around its software industry, and this makes Belady the "godfather" of the Austin Software Council (ASC). The second spur to the formation of the Council occurred during the conference's closing panel with Ray Yeh, Wolf Metzner, Ed Taylor, and Peter Zandan, and in the general discussion following it. In this discussion, Angelos Angelou first shared the information that, in terms of number of companies, software had become Austin's biggest industrial sector. Most of this (except for a portion of Belady's talk which somehow was not captured on tape) appears verbatim in the proceedings of the conference (Goldgar, Orth and Phillips 1992).

But there was as yet no Software Council. Shortly after the conference, I began to get phone calls from people who wanted to follow up on Belady's suggestion and the recommendations from the panel session. A group started to meet every week or two, hosted by Gary Hamilton at the law offices of Pravel, Gambrell, Hewitt, Kimball, and Kriger. The core of this group were Rick Goldgar, Jim Ronay, Gary Hamilton, Paul Toprac, Ed Taylor, Wolf Metzner, Mary Ann Baker of Dresser Industries, Richard Denney of Schlumberger, Al Bhimani of the Hill Country CASE Users Group, Madison Cloutier of the Texas Information Technology Association, Joe McCall, and Fred Phillips. Discussion centered on aims for an ongoing group, and on organizational models provided by similar associations. Jim Ronay brought material on the Software Association of Oregon, the Boston Computer Society, and other efforts around the country. Goldgar and Phillips began to do the networking, note-taking, list-building and phone-calling.

Walter Bissex had attended some of these meetings, and for whatever reason (he may have noted that we were talking much and accomplishing little) went to George Kozmetsky to enlist George's clout in moving a new association forward. George saw that having the university host the new organization would be an expeditious way to get it started.

From that time, organizational meetings moved to the IC^2 Institute seminar room. They were attended by a wider group of people, and were chaired in turn by Jim Ronay, Rick Goldgar, and Fred Phillips.[1]

Ramiro Wahrhaftig, Vice Rector of the Pontificia Universidade in Curitiba, Brazil, was then a visiting scholar at IC^2. He observed the meetings. This led to the establishment of the Curitiba Software Council, the move of Polo de Software to Austin, and several software business connections between Austin and Brazil.

At this time, standing committees were formed, for monthly programs, conferences, finance, membership and so on. Brian Massey became membership chair and Joe McCall was program chair. Fred Phillips remained UT's liaison to the group, which had not yet been formally chartered. During this time, a second conference was planned and held. It was organized by Samia El-Badry and Rick Goldgar, and its proceedings were published as (Desai and Phillips 1993).

The planning group had included people from the nearby Texas cities of Waco and San Marcos, and the second conference drew attendees from Mexico. This advanced ASC's goal of building Austin's strengths while benefiting the entire corridor region.

Though most people remember the formal start of the Austin Software Council as happening in 1993 (with a press conference at IC^2 featuring Mayor Bruce Todd and Chamber of Commerce President Glenn West), the proceedings of the first conference were put out in 1992 as a publication of the Council, as we anticipated its charter would proceed smoothly.

This did happen. Jim Ronay was elected President of the Council, and a board of advisors was formed. Although starting ASC inside UT did speed the formation of a new council that had no money for rent or publicity, it did result in some frustrations. Lines of authority were blurred, for example. But it was soon realized no one wanted any authority as long as the jobs got done, and ASC volunteers were great at getting the jobs done. More seriously, UT seemed to be able to accept money (for instance, ASC dues) under pretty much any circumstances, but could disburse money only under very restrictive rules. Thus, ASC officials often could not authorize spending money for ASC programs. During this time, Jim Ronay, Ashby Wolff and Fred Phillips met quietly and often to find ways to navigate the labyrinthine rules and keep ASC's progress on track.

George Kozmetsky transferred UT/ASC liaison duties to Jamin Patrick, and a third conference (Culbertson and Phillips 1995) was held. This was one of the earliest conferences on electronic commerce. It was also distinguished by people confusing it with a conference on a similar topic that occurred two weeks later at the UT Business School, and by a bus tour of local software companies that left a few out-of-town attendees stranded at night out in the Hill Country.

Monthly dinner meetings were held at the Microelectronics and Computer Consortium (MCC). Their format – a presentation in the auditorium before dinner, then a buffet dinner with tables marked for people who wanted to discuss marketing, finance, and so on – was creative. A successful strategic planning exercise was completed. The ASC website was born. Constructive relationships were built with the Software Quality Institute and the Austin Multimedia Alliance.

In fall, 1995, this author resigned from the ASC board and moved to Oregon. Shortly after, ASC reached a membership of 800 and changed its name to Austin Technology Council. Paul Toprac and then Les Belady (by then retired from the presidency of Mitsubishi Electric Laboratories and living in Austin) succeeded Ronay as President of the Council. Former Microsoft Executive Vice President Mike Maples, also retired in Austin, was instrumental in moving the Council's goals forward in the late 1990s.

ATC's activities continue to expand and influence; see www. austintechnologycouncil.org for current information.

Note

1. The expanded planning group, according to the address list from that time, were generally Herb Krasner, Al Dale, Miller Hicks, Theresa Sullivan, George Kozmetsky, Angelos Angelou, Samia El-Badry, Becky Taylor, Norm Gelfand, Jarl Aalbu of Scientific & Engineering Software, Cheryl McManus Burtzel from the Texas Attorney General's office, Bill Boreing of MAKO Computer Corp., Bill Broussard, John Brubaker, Joseph Coffee of the Texas Dept. of Health, Lee Cooke, Robert Culbertson, Chuck Denman, Andrew Donoho, Bruce Gardner of US-Japan Translations, Darrell Glasco from Greater Austin Chamber of Commerce, Reiner Krumme of TUV Rheinland of North America, Charles Laritz of Texas Department of Mental Health & Mental Retardation, Patricia Mack of Expert Application Systems, Brian Massey of Paxson Enterprise, Kay Matthews, Joe McCall of Prudential Securities, Margaret Lewis of Novell, Tom Nelson of Nelson Investments, David Phillips of NETSERV, Lon Rankin Jr. of IBM, Alan Salisbury of MCC, Jay Schutawie of Dresser Industries, Sharon Strover of UT's College of Communications, Kellye Stuart of Bank One, Martin Wilbanks of IBM, Mike Byrnes of Hibernia Bank, Jennifer Sullivan-Whitney of Price Waterhouse, Ed Taylor of Pencom Software, Paul Toprac of Texas Direct Consultancy, Jan Triplett of the Entrepreneurs' Association, Jim Truchard of National Instruments, Keren Ware of Discovery Hall, Glenn West of Austin Chamber of Commerce, William T. Willis of Price Waterhouse, Peter Winstead of Winstead, Sechrest and Minick, and Ashby M. Woolf.

3
The Austin Experience: Behind the Success Factors

Fred Phillips

In a speech to the National Association of State Venture Funds, I conveyed this general background (Table 3.1) on the evolution of the Austin.[1]

In the same speech, I listed the Austin technopolis' critical success factors. Among them were awesome networking (everyone talking to each other) and a common vision (all parties telling the same story to entrepreneurs and to relocating companies). See Table 3.2.[2]

A thoughtful NASVF member from San Diego asked me, "Yes, but what made *those* factors possible?" Part of my answer was that Austin's networking stemmed from a social capital that would make Fukuyama proud: The organizations in Table 3.3 had frequent meetings, overlapping membership, and a tradition of welcoming outsiders. As a result, communication was facilitated, phone-tag was reduced, outside influences were given a fair chance, and external connections were made.

On behalf of the Software Council, Alison Raffalovich (1996) interviewed dozens of top executives from a cross-section of Austin's technology companies. Responses clarified Austin's advantages and disadvantages. They are summarized in Table 3.4.

Fate and good timing provided additional answers for the thoughtful NASVF member. George F. Will published a timely column asking why, when historic Asian and African cultures developed huge wealth and creativity, it was Europe that created the modern technological age. He conjectured that the Christian, and specifically the Protestant, notion that each person is responsible for his own salvation – that actions taken in this world have consequences in the next – encouraged commercial innovation even outside the ruling classes.[3] Now this may be nonsense, and in any case would be very hard to prove or disprove. But it did lead me to consider how social psychology might affect the growth of technopoleis.

22

Table 3.1   Timeline of the Austin technopolis: broad scale

1960s	Austin industry is State government and higher education. The times they were a'changin'; social tensions.
	Beginnings of a major music city are seen.
	Air conditioning, jet planes enhance prospects of all southern cities including Austin.
	President Johnson steers a few useful development projects (for example, Colorado River dams) our way.
	Low prices, great quality of life.
	George Kozmetsky touts technology innovation as the driver of economic development.
1970s	Austin's wealth, like rest of Texas', is still land, cattle, and oil.
	But Austin is known worldwide for music.
	Social tensions ease; hippies and rednecks enjoy the same music in the same clubs.
	College grads want to stay in Austin, but are underemployed – lots of Ph.D. cab drivers.
	'Energy crisis' attracts rust-belt refugees to Austin.
1980s	Decade starts with wide skepticism about prospects of high technology.
	But oil, real estate and cattle industries tank almost simultaneously in mid-decade.
	MCC comes to Austin, symbolizes the high-tech future.
	Investment in UT results in soaring reputation for the University.
	Texas investors start to embrace high-tech; companies absorb the excess skilled labor.
1990s	Many technology development alliances formed to nurture Austin's high-tech transformation.
	Strengths in music, electronics, software combine to form major multimedia development center.
	Austin known worldwide as a great place to start a high-growth company.
	IC^2 Institute personnel consult worldwide on technopolis formation.
	And by 1991, there were 400 companies in Austin in the software sector alone (see Figure 3.1).
2000	Austin Technopolis well-established. Less demand for development alliances.
	Less community unity: All boats have been raised, now each boat is jockeying for position.
	Labor market tapped out, even with enormous university graduating many engineers each year.
	Traffic problems increase, housing prices 'way up.
	But Austin is showing all the bright signs of optimism and prosperity.

Fate struck again on the eve of the full moon. On this evening every month, Charles McInerney leads a yoga class on Austin's Mount Bonnell. I happened to be in town that night, and Charles told this story.

A psychology professor put human subjects, one at a time, in a "waiting room" with an unpleasant temperature and noise environment. A second

Table 3.2 Austin technopolis critical success factors

Skill in networking – passion for networking – getting everyone to talk to each other

Across organizations, across sectors, across industries
    Linking entrepreneurs, capital, technology, and management experience
    Ability to engage communities from Dallas to Monterrey

A common vision – everyone "on the same page"
    "More so than anywhere else I've seen." – Former Austin City Manager
    Dr Camille Barnett
    "Taxes may not be the lowest here, but it's the only city where I get the same story from the Mayor, the Chamber, and the university." – CEO of a company relocating to Austin

A passion for measurement – always knowing where we stood. Statistics published by:

    Chamber of Commerce
    UT Bureau of Business Research
    IC^2 Institute

Texas Research League

Luck
Quality of life
Texas wildcat tradition
Timely crisis in traditional industries
Texas pride and determination

    Tradition of "the biggest & the best" benefited the University and the community
    Determination to maintain high quality of life
    Many public-spirited NGOs, NPOs, public-private alliances

IC^2 Institute – keeper of the vision. Furthered by organizations started by the Institute:

    Austin Technology Incubator
    The Capital Network
    Austin Software Association

Research on commercialization & entrepreneurship

Table 3.3 Technology-oriented civic, trade, and professional organizations and event hosts in Austin, 1990s

---

IC^2 Institute	Entrepreneurs Association
Student Entrepreneurial Society	Technology Advisors Group
Austin Software Council	Chamber of Commerce
Entrepreneurs Council	Software developers groups
American Electronics Association	User groups
Information Technology Management Association	Rotary
Women in Management	Metropolitan Breakfast Club
Women in Computing	Price-Waterhouse High Tech Luncheon
Software Quality Institute	Ernst & Young entrepreneur awards

Table 3.4 Austin's success factors and disadvantages

	Austin's advantages	Austin's disadvantages
Quality of life	• Climate, scenery, and environmental ethic • Low cost of living • Ethnically mixed community • Active arts scene • Sophistication and intellectual level • Friendliness	• Traffic congestion • Lack of rapid transit Limited non-stop flights • Texas as a whole exerts negative halo effect on Austin's otherwise good image • Growing income gap • Not enough opportunities for continuing education
Technology business	• Pool of technical talent • Ease of attracting new talent to Austin • Existing critical mass of technology firms • Upbeat attitude • Energetic external networking • Collaborative environment • Clean industries with good jobs	• Petty politics at city, state levels • UT's failure to reach out to business community • Increasing competition for experienced talent • Relative to Silicon Valley, less legal, financial, marketing talent to support tech industry • Limited coverage by industry analysts [since remedied] • Vulnerability to economic downturns

Source: Adapted from Raffalovich (1996).

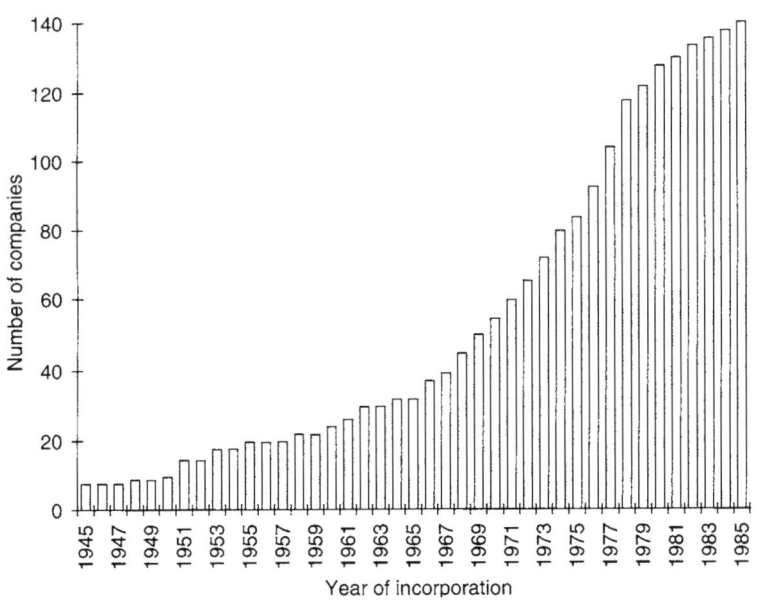

Figure 3.1 Early growth of technology companies in Austin
Source: UT Bureau of Business Research.

group was kept waiting in similar conditions but with an obvious control on the wall for the heater and its noisy fan. When asked about the conditions of their wait, members of the first group used words like "unbearable." The second group described it as "not bad" – *even when they had not used the controls.*

This could simply mean that stress is less when we feel we are in control. However, there was a second phase to the experiment.

The researcher asked the subjects to fill in a "post-experiment" questionnaire in a different room. The subjects didn't know the experiment was still in progress! There was a bright light shining into the subjects' eyes as they filled out the form. Many of the second group of subjects, who had had control in the waiting room, asked for the light to be turned off. None of the first group did.

The psychologist called the first group's behavior *learned helplessness.* Denied a choice in the first instance (the waiting room), they presumed they had no choice in the later situation (the questionnaire room). The other subjects, who had control in the waiting room, took control in the questionnaire room.

I had mentioned to the NASVF group that a large number of university graduates – including all those Ph.D. taxi drivers – had stayed in Austin after graduation even if it meant underemployment. Theirs was a lifestyle choice. It would be wrong to dismiss all these folks as slackers. Many were active in community organizations. Others comprised the labor pool that served the early waves of high tech companies in Austin. Still others started writing and selling software, and so on. All contributed to or helped perpetuate the unique Austin social culture.

These people – let's call them the *educated choosers* – were in a position to make and influence the choices that transformed Austin's economy. Having made one choice (to live in Austin despite career tradeoffs), they felt empowered to make further choices.

I will surmise (surmise means asserting with little data but much confidence) that the citizens of less transformative regions have learned helplessness; they believe that transformation either happens to them or doesn't – not that they make transformation happen.

This may sound as transparently self-congratulatory as George Will's pean to the Protestants. It is, though, supported by Hall's (1998, p. 26) remark about Athens of old: "Democracy could have happened only in a place in which people had confidence in their own independent judgments and therefore demanded the right to control their own destinies." And if it is true ... well, no one gets off scot-free after making only two choices. We've got more choices ahead of us.

The educated choosers (ECs) are now distraught about traffic, real estate prices, and malls and sprawls. They are irritated by the quick buck artists who, lacking any appreciation for what Austin is all about, now seem to make up so much of the city's population. One of my oldest EC friends, an Austinite for thirty years, is so fed up he's ready to leave Austin. "I have to fight my way through miles of strip malls full of useless national chain stores, just to get to Antone's or Waterloo," he said, referring to two homegrown music stores.

One further choice I would urge on him and all the other ECs: Don't leave! I emailed my friend: "Good to see you, don't get depressed about Austin, the uncultured scum will eventually depart and leave behind lots of useful infrastructure that will house future branches of Antone's and Waterloo Records."

Notes

1. A finer-scale Austin technopolis timeline is shown in Table 17.2.
2. Hall (1998, p. 18) presents an alternative list of "critical prerequisites for the development of such creative milieux: a sound financial basis, but without tight regulation; basic original knowledge and competence; an imbalance between experienced need and actual opportunities; a diverse milieu; good internal and external possibilities for personal transport and communication; and structural instability – a genuine uncertainty about the future within the general scientific and technical environment."
3. This notion was originally put forth by economist-sociologist Max Weber in *The Protestant Ethic and the Spirit of Capitalism* (1904).

4

Toward an Intellectual Foundation for "Shared Prosperity"

Fred Phillips

"The challenge of technological innovation in the new globally competitive era can be stated as follows: How can each organization, region, and nation, individually and in concert with others, manage technology creatively and innovatively to reap the benefits of sustained economic growth? Those organizations and regions most able to accomplish this objective will play key roles in resolving the paradox of global competition and collaboration."

> —*George Kozmetsky, Founder, IC² Institute of the University of Texas at Austin*

An Introduction to shared prosperity

National Medal of Technology recipient George Kozmetsky saw technology and ideology as the dual drivers of economic change. In his later years, Kozmetsky, an internationally renowned academic and industrialist, enunciated a philosophy of "shared prosperity at home and abroad (Kozmetsky, 1997; Kozmetsky, Jackson and Boyd, 2001; Kozmetsky and Williams, 2003)." Kozmetsky's speeches on this topic inspired many developing regions to network internally (across economic, social, and government sectors) and with like regions elsewhere. The effects were notable and positive. National governments, international bodies, and NGOs have adopted the term "shared prosperity" as a banner.[1]

The shared prosperity concept cannot survive simply as an inspirational phrase, nor, now that he is no longer with us, on the basis of Kozmetsky's charisma. If it is to continue to do good work, "shared prosperity" needs an intellectual foundation and the beginnings of a theory, with both firmly established in the literature of a number of disciplines.

Because shared prosperity involves many disciplines and activities, and because the concept is still evolving, these foundations have not yet been written down.

However, we do know this: Shared prosperity involves the building of industry clusters and social capital, and action-oriented communities that can embrace change. Shared prosperity requires new approaches in every activity from education and workforce training to income inequality, political stability, technology transfer and international trade. Shared prosperity is not a naïve give-away of competitive advantage, nor is it a simple-minded trickle-down economics. Instead, it is a sophisticated means of networking, knowledge-sharing, and partnerships that enhance the comparative advantages of regions. It is clear that no existing theory of political economy (and few currently practiced government policies) truly matches Kozmetsky's concept.

Overview

This chapter urges the establishment of a roadmap toward intellectual and theoretical foundations for a political economy based on "shared prosperity at home and abroad." The sections that follow:

- Briefly establish the need for a new approach to political economy, and further elaborate the shared prosperity concept and its origins;
- Identify from current literature and analyze some promising conceptualizations of shared prosperity;
- Describe the process of shared prosperity initiatives as they are practiced at two institutions (the IC^2 Institute and Maastricht School of Management), with specific cases, and compare these processes to those garnered from the literature;
- Summarize what we know so far about shared prosperity, set forth some research priorities, note obstacles to the research due to data limitations, and suggest feasible next steps.

Shared prosperity and its policy relevance

Former US Labor Secretary Ray Marshall (1998) described "America's long period of broadly shared prosperity before the 1970s" and defined this phenomenon in terms of real wages, high employment levels, and lessened inequality of wealth and income. He remarks that shared prosperity in that period was due to abundant natural resources, economies of scale in mass production, and pragmatic public–private cooperation for built infrastructures and social support systems – all factors that either no longer exist at the federal level in the US or are no longer the most relevant for creating a nation's wealth. "It is doubtful that existing public and private policies can sustain growth while improving opportunities for the majority of Americans who have not participated in economic growth for the last twenty years," Marshall concludes, "The policies and institutions responsible ... require a new national and international economic policy paradigm."

The idea of renewed shared prosperity in regions has roots in the work of the late George Kozmetsky, founder of Teledyne Corp., longtime Dean of Business at the University of Texas at Austin, and founder of the IC² Institute. Through Kozmetsky's and Marshall's influence, the term "shared prosperity" has been adopted and used, for example, by Futurist Alvin Toffler and former World Bank President James Wolfensohn; international agencies and organizations like ASEAN, APEC (2003), UNCTAD,[2] OAS (2002), ISO and IMF; and regional and national governments and NGOs in Canada, Silicon Valley, and San Diego.

It is clear, though, that many use the phrase for its warm sound and emotional appeal, with little denotative meaning.[3] In other communities of practice, however, and particularly within the global IC² community, "shared prosperity" has a specific meaning, and promises specific benefits to interested regions.

At a time when many question the validity of national policies behind new free trade treaties (Magnusson 2005), US relations with the Muslim world and China, or military action in the Mid-East, "shared prosperity" offers a new well from which positive alternative policies may be drawn. Some of these policies might lead to different decisions than would current doctrines, and some might lead to similar decisions; in general we cannot say, until we have progressed further toward a theory of shared prosperity. The non-partisan IC² Institute and the shared prosperity notion have no political agenda per se, but are aimed at equitable, innovation-driven betterment of quality of life and standards of living, and outstanding economic incentives for innovators.

Shared prosperity cannot have policy relevance, however, without at least some agreement on its meaning. Let us look at several recent usages in policy speeches, the popular press, and the scholarly literature.

Concepts of shared prosperity: examples from the literature

Marshall (1998) cites the following as essential considerations in a new paradigm for shared prosperity: capital investment, educational opportunities, decentralized management systems, positive rewards for value added, continuous individual, group, and organizational learning, leading-edge technologies, health care, "policies to provide independent power to all stakeholders," and social capital. His mention of social capital reinforces Fukuyama's (1995) connection of social networking with wealth creation and foreshadows this chapter's emphasis on networking for shared prosperity.

Other sources provide pointers to additional essential considerations for shared prosperity. From each of the following sources are abstracted the initiative's:

- Definition of shared prosperity
- Networks of entities leveraged to achieve shared prosperity
- Geographic scope of the networks
- Aims of the project(s) and
- Organizational mechanisms for achieving the aim.

Single-neighborhood or single-issue initiatives

Some shared prosperity initiatives may be dismissed immediately, their scope too narrow to suggest regional or national policy principles; nonetheless, we can see in these initiatives the same networking approach and the same desire for open, transparent processes that characterize the more exemplary initiatives discussed later. Instances of such narrow initiatives include single neighborhoods in New York[4] and Philadelphia,[5] in which residents and local associations argue against gentrification and in favor of block refurbishments that encourage shared prosperity across more diverse income groups, and Citizens United for Shared Prosperity, a coalition of organizations committed to getting a "living wage" ordinance passed in St Petersburg, Florida.[6]

At a slightly broader level, a writer from the Mongolian National Center for Standards and Metrology expressed a view of shared prosperity that involved raising the level of her country's adherence to international standards (plug voltage, food safety, and so on) in order to prepare for expanded international trade.[7]

Also dismissed without consideration are the instances of "shared prosperity" used as an undefined term in a political slogan. Examples include the Canadian Edinburgh Commonwealth Economic Declaration,[8] and the 10th Chinese National People's Congress (Hamrin 2003). Ditto for its use as an undefined term in an economic argument (Mann 2002, or Joint Venture Silicon Valley, 2002 which uses "shared prosperity" in apposition to "lifting the living standards for everyone and limiting the displacement of ... individuals and families").

Single metro area initiatives

In the UK, the Cheshire Partnership[9] forms alliances across the metropolitan region for multiple initiatives to increase the quantity and quality of employment opportunities. Emphasizing access to learning-for-employability for all residents, Cheshire creates inter-sectoral networks to attract companies and encourage entrepreneurship and infrastructure development.

Working Partnerships USA (WPUSA)[10] was formed in 1995 in response to the income disparities among Silicon Valley, US residents. The organization networks labor unions, religious groups, educators and community-based organizations, coupling economic research and policy development with organizing, advocacy and public education. Curiously, though WPUSA claims a regional role, its critique of San Jose's Redevelopment Agency mentions no causes or effects outside San Jose city limits. The Partnerships and the Agency both emphasize job creation and housing for every income level. The Partnerships, however, hope to see more networking of diverse community elements, more transparent redevelopment processes, and ultimately that "all community elements receive ROI on tax funds."

San Diego's Center on Policy Initiatives defines shared prosperity in terms of job quality, job quantity, and health coverage. Recognizing the importance of industry clusters to the city's improvement on these dimensions, the Center's report (Marcelli, Baru and Cohen 2000) fleshes out this definition by analyzing the occupational composition of local clusters, average incomes, educational requirements for employment, earnings by cluster, the mix of full-time versus part-time employment, the clusters in which firms are likely to provide health insurance, the location of firms, and the size of firms in cluster and non-cluster industries.

Cross-border, regional supra-national, and inter-regional initiatives

Indian External Affairs Minister K.N. Singh[11] defines shared prosperity via an emphasis on demilitarization with diversion of funds to the civilian economy. His networking vision commits India and Pakistan to cooperation on business services, an oil pipeline, and nuclear non-proliferation. Morocco's King Mohammed VI[12] wishes for shared prosperity across the Maghreb. In 2004 he noted, "It would be unrealistic to speak of shared prosperity, solidarity and globalization with a human face" unless "priority is given to training skilled labor in the countries of the South, and unless substantial investments are made to help these countries in their development effort."

The ASEAN–India Partnership for Peace, Progress and Shared Prosperity[13] enunciated goals of peace, stability, development and prosperity. Objectives serving these goals include poverty alleviation, reduction of social disparities, wide access to opportunity, regional infrastructure, cooperation in science and technology, and preservation of cultural heritage. Networking with ASEAN, WTO, and "other multilateral fora," the Partnership emphasizes multidimensional links dealing with civilization, culture, economic and social interaction, and development of human resources, especially among youth, for natural resources, and for high-tech and knowledge industries.

Enterprise Europe[14] (specifically, EU Commissioner for Enterprise and Information Society Olli Rehn and Member of the European Commission Ján Figel) emphasize SMEs, microcredit, entrepreneurship, corporate social responsibility, standards, and knowledge-sharing networks with the US and North Africa.

The Asia Development Bank/APEC Forum on Shared Prosperity and Harmony[15] hopes to mobilize constituent countries in the region to reduce socioeconomic disparities and poverty, reduce the knowledge gap, and encourage cyber education, HR development, and technology transfer.

The recently announced Security and Prosperity Partnership of North America[16] hopes to mobilize several cross-sectoral Mexico–Canada–US networks, leveraging the NAFTA organization, ministerial working groups, and ad hoc interactions of the three national governments. The announced aims are: protecting against internal and external threats to health, infrastructure and environment; making trade efficient; and "economic dynamism." Though intelligence sharing is mentioned, no specific mechanisms are noted, and at some time in the future, "working groups will set" objectives for the Partnership.

Worldwide initiatives

International Monetary Fund Managing Director Horst Köhler proposes networking nations via the WTO, IMF, and World Bank.[17] The aim would be worldwide economic growth with the US economy as the driver. Mechanisms would focus on protecting property rights, the rule of law, and shared values, and on fighting corruption (Kohler 2004).

Speaking at the Progressive Governance Center in Hungary, 2004, Canadian Prime Minister Paul Martin adumbrated a vision combining the "progressive governance philosophy" ("forging new approaches to equality of opportunity and securing them for the years to come both at home and around the world") with fiscal conservatism.[18] His vision involves cross-sectoral networks within and among twenty developed and developing countries to advance four thrusts: Protect the rule of law, Deny proliferation of weapons of mass destruction, Respect human rights, and Build infrastructure and institutions. Martin emphasizes growing national economies while investing in cities and communities. He further emphasizes lifelong education, entrepreneurship, and putting "common humanity at the center of international policy" for "collective, strategic and responsible" action.

Related thoughts come from the World Summit of Young Entrepreneurs[19] of the World Trade University (a UN initiative), networking "peoples and institutions" (4800 entrepreneurs in 185 countries) "to enhance the capacity of the present and to develop the potential of future trade leaders to better manage the challenges of the multilateral trading system so that prosperity is shared," and the OECD Employment Outlook 2004.[20] The latter publication defines shared prosperity simply as high employment rates. Its network is the OECD nations, and through statistical analysis, it "urges governments to combine job strategies with other social objectives," for example, job training, leveraging informal employment systems, and understanding tax evasion.

Table 4.1 extracts the common elements of the initiatives described by all these speakers, writers and documents. Some of the initiatives are clear in their objectives; others are not. Some are open to new or multiple mechanisms for achieving their objectives. Others are wedded to the mechanisms of the newer free trade agreements (NAFTA, WTO) – though it has been convincingly argued elsewhere (Marshall 1998; James 2002; Phillips 2004) that these agreements are designed to preserve, rather than reduce, existing inter-regional income disparities.

Table 4.1 Common elements of shared prosperity concepts from diverse sources

1.	Interlocking networks
2.	Multiple social, economic and military issues
3.	Multi-lateral active cooperation
4.	Reduction of income and knowledge disparities
5.	Clear-eyed financial approaches
6.	Creation of jobs via technology entrepreneurship
7.	Respect for persons and groups
8.	Preservation of cultures and the rule of law
9.	Education and development of human capital
10.	Regional (metropolitan regions and cross-border regions) approaches
11.	Ensuring progress in the home region *and* in partner regions
12.	Transparency and inclusiveness

One element that is notably and rightly absent from Table 4.1 is *consensus*. Shared prosperity seems to rest on the *initiative* of individuals or organizations, on *idea leadership* ("run it up the flag pole and see who salutes it"), and on *inclusion of the committed*, regardless of whether committed participants bring ideas, funding, a good rolodex, or just a sincere desire to learn. This does not mean that broad consensus may not emerge.[21] Similarly, shared prosperity initiatives need not be explicitly supported in law. However, they benefit by being eligible for, or influential in creating new sources of, government funding, and it is important that no laws actually prohibit the constructive directions the initiatives may wish to take.

Table 4.1 implies that shared prosperity initiatives need not meet Paul Martin's criteria of "collective, strategic and responsible." Certainly shared prosperity efforts should be responsible. As decentralized, network-based alliances with memberships shifting according to the quality of ideas and the energy of their implementation (see Romer 1993), shared prosperity efforts need not be collective in a universal sense. While shared prosperity efforts can be expected to be strategic for their networks and their regions, they are not "strategic" in the older sense of a national government identifying "strategic industries" to favor via public investment and favored tax treatment.

The shared prosperity initiative process at two international institutions

This section focuses on activities of the IC^2 Institute and of Maastricht School of Management, noting how these two institutions' initiatives agree or differ from the varied shared prosperity programs and partnerships noted earlier.

In the literature cited earlier, "shared prosperity" is sometimes used as a synonym for free trade, for an increased minimum wage, or for the reduction of income inequality within a single nation. In George Kozmetsky's view, these are misuses of the term that capture only a part of the concept's true scope. I will illustrate, before going on to real cases, with a narrative of a fictitious but typical initiative.

Kozmetsky and his network of influential, well-informed contacts identify an issue of emerging or near-future importance – say, the growing criticality of the software industries, factory robots, or the need for education to bring disadvantaged youngsters into the technology work force. The subject is one that has not been widely addressed heretofore, and one that involves creating new wealth or increasing equity by leveraging technological innovation. A conference is organized. The contacts – and their contacts – are mined for expert speakers. Some are from the local area, and others are from other states and countries. Grant funds may be raised to support the conference and its resulting publication. Officials and members of civic and trade organizations are invited to attend and support the conference, as are city, county and federal officials, corporation executives, and leaders from communities nearby and around the world for which the subject at hand is also of importance.

If the conference attendees are enthusiastic about the potential for further constructive collaboration on the subject, volunteer work groups are formed. (If they are not enthusiastic, the idea is dropped without regrets, and the process re-started with a different subject.) Attendees form a new network of communication on the topic. Attendees and work groups from the contiguous region (in Austin's case, this was often the corridor between Dallas, Texas, and Monterrey, Mexico, or the states of Texas and New Mexico) decide on an implementation project and/or a new, standing organization, built around the conference topic, that will advance the goals of new wealth and greater equity. Attendees from more distant locations, using what they have learned at the original conference, re-start the process back home, building their own conferences and regional networks, but staying in touch. New knowledge is generated, new companies and relationships are formed, and new, sustainable jobs are created.

This narrative shows it is not just skills (as the new growth theory of economics would have it) that are transferred across regions, but also:

- Early warnings of emerging trends;
- A sense of the possibility of new kinds of actions; and
- The sense of permission to take such actions.

The IC^2 Institute

This description of the Institute is reproduced from its website, www.ic2.org:

> The IC^2 (Innovation, Creativity & Capital) Institute is an international, trans-disciplinary "Think and Do" tank devoted to solving unstructured problems to accelerate wealth and job creation and shared prosperity at home and abroad. A research unit at the University of Texas at Austin, IC^2 is focused on knowledge exploration, dissemination, and application, across a broad range of academic and applied areas. IC^2's research is disseminated through educational programs, conferences, and publications.

IC^2's early experiments such as the Austin Technology Incubator (ATI), The Capital Network, and the Austin Technology Council, continue to contribute to the Austin region's tech-based growth, and continue to serve as "experiential learning laboratories" nationally and internationally. IC^2 has engaged in a myriad of projects to assist emerging regions or regions in transition in the development of their private sectors through a focus on entrepreneurship as the engine for growth and technology commercialization as the vehicle.

IC^2 has worked with the World Bank, the US Agency for International Development (USAID), the Eurasia Foundation, investment resources, and corporations with business interests in a region.

The IC^2 Institute has appointed over 200 Fellows from 18 nations. The Fellows are a knowledge network of premier talent from academia, business, and government sectors around the world, and include Nobel Laureates, Medal of Technology winners, and Fortune 500 leaders, as well as younger professionals and professors. Renowned experts in areas such as econometrics, marketing, business strategy, regional economic development, technology transfer and commercialization, chaos theory, creative and innovative management, alliance building, and globally networked entrepreneurship, the Fellows provide contacts and intellectual backing for shared prosperity projects. The projects, in turn, introduce the Institute to additional experts who may be appointed as new Fellows.

The Institute believes "the key to regional prosperity is the strategic combination of technology, entrepreneurship, and education. The IC^2 Institute works with a region's policy makers, educational institutions, local and international investors, and new and existing ventures to accelerate and sustain technology-based economic development."[22]

The contributed essays in Marshall (1999) present sound but scattered ideas for a new paradigm of shared prosperity, as do many of the policy initiatives mentioned earlier in this article. I propose that the IC^2 Institute process described above is a useful lens for focusing these varied ideas. (The "Current Knowledge and Needed Research" section below, culminating in Table 4.3, gives structure to this proposition.) An excellent example of the success of IC^2's process is the Institute's CBIRD project.

Case 1: Cross-Border Institute for Regional Development

The Cross Border Institute for Regional Development[23] (CBIRD) is a bi-national collaborative initiative for the border region between South Texas and Northeastern Mexico. CBIRD promotes a regional vision and a mission to transform and diversify the economic and social conditions of the region, through deployment of better technologies for manufacturing, business, services, and health care.

CBIRD is a neutral catalyst, bringing together capital, technology, knowledge and talent to facilitate greater and more integrated bilateral cooperation and coordination. It functions as a "think tank" and "do tank," providing a forum for debate and decision. CBIRD's goal is to create wealth and equitable prosperity for the region by attracting twenty-first century domestic and foreign industries, businesses and services. Its objective is to empower local grassroots communities to shape their own future. CBIRD offers an opportunity for "cooperation and collaboration among all regional stakeholders [for] civil and social entrepreneurship."

CBIRD was created to meet the following challenges:

- Integrate the border region and its infrastructures [with the] global knowledge-based economy to maintain competitiveness and to maximize prosperity and growth for all residents on both sides of the border.
- Create higher-paying technology-based jobs to reduce the per-capita income gap between Texas and the Border region.
- Create an environment based on cooperation and collaboration in this bi-national, bi-literate and bi-cultural region.
- Improve each individual's standard of living and the quality of life, and to protect the local environment.[24]

Following the principle that a successful demonstration project is the best advertising, CBIRD initially concentrated its efforts on sub-region consisting of the northern part of Nuevo León and Tamaulipas states, and the lower South Texas region. CBIRD had two headquarters, one at The University of Texas at Brownsville, and the other at the Instituto Technológico de Estudios Superiores de Monterrey. CBIRD has a Bi-National Advisory Board, with equal number of members from each country, with representatives from academics, business, industry, government, and NGOs.

CBIRD has supported the leadership of the region's grass-root communities to achieve its vision and mission. Having successfully introduced its constituents to information sources and to the principles of networking and self-empowerment, a smaller CBIRD office now resides at the Lyndon B. Johnson School of Public Affairs at the University of Texas at Austin. Its constituents in the Rio Grande Valley may continue to call on the universities for advice.

Case 2: Belize Enterprise, Science & Technology (BEST) Park Project

At an IC^2 Institute planning meeting, noting the improved international relations in the region and the future prospects for Cuba, the present author suggested an extension of the CBIRD model into the Caribbean Basin. Others at the Institute took the initiative to launch a project in Belize (Gibson, Cotrofeld *et al.* 2004).

Unlike hit-and-run incubator consultants, the IC^2 Institute becomes an ongoing networking resource for its clients. The Institute identifies the client's best networking partners. In the case of Belize, Trinidad/ Tobago was chosen as a partner due to its comparable size, common language (English is spoken in both nations), and complementary needs.

In keeping with its shared prosperity and technopolis focuses (Conceição *et al.* 1999; Jarrett *et al.* 2002; Kozmetsky *et al.* 1988; Malecki 1997; Nishiyama 1999; Phillips Roberts *et al.* 1999; Smilor, Wakelin and Kozmetsky, undated; Gibson and Stiles, undated), the Institute kept the project centered around metropolitan regions and the linkages among them. The Institute benchmarked nearby regions comparable to Belize City, including cities in Costa Rica, Jamaica, Yucatan, and Panama. It mapped the Austin connections that could be of use to Belize.

The Institute considered possible interactions among Belize's art, culture, tourism, and technology sectors. It paid due regard to historic ethnic tensions, border disputes, and so on.

Project leaders hope to have Belize's results serve not only to benefit Belize, but also as a role model for further initiatives in the region. Participants coined an inspiring yet practical philosophy, "Hope plus extraordinary vision [leads to] sustainable reality."

Maastricht School of Management

Maastricht School of Management is the oldest and largest management school in the Netherlands, having begun in 1952 as the management-training arm of the Technical University of Delft. With partner institutions in each location, MSM offers MBA programs in about 30 cities (Cairo, Haikou, Jakarta, Kuala Lumpur, Ho Chi Minh City, Lima, Maastricht, New Delhi, Singapore, Changsha, Dhaka, Shanghai, Shekou, Malta, Ulaanbaatar, Jeddah, Amman, Windhoek, and Almaty), and doctoral programs in Maastricht and in six outreach locations (Hainan, China; Djakarta, Indonesia; Lima, Peru; Almaty, Kazakhstan; Cairo, Egypt; and

Dingli, Malta). More partner locations are added yearly, with new ones expected soon in India and the new EU nations of eastern Europe.

Under a "flying professors" model, at least half the credits in each program are taught face-to-face by regular faculty from Maastricht School of Management, with the remainder taught by faculty of the local partner institutions. This model pleases students, keeps the educational alliances strong, and effects skills transfer as a "contact sport." (See Figure 4.1.)

All MSM outreach degree programs are targeted at working professionals. As a result, MSM is connected to the partner institution, to local students and faculty, and to students' employers in each location. Via summer conferences in Maastricht and some faculty and student exchanges, MSM "makes the network dense" by connecting the farflung students, faculty, institutions and employers *with each other* as well as with MSM. MSM's 1600 worldwide alumni have attained influential

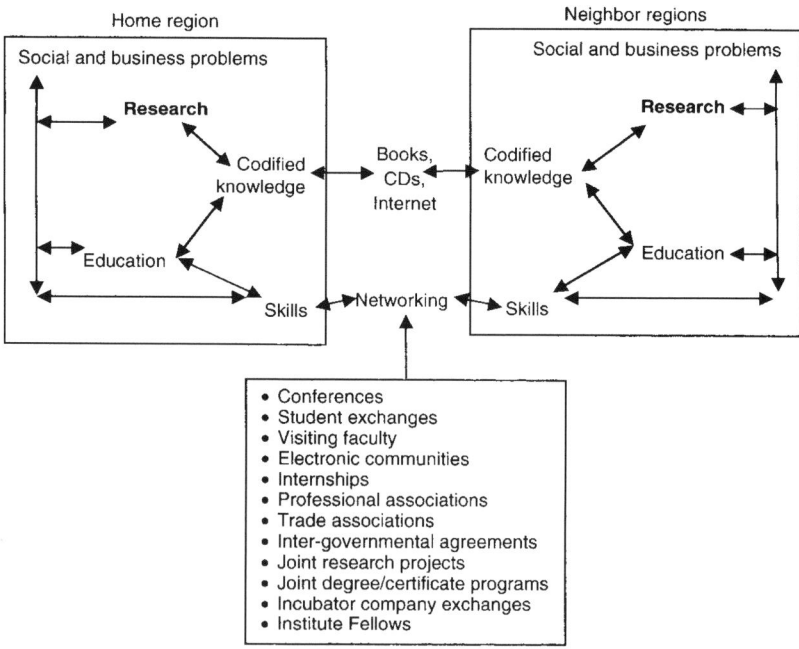

Figure 4.1   Networking for inter-regional skills transfer

Notes: [a] Note the multiple networking mechanisms at the bottom of the Figure.
[b] Additional possible networking mechanisms are noted in Agiplan (1999).

positions in their countries' public, NGO, and private sectors; MSM's alumni network is remarkable in its influence and geographic coverage.

MSM's mission, research, and teaching emphasize development economics and business–government cooperation for advancing newly emerging economies. Indeed nearly all the outreach partnerships are in locations fitting that description, mostly in Africa, the Middle East, Latin America, and Southeast Asia. With funding from the EU and various Dutch ministries and international agencies, MSM's Projects Department engages in numerous capacity-building projects in these and other emerging economies. Often these projects involve building new universities, management schools (current projects are doing this in Ethiopia and Yemen), or local research programs in established universities.

MSM leverages the funded projects with its existing educational programs:

- Personnel from project countries visit Maastricht as executive education students and sometimes as MBA students, doctoral students, or visiting scholars.
- MSM alumni in-country provide valuable advice, introductions and access to data. This makes the projects more effective, and increases MSM's ability to win more international funding for further projects.
- New schools and universities created with the help of the projects may turn into new outreach locations for MSM's MBA and doctoral programs.

Like the IC^2 Institute, Maastricht School of Management finds that interesting things happen on and near borders. Malta will serve as home to an MSM-Malta Institute of Management Mediterranean MBA, drawing students from Italy, Libya and the Maghreb region. MSM is involved in creating new business incubators where Eastern Europe meets the west. As with Austin and its proximity to the Mexican border, Maastricht, with close proximity to Germany, Belgium and Luxembourg, enjoys a particular cultural vitality which encourages innovation. The two universities wisely take advantage of this.

Shared prosperity: current knowledge and needed research

I have presented these narratives briskly, but any number of practical difficulties lurk behind them. Are there enough of the right kinds of companies or entrepreneurs in the region to advance wealth or equity along the dimensions addressed at the conferences? Will people in the region tolerate change in this dimension? How can they be persuaded to do so without violating precious cultural values? Is there a propensity to join civic organizations, to communicate among such organizations, and to form new ones? Is there communication across the university, corporate, non-profit and government sectors? Are there peacemakers who can overcome the inevitable conflicting interests of involved parties? Are there savvy political minds who can delineate what those interests are in the first place? Who can take on the role of "Dr Kozmetsky" in other regions and now in Austin itself, and what are the optimal characteristics of such a leader?

Will city and rural infrastructures support the needed/resulting growth? What constitutes a critical mass for self-sustaining economic activity, and how can this mass be achieved? What cultural factors are essential to the success of the venture? (e.g., in the US, environmentalism is seen as an individual virtue; in less developed regions, environmentalism is seen as a key to community survival, because it maintains local soil and water quality, attracts tourists, and so on) What are the expected impacts of new technological developments? In cross-border regions, how is the objective affected by globalization, WTO rules, and newly interdependent capital and labor markets?

What are the critical success factors in this sequence, and what is dispensable window dressing? Decades of project experience give ample clues to the answer to this question. One is shown in Table 4.2, due to Gibson and Conceição (2003). The cases described in this paper, together with Table 4.1 and Table 4.3, comprise additional pieces of the answer. However, further scientific validation is needed in order for shared prosperity to become entrenched in the ecology of ideas.

Gibson and Conceição (2003) focus on the distinction between codified knowledge and skills. Codified knowledge is transmitted among people and regions via books, CDs and other archival means. Skills are transmitted face-to-face: thus the phrase, "Technology transfer is a contact sport." Gibson and Conceição conclude, "The purpose of networking is to transmit skills." Figure 4.1 adapts this view to create a schematic of regional networking for shared prosperity.

Table 4.2   Influencers for regional/community cooperation

1st Level Influencers/Visionaries
2nd Level Influencers/Champions
Regional Networking Organizations

Table 4.3 Shared prosperity initiatives compared with conventional aid efforts

Old political economy approaches	Newer shared prosperity approaches
Paternalistic; one-way initiatives and flows	Multilateral initiatives
Strategies imposed from top down	Multiple networked initiatives
Driven by a single issue or problem	Multidimensional, attacking related problems
Rigid	Flexible
Expensive	Inexpensive
Large-firm orientation	Entrepreneurial orientation, with the participation of large firms
Single industry/agency	Multiple sectors, diversified funding
Initiating entity and receiving entity seen as separate and independent	Presumes present or near-future interdependence of participating regions
"Developed and undeveloped economies" view Strict accord with international product life cycle theory	Acknowledges tech leader and tech follower regions, but understands that useful innovation can come from anywhere.
Program-based	Relationship-based; better able to respect and leverage cultural differences
Large-agency programs are prone to bureaucratic inertia and resistance to change.	Network initiatives attract innovators and influencers in each region.
Fixed or inappropriate metrics for success; often discipline-bound.	"Fuzzy goals"; interdisciplinary, multiple-perspective, or transdisciplinary.
Money-focused	Financially responsible, but recognizes that knowledge creation, knowledge management, and sense of empowerment are as important as money to emerging regions.

Challenges of data and metrics

Recognizing that shared prosperity (like other questions addressed by his Institute) could not be resolved using the existing theory of any single discipline, Kozmetsky called it an "unstructured problem," and insisted on attacking it with teams of researchers representing many disciplines. Following McWhinney (1992), Mitroff and Linstone (1993) prefer the word *issue* to denote such an "unbounded, ill-defined, over-whelming complex of [interlocking] problems." They cogently illustrate that disciplinary approaches are not only inadequate, but dangerous:

> Consider ... the problem of drug use and addiction. ... [To an educator] the problem is one of educating young people and their families to

the dangers of drug use. ... In the language of economics, the problem is the huge profits associated with the production and consumption of illegal substances. ... In the language of social work, the problem is the breakdown of the family, the lack of male role models, and so on. In medical terms the problem is one of treating the physiology of drug addiction. For the criminal justice system, the problem is ... money for policing. For psychology, [it] is the despair of people in inner cities and the associated problems of low self-esteem. ... Each [discipline] uses different variables to structure the 'problem,' and consequently collects very different kinds of data.

Mitroff and Linstone emphasize not only that one group of researchers cannot use the others' data, but that action taken to advance one group's success metrics will exacerbate the problems as they are seen by the other groups. The social worker's free meal center for street addicts will, from the perspective of the city planner, make an already undesirable neighborhood even less attractive to business investment, and, to the economist, create a disincentive to gainful employment – notwithstanding that neither the neighborhood nor the addicts respond to positive incentives for change.

Marshall (1998) points up the relevance of this to shared prosperity. The economic trends driving the decline of America's mid-century shared prosperity are, he says, "fragmenting the country politically and exacerbating such serious social pathologies as crime, family disruptions, suicide, and mental and physical health problems." Marshall's statement supports the value of interdisciplinary approaches, of course, but also supports another principle that Kozmetsky forcefully advanced, that of "fuzzy objectives."

It is clear that in the context of an issue (or a goal) like shared prosperity, objectives of the political-slogan ilk, like "a chicken in every pot," are too slippery for constructive policy-making. What Mitroff and Linstone have made equally clear, however, is that very specific, measurable objectives such as may be advanced by any one variety of social scientist are also unusable. Kozmetsky advocated a middle path, that is, fuzzy objectives that allow a team:

- To see which direction to go;
- To redefine or reprioritize the objectives when technological change alters the situation (that the latter will happen is itself both an assumption and an objective of every shared prosperity initiative);
- To know when it is getting closer to a fuzzy objective;
- But perhaps not to know how much closer it is getting.

Unfortunately the concept of the fuzzy objective is neither mathematically precise[25] nor recognized by granting agencies or policy evaluation professionals. Fortunately, however – for they seem essential to any truly effective approach to shared prosperity – fuzzy objectives can be practical in the kind of decentralized, network-based, politically non-partisan initiative exemplified by the IC[2] Institute's research/project process. Kozmetsky habitually explained the concept to visitors by drawing co-ordinates, with time on the horizontal, and the vertical representing direction in a vaguely defined strategy space. On the right-hand end of the diagram, he drew cloudlike objects representing the fuzzy objectives. A point designated "here and now" became the apex-origin of a cone of possible strategic directions, that would intersect the cloudy targets. The Austin Software Council actually instantiated this diagram, to exhibit its own early networking strategy (Figure 4.2).

Another data problem facing shared prosperity initiatives is a bias due to the life cycle of these initiatives. Sölvell *et al.*, (2004) surveyed 239 industry cluster initiatives around the world. (Cluster initiatives are a good proxy for shared prosperity initiatives of the kind that concern us here, because they often utilize the same kind of decentralized public–private networking.) Though a very few responding initiatives were as much as twenty-five years old, 195 of the 239 had been launched within the six years ending in 2002. That is, most older initiatives had failed, run out of funding, or disbanded for some other reason (possibly

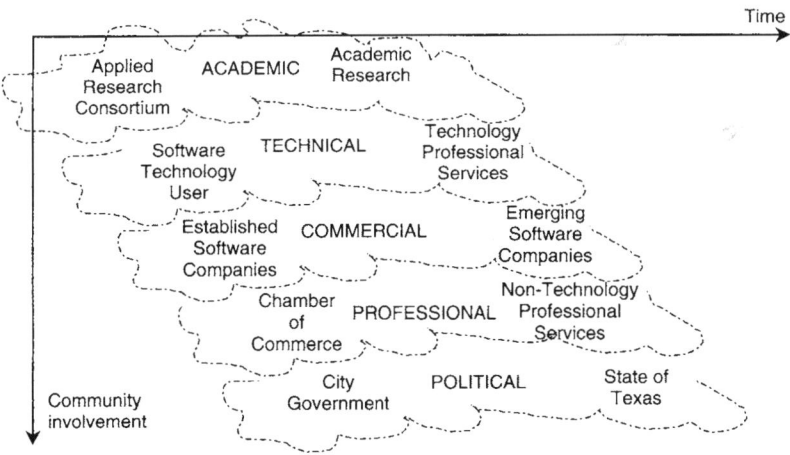

Figure 4.2 Fuzzy objectives for diverse participation in the early Austin Software Council (from an ASC planning document, c. 1994)

including success), and the newest initiatives did not yet feel confident to report on their activities.

Of course, other measurement problems for shared prosperity include the well-known difficulties of disaggregating national and state data to regional levels, and disaggregating industry data from Standard Industrial Classifications (SICs) to distinguish knowledge-based growth technology sectors.

Conclusion

Hall (1998) remarks on the "solid middle class" that made fourth century Athens a creative, booming economy, and on the high degree of social mobility that characterized the same kind of economy in renaissance Florence. Inose (quoted in Kameoka 2004) rejects the definition of competitiveness as trying to win the game by beating another; noting the Latin roots of "compete" mean "pursuing together," Inose conceives regional and industrial competition as a process wherein players correct other's weaknesses, acknowledge each other's strengths, and spur each other to greater achievement in a never-ending game. Hall's and Inose's observations are in line with the philosophy of shared prosperity.

What is the potential of shared prosperity as a school of scientific thought that will influence policy makers? Clearly, Kozmetsky's and Marshall's concepts of shared prosperity are not simply economic notions, but interdisciplinary constructs. Some of the disciplines to be tapped are shown in Table 4.4.[26] How can the walls of individual scientific

Table 4.4   Some IC[2] fellows: their expertise and affiliations

Everett Rogers[a]	Communication and Innovation Diffusion	University of New Mexico
Ken Land	Sociology	Duke University
William Barnett	Evolutionary Economics	Washington University
John Butler	Entrepreneurship	University of Texas
Steven Gomes	Alliances	Cal State Northridge
Angelos Angelou	Economic Development	Angelou Economic Advisors
Miroslav Benda	Supply Chain Management	Amazon.com
Corey Carbonara	Telecommunications	Baylor University
Xuelin Chu	Business Education – China	University of Science & Technology, Hefei
Kenneth Eickmann	Construction	University of Texas
Kenneth Flamm	Political Science / International Affairs	University of Texas
Antonio Furino	Health Care Policy	University of Texas
Kiyoshi Niwa	Systems Science	University of Tokyo
Seigfried Hecker	Technology Policy	Los Alamos National Laboratory
Laurence Hurley	Biotechnology	University of Arizona
Rustam Lalalka	Development Economics	Business & Tech. Devel. Strategies Inc.
Nikolay Rogalyev	Innovation in Russia	Moscow Power Engineering Institute
Tae Kyung Sung	Korean Technology Development	Kyonggi University

Note: [a] Pioneer communications theorist Everett Rogers passed away in 2004. Chapter 22 remarks on Rogers' roles in technopolis development.

disciplines be breached to instigate ongoing cross-disciplinary dialog for shared prosperity?

These questions are important because, inter alia, the domestic and foreign policies of national governments should encourage stability. Foreign policies should not, however, encourage the false stability of autocracy and extreme income inequality. They should support the kind of stability that comes from a democratic process and a large middle class that is educated to use and value the democratic process. No existing theory encompasses the latter kind of policy.

A new theory of political economy is needed. It is my hope that it will be called "Shared Prosperity," that the IC^2 Fellows will continue to write books and articles that will be widely discussed,[27] and that a well-considered and well-defined concept of shared prosperity will become as fundamental an economic notion as free markets or international trade. The right-hand column of Table 4.3 summarizes the current, fledgling status of this theory. This chapter has also set forth some guidelines for axioms of a future formalization of "fuzzy objectives," anticipating that this will be a needed part of any shared prosperity theory.

"Two key realities can change everything," said Kozmetsky, "The distance-canceling power of internet and web-based communication [increase] the possibility of global access to talent, technology, capital, and know-how. The objective is wealth creation and shared prosperity: Networking society for social, economic, political, scientific, and technological development."

Notes

1. George Kozmetsky passed away in April, 2003, leaving hundreds of colleagues, students, and Fellows of the institute he founded (the IC^2 Institute at the University of Texas at Austin) wishing to carry on and extend his work. To that purpose this chapter is respectfully dedicated.
2. http://r0.unctad.org/ecommerce/event_docs/estrategies/mann.ppt
3. Though buying into the ideal of shared prosperity, Sachs (1998) takes a negative view of the way the phrase has been used to date: "America has wanted global leadership on the cheap [and] that pressures on the rich countries to do more for the poorer countries could be contained by the dream of universal economic growth." This results, he says, in "a phony Washington consensus on how to achieve shared prosperity." Sach's comments are best interpreted simply as fair warning that any idea can be misused, with possibly dire social consequences. The present paper, in any event, emphasizes that a constructive framework for shared prosperity is more complex than the simplistic trickle-down economics that Sachs was attacking.
4. http://www.picced.org/publications.php

5. http://www.phillyimc.org/article.pl?op=EmailStory& sid=04/10/14/1438218&mode=thread
6. http://spcusp.org/
7. http://www.iso.ch/iso/en/commcentre/pdf/WSD0010.pdf
8. http://www.dfait-maeci.gc.ca/foreign_policy/commonwealth/ imoc315-en.asp
9. http://www.thecheshirepartnership.org.uk/Shared_Body.htm
10. http://www.wpusa.org/index.pl
11. http://www.defenceindia.com/14-feb-2k5/news17.html
12. http://news.marweb.com/morocco/icc_marrakesh.htm
13. http://www.embassyofindia.com/12_IndiaNewsDecember2004/page4.html
14. http://europa.eu.int/comm/enterprise/library/enterprise-europe/ issue17/articles/en/topic1_en.htm
15. http://www.adb.org/Documents/Speeches/2000/ms2000021.asp
16. http://pnwer.org/links/North%20American%20Leaders% 20Unveil%20Security%20and%20Prosperity%20Partnership% 20-%20US%20Department%20of%20State.htm
17. http://www.imf.org/external/np/speeches/2004/011204.htm
18. http://pm.gc.ca/eng/news.asp?id=284
19. http://www.unctadxi.org/templates/News_853.aspx
20. http://www.oecd.org/document/62/0,2340,en_2649_201185_ 31935102_1_1_1,00.html
21. Consensus emerges conspicuously often in the Netherlands, where it is therefore a feasible criterion for public and private initiatives.
22. www.ic2.org
23. http://www.ic2.org/main.php?a=2&s=6. This description of CBIRD is paraphrased from the web site.
24. Ibid.
25. A step in the right direction is the "fuzzy cognitive map" proposed by Cordero and Pelaez (2002); see also Xirogiannis and Glykas (2004). When policy variables are involved, fuzzy cognitive maps could be a useful adjunct to or substitute for Porter's "cluster dynamics."
26. The present author is also a Senior Fellow (and former Research Director) of the IC^2 Institute.
27. A committee of the IC^2 Fellows met in Mexico in June, 2003, and clarified the following: All are committed to carrying on the Kozmetsky legacy, but they also take seriously their scholarly leadership in their respective fields. That is, they would not research and write about shared prosperity solely as a tribute to Kozmetsky. Rather, the subject interests them because of its real potential for structuring, verification, and policy impact.

5
The Business School in a Time of Transition

Fred Phillips

The first new faculty chairs endowed under a technopolis initiative tend to be in the engineering and biosciences departments. Then the university's Patent and Licensing Office is beefed up with lawyers and brokers. The business school, as some techno-regions have proved, may be relegated to hind teat or excluded from the banquet altogether. This may be the fault of university administrators who underestimate the b-school's potential contributions, or of engineer-entrepreneurs who have not yet learned to respect marketing. But it may just as possibly be a result of the b-school failing to show interest and initiative.

How can an ambitious graduate school of business capitalize on its reputation, conduct itself as a leading educational institution, and further increase its stature as a school of top rank? The business school in the technopolis faces new and exciting challenges. Each school must refine its strategies for serving local, regional and global constituencies; for excelling in research and education; for attracting and retaining faculty; and for systematic long range planning.

These challenges involve both the business school's own initiatives and the ways in which the business school helps the university pursue its mission. What will it take for a school to meet its challenges and enhance its leadership position? Vision, creativity, energy and daring will separate the ongoing and future leaders from the has-beens. This chapter looks at the several roles of a business school in an aspiring techno-region.

Local, regional, and global roles: the case of the University of Texas' McCombs School of Business

The University of Texas is one of Austin's largest employers. As a state university, UT has a public purpose ("to transform lives for the benefit of society"), further accentuating its responsibility as a corporate citizen. The McCombs School and the university serve the Austin community as direct providers of jobs and knowledge, instruments for the realization of minority communities' economic aspirations, as well as those of the community at large, and creators of new enterprises and economic development based on university knowledge spin-off.

UT-Austin's role as the University of Texas System's flagship campus must not distract the McCombs School from its responsibilities to the local economy.

The School's responsibilities, of course, do extend to wider geographies. Austin is the hub of a vital region that includes Texas, New Mexico, Chihuahua, Coahuila, Nuevo León, and Tamaulipas. This region boasts a population in excess of thirty million, several eminent engineering and business schools, major commercial cities and ports, important national laboratories, and great centers of art, music and tourism. In short, all the ingredients for vigorous economic growth.

These ingredients were present thirty years ago, proved themselves in recent decades, and are still producing technology and business growth. One might ask, what is different now? The answer is that while there are still tensions between the region's ethnic communities and tragic histories to live down, the tide has turned. The interface between cultures is now more positive than otherwise, and we see tremendous cultural vitality in Texas and environs. One of the next great world cultures is arising in the areas surrounding the Gulf of Mexico and the Caribbean. Two capitals of this new culture will be Miami and the Austin-San Antonio metro.

More recent tragedies prove the global arena cannot be ignored. If UT is to maintain and expand its leadership role in Latin America and in other world regions, the McCombs School must be highly experienced and active in international affairs. Violent factions in the Middle East believe that globalization – which they clearly equate with Americanization – not only fails to benefit them, but harms their economy and endangers their way of life. The same belief can be found, and sometimes justified, in Latin America. What part of Latin America will be the next Afghanistan? How can better business practices prevent a violent conflict there? As the US embargo on Cuban trade quietly ends, we should remember that our support of that nation's dictator led to a revolution and the exclusion of American business activity there. The establishment of a new relationship with Cuba is a rich field for policy discussion within the McCombs School of Business, as is the financial volatility in Argentina.

Social stability serves the interests of business, and US policies should encourage stability. (In the past, disruption was also good for business, but in a globalized economy this is less true. Analyses in the press indicate the current war against terrorism did nothing to ameliorate the recession.) Our foreign policies should not encourage the false stability of autocracy and extreme income inequality. They should support the kind of stability that comes from a democratic process and a large middle class that is educated to use and value the democratic process. There is no name for the latter kind of policy, because no existing theory encompasses it; a new theory of political economy is needed.[1] Business schools can help formulate it with colleagues from liberal arts, public policy, and humanities departments.

Corporations must compete globally, and need to spread product development costs over a global customer base. They need new growth opportunities, and generally speaking, want to acquire them ethically and with care for the environment. The earth is home to six billion people, and cannot support a large number of people consuming energy and materials at the rate Americans (a quarter billion of us) do today. By 2025, according to UN forecasts, two billion people will have disposable income. They cannot use the high-energy, high-waste products on the market today, but rather will want and buy products that fit their needs and budgets. There are immense growth opportunities in products that:

- Use reduced energy to produce, distribute, consume and recycle.
- Fit the needs and lifestyles of developing markets.
- Protect populations, markets, and the Earth for the long run.

I advocate a business school curriculum that offers students the chance to pioneer these products and markets.

The globalization movement seeks to accord greater powers and greater protection to corporations that operate across national boundaries. This will shift power away from sovereign and local governments. We don't yet know whether this is good or bad, but it implies an urgent task for universities and business schools, namely, to re-examine the role of the corporation in society.

Research

In a business school, not all faculty research requires daily interaction with businesses. It is absurd, though, for faculty to be out of touch with industry's people, problems and resources. Industry cooperative research is an important growth area for b-schools, especially as federal research funds diminish. It is the responsibility of the School's leadership to find and foster the right kinds of faculty–industry interaction.

During the "mathematical revolution" of the 1950s and 1960s, quantitative methods originating in business schools had a terrific impact on operations, finance and marketing in industry. These very powerful advances in methodology put universities in the position of bestowing knowledge on industry. Now, however, the major benefits from the mathematical revolution have been realized. New business problems have arisen – globalization of markets, the rise of high-tech companies, newly multicultural workforces, and so on – that are not amenable to solution by these methods. In the 1990s, many professors describe industry best practices, and show "follower" companies how to apply the best practices. However, new theory, new methodology, new data, and new problems are always playing leap-frog in every scientific discipline. Eventually the time will come when theory and methodology, the strong points of the university, will rise in importance again.

Meanwhile, every leading university must find a way to lead! Industry does not lead in every area of knowledge formation, and it is incumbent on the b-school to lead in those niches where the university can lead. The b-school can also take the lead in initiating new, cross-sector alliances that leverage the university's research strengths for worthwhile programs. Examples include public–private business incubators, internship programs, and knowledge exchanges with foreign cities for purposes of economic development.

Leading business schools should lobby governments and foundations to initiate research policies that allow important projects like these to move forward quickly.

Ethics and complex systems

Lifelong learning and corporate training needs, the rate of change in educational and other technologies, adult versus adolescent learning styles, competition for students, and many other forces generate challenges for business educators.

Physicians take an oath, after Hippocrates, to do no harm. Lawyers swear to uphold the US Constitution. What of MBA students, who have an equal impact on our society? They graduate if they get adequate grades in their technical courses, and are not required to swear to a single thing. Especially after a debacle like the fall of Enron, we must wonder why this is so. Business schools, perhaps via the accrediting bodies AACSB and EQUIS, would do well to design an oath for business students that will remind them of their responsibility to society, and that will be widely adopted by schools of business.

We must go beyond teaching students to tolerate diversity, and teach them to comprehend the opportunities and limitations implied by the enormous complexity of the globalized business environment, as well as the practical skills to manage multi-country alliances and projects. Maastricht School of Management Dean Ronald Tuninga says,

> We at MSM strongly believe that bringing people together from all over the world helps create a better understanding among people from different cultures and helps us to build safer societies and more socially responsible businesses. As we have seen in world events in the past two years, people educated in the tradition of Maastricht School of Management are more necessary than ever before. Culturally sensitive, tolerant and ethically and socially responsible managers can help build companies that are responsive to the needs of many stakeholders and society.

Indeed, academics do a better job than business people when it comes to handling multiple stakeholders. Only academics can keep students, parents, faculty, trustees, corporations, donors, legislators, and funding agencies happy all at once, and juggle multiple product lines at the same time.

Nor are "safer societies and socially responsible businesses" simply platitudes. In 1992, Francis Fukuyama (the afore-cited author of much useful work on social capital) wrote a book called *The End of History and the Last Man*. In it, he theorized that while further regional conflicts are probably inevitable, the globalization of liberal democratic capitalism was "the final resting point of history." Now, globalization means that all parts of the world are connected. I wonder whether Mr Fukuyama was aware of something Marshall McLuhan said in *1962*:

> We shall at once move into a phase of panic terrors, exactly befitting a small world of tribal drums, total interdependence, and superimposed coexistence. ... Terror is the normal state of any ["oral" or connected] society, for in it, everything affects everything all the time. (Davis 1998, p. 302)

Indeed, today's unrest is greatest in parts of the world that have few extra resources to buffer the region against the tight connections of globalization. Fukuyama understood the complexities of his argument and the exceptions to it, but in light of the September 11 and March 11 tragedies, we must conclude that the main thrust of his thesis was naïve.

Vaclav Havel, the playwright who became the first post-Soviet president of the Czech Republic, perceives that global technological civilization, though here to stay, is only a "thin veneer" over an unchanged human nature, over an "immense variety of cultures, of peoples, of religious worlds, of historical traditions and historically formed attitudes." Havel goes on[2] to note that

> even as the veneer of world civilization expands ... ancient traditions are reviving, different religions and cultures are awakening to new ways of being, seeking new room to exist ... and to be granted a right to life ... [and] a political expression.

At the same time, the secretary general of the United Nations has asked the international business community to embrace sustainable development, social development and human rights. Tuninga notes, "The Secretary General's implication that international business is best placed to help the international community bring about such long term aims of global development underscores the important role and social responsibility of the business community. At MSM, we have recognized this responsibility, and have broadened the curriculum to include corporate social responsibility and the ethical values and norms which are essential in the global economy of the 21st century."

Ultimately it is on the basis of these norms and values that trust relationships, which enable international commercial cooperation can be further developed and nurtured.

Vaclav Havel sees this as a central challenge to every part of today's world,

> to start understanding itself as a multicultural and multipolar civilization, whose meaning lies not in undermining the individuality of different spheres of culture ... but in allowing them to be more completely themselves. This will only be possible, even conceivable, if we all accept a basic code of mutual co-existence ... one that will enable us to go on living side by side. ... Yet such a code won't stand a chance if it is merely the product of the few who then proceed to force it on the rest. It must be an expression of the authentic will of everyone, growing out of ... our original spiritual and moral substance, which [in turn] grew out of the same essential experience of humanity.

McLuhan's vision implies that terrorist bombers are somehow inevitable in a connected world – an integral expression of the nature of this world, rather than an external threat to it. Nevertheless, each of us will decide as individuals whether to be part of the problem or part of the solution.

Havel asked whether his idea of a new, common creed was "hopelessly utopian." Business professors and students know that new products – and a new idea can be considered a new product – penetrate the market because there are "innovators" and "early adopters." Thus, we may reply to Vaclav Havel, it *is* utopian to expect everyone to accept a code of mutual co-existence all at once. At first, and at any stage, some people will, and some people won't. B-schools may urge students to be innovators in seeking the common spirit that will unite us.

What does that mean? What, specifically, can each of us do?

In 2004, four American business deans (Bisoux 2004) offered answers to this question. Their answers are:

- Social entrepreneurship.
- Post-conflict planning studies.
- Affirmative inquiry.
- Personal relationships.

To freely interpret each these:

Social entrepreneurship. The best-known instance of this phenomenon is micro-loan programs, which provide both an ROI for the investor and sustenance for the needy. Even beyond those worthy results, however, these programs show young people that there are paths out of poverty that do not involve the taking up of arms.

Post-conflict planning studies. These efforts allow participants to form a positive vision in which their regional conflict is not unending, and in which desirable things will happen after the coming of the peace.

Affirmative inquiry. Guided discussion that focuses on the positive changes that can be made, rather than on blame and the negative aspects of current realities. Affirmative inquiry also involves building a classroom environment in which world political conflicts are not assumed to be "ongoing," and in which students feel empowered to ask, "How can I make a difference?"

Personal relationships. Classroom projects, summer institutes, and entire new schools are built around joint efforts of students from both sides of a conflict. Worthy social entrepreneurship projects are often the result.

I will add that at MSM, we insist on mutual courtesy and respect among all the ethnicities represented at our school. This is not because we naively believe that commerce and trade are the common factors that will create peace in the world. Rather, we believe along with Vaclav Havel that displaying respect in this way is simply right – a central part of the code of co-existence that will allow us to survive and thrive.

Faculty

It is a networked world now, and the school must provide faculty with technology for research collaboration with distant colleagues, access to teaching assistants from other universities, and the wide-area sharing of curriculum. Any inter-institutional agreement that is needed for faculty collaboration should be facilitated and given every opportunity to prove its value. Networking also means helping external constituents, including donors, see the value of the faculty's work.

The school's mission presumably includes educating undergraduates, MBAs, Ph.D.s, and working executives; serving the community and region; and providing the research base and Ph.D. graduates that will form the next generation of business faculty. To these ends, the school's faculty must have high morale and great commitment. These come from a shared excitement about the future, and from fair and frequent recognition of achievements.

The Dean must link the School's strategy to individual incentives and accountability. This is not incompatible with maintaining high morale, especially when there is open sharing of information about finances and incentives.

Business schools will continue to generate new knowledge. There will be rules, pressures, and opportunities for the school to profit by treating the new knowledge as "intellectual property," but faculty researchers must retain the choice to freely disseminate their discoveries when it is legal to do so. Even "free" knowledge published in books and journals yields positive returns to the university from seminar registrations, publication sales, and enhanced reputation. The b-school must vigorously market the intellectual output of business professors, whether "free" or "IP." This requires increasing staff support for editing, marketing, multimedia production, public relations, and liaison with the university's intellectual property office.

The future of the business school

Michael Dell has aptly stated that US businesses have completed no more than ten percent of the transformations that new technologies have made possible and necessary. Dell is referring to productivity gains from information technology, and the potential of these gains to transform business. Beyond this, new industries will soon arise from biotechnology, nanotechnology, quantum devices, and space technology, in addition to the world-products industries mentioned earlier. Top business schools face still-unimagined changes in the near future, as they design and deliver curricula to prepare students to lead in these new industries, and in extremely computer-augmented traditional industries.

For this reason, a business school would be well advised to initiate a standing skunk-works/planning team, with a mission to create and feasibility-test scenarios for the future of the school. Joint curriculum with the engineering school can give business students overviews of new industries' technological underpinnings, and personal connections with the technologists who will make those industries' products. Scenarios for the technological future must also include instructional technologies that are best suited for teaching business.

As state funding decreases and compliance burdens increase, some leading schools are looking at alternative organizational forms, including privatizing some or all of the business school operations. These options must be examined – with great caution.

A pre-eminent school must make plans that are big, bold and worthwhile – and back up the plans with resources and competent people. The plans require intensive fundraising, and intelligently spending funds that have already been raised. They require leading local, regional, and global constituencies toward change while learning from them and remaining attentive to their sensibilities. They require pushing the envelopes of research, education, and service. They require taking charge of issues that lesser institutions think of as beyond their control.

The technological future means new markets and opportunities for ethical b-schools

This section highlights three new opportunities for initiative in business education. They represent the long term, the middle term, and the short term. These are, respectively, the space program; maintaining scientific/technological competence; and the AIDS crisis.

Systems without back-up are rarely fail-safe. As long as the human race is confined to planet Earth, we are vulnerable to plagues, roaming asteroids, or other environmental disaster. The only truly sustainable development open to us is manned space flight.

The space program is a striking example of a powerful principle: Technological change both causes and responds to social change, and in either case, new markets are created. The program's progress reflects the sociopolitical events (Second World War rocketry, the international tensions leading to Sputnik and the US moon landing of 1969, and the shuttle disasters) that fire our imagination and our will. The space program also drives popular culture (e.g., the *Star Wars* films), and serves as a frame for popular conceptions of our future and our psyche (*Star Trek, Alien*). The business opportunities are not just in entertainment and lifestyle products, of course. There are consumer and healthcare product spinoffs, famously Tang and medical telemetry. There is the potential of mining space for energy and materials. There are current commercial battles for control of the satellite bandwidth that serves our telephony, television, and global positioning systems. There is a market for experimentation and prototype production services on the space station. There will be unimagined markets created by as yet undiscovered knowledge "out there." Meanwhile, the current phrase "low-orbit economic zone" inspires hope for the future of the human race as well as profit calculations.

The low-orbit space shuttle also exemplifies the middle-term issue: maintaining scientific and technological competence. The engineers who worked on high-orbit and lunar Apollo projects are retired or deceased. They did not transmit their knowledge to a younger generation; high-orbit technology will have to be rediscovered at huge and unnecessary expense. Declining public and private funding of science in the United States also endangers the continuity of competence, *inter alia* because this funding supports Ph.D. students. Other dangers are the outsourcing of technical jobs overseas, and the new difficulties faced by those seeking visas for graduate study in the United States. These connect with the value placed on science within the current social worldview, and the consequent motivation, or rather de-motivation, of American youth to seek careers within and around the lab-to-market pipeline (e.g., in science, engineering, product design, policy, sociology, finance, health care, civics, alliance management, and economic development) pictured in Figure I.1 "The innovation arrow."

A hundred years ago, funding for science (then mostly from wealthy individuals) and the public's need for science were both haphazard. In the more complex society of the mid-century, science (specifically, radar, cryptography, the Manhattan project) saved the day. The ensuing social contract with the Manhattan scientists, which led to decades of public support for university research, is now expiring. Globalization, and its resulting pressure for short-term bottom-line performance of corporations, is reducing private R&D expenditures. Society grows more complex rather than less, and will turn to scientists and engineers for solutions to the problems of complexity (as is the case now with health care and bioterrorism) regardless of the facts of fewer dollars and fewer scientific and engineering personnel. Thus does science interface with trends in taxation and public finance, international trade, ideology, security, and the US role in the post-Cold-War world. I hope it will continue to do so, despite the present loss of knowledge and people. Where do business schools enter this picture? With new knowledge-management and expert system products, and new business models that find and deliver value to people willing to pay for the preservation of knowledge.

Terrible though they are, terrorism and traffic accidents kill very few people compared to AIDS. Worldwide, AIDS takes fourth place among causes of death, according to the World Health Organization, and is now the number-one overall cause of death in Africa. One in four African children are now orphans, and the number of orphans will double in the next seven years. Scientifically, the problem involves epidemiology, virology and immunology. Technologically, it involves design, production, storage, transportation and delivery of anti-retroviral therapies. Sociologically, attitudes about therapies, condom use and relations between the sexes; education and dosage design to ensure patients of varied cultural backgrounds and literacy levels follow their therapeutic regimens; training of health care personnel; political leadership; and protection of drug patents are merely the tip of the iceberg. Parentless children will create new social structures (surrogate families), strain old ones (fostering and adoption), and exacerbate existing tragedies (youth gangs, civil wars fought with child-soldiers). AIDS is the leading cause of death for teachers in South Africa and elsewhere in the continent, and students must drop out in order to care for ailing parents. The crisis will be faced, then, by a less-educated African populace. In America, AIDS appears to be the leading cause of death in inner cities, though this statistic is confounded with numbers describing drug use. Drug users are more susceptible to contracting and suffering the worst consequences of HIV, and so in the United States the technical and social problems of HIV/AIDS are bound up with a host of drug-related issues.

Business schools can address the technological and sociological aspects of the crisis, because these aspects imply markets and products. B-schools have the tools, too: Logistics, alliance management, design of training programs, intellectual property management, non-profit management, and so on. Why do we not see more b-school programs aimed at the big questions? The schools that attempt it will earn distinctive recognition.

The university's unique strengths

Our intellectual property and venture capital systems do not deal with the very long term. Universities are well-practiced in the long-term orientation. Thus the university should deal with the long-term issue of our space and interplanetary settlements. For exactly the same reasons, the b-school should engage with the AIDS crisis: Intellectual property considerations can work against the wide availability of cheap therapies, and the "market" of AIDS sufferers in the world's poorest communities does not attract investors. The school should work with non-profits, foundations, and NGOs to find better, cheaper, and more culturally acceptable ways to ameliorate this terrible situation – and, perhaps, to find creative ways to structure solutions as attractive investment opportunities.

As for maintaining scientific and lab-to-market competence, there is no better place to do this than an institution of higher education that is dedicated to stewarding knowledge as well as creating and disseminating it. The university, however, cannot do this alone. It must reach out to national laboratories, economic development agencies, and others who have incentives, resources and expertise to portray science as important for society's future, and mentors to transmit tacit knowledge in a timely way.

Notes

1. Chapter 4 herein suggests the name "shared prosperity."
2. http://old.hrad.cz/president/Havel/speeches/1995/0806_uk.html

6
Anointing a "City of Light and Wisdom"

David Gibson

The concept of technopolis was introduced to Austin more than a decade ago.

The setting was an international conference in March of 1987, hosted by the University of Texas' IC^2 (Innovation, Creativity, Capital) Institute. Participants came from Japan, China, England, France and the silicon centers of the US to present their views on emerging issues in technology commercialization and economic development.

But the roots of technopolis – a Utopian, radiant city based on science and technology – sprang from the humanistic mind of the Renaissance. The first example was T. Campanella's 17th-century vision of a "City of the Sun." This was a culturally diverse, polytechnical city – a showcase of science and continuing education. There, science was not just for an aristocratic elite. Philosophers, political planners and social prophets were intrigued by the idea of creating a "city of light," designed and ruled by wise scientists, where research and innovation were a way of life and invention and creativity were venerated. These ideal cities were to be the poles around which the economy of nations would grow and society would progress.

The modern "technopolis" – "techno" for technology and "polis," Greek for city-state – combines scientific research and invention with the practical applications of technology through innovation.

The Japanese brought the ancient technopolis concept into modern terms in the early 1980s, when their trade ministry envisioned a techno-state of research cities. These regions, known as technopoleis, were to become the center of Japanese scientific and technology-based research in the 21st century and they would include universities, science centers, industrial research parks, research and development consortia, venture capital foundations, offices, convention centers and new towns.

This could be a description of Austin, 1999.

In a technopolis today, the emphasis is on collaboration among business, academic and government sectors at the regional level to speed economic development and improve quality of life. The concept emphasizes that we are living in a profoundly different world, more than we were even a decade ago. Technology is dramatically altering the shape and direction of society and the world's economies, and the way people think and act.

No matter what field we are talking about – advanced manufacturing, aeronautics, electronics, genetics, medical, education, entertainment and the media, the environment and education – the digital economy and the global marketplace are creating revolutionary opportunities perhaps not seen since the Renaissance.

"Technology continues to shrink the world. There is no choice other than to participate in the global community ... This is what the 21st century is all about," said Dr George Kozmetsky, a successful entrepreneur, former dean of UT's College and Graduate School of Business and founder of the IC^2 Institute.

We still have a lot to learn about how to make these sustainable cities of light and wisdom. The world's two most mature technopoleis – Silicon Valley and Route 128 in Boston – developed rather spontaneously, and they didn't even get much attention until the early 1970s. Throughout the last decade, academic, business and political leaders from around the US and the world have come to Austin to study and learn from "The Austin Model" that accelerated technopolis development. These leaders want to know how Austin built such a successful technopolis in about 15 years, considerably faster than other regions of the world.

While there's no step-by-step formula for success, there are several important factors:

- Quality education at all levels, from kindergarten to the graduate student and beyond.
- Visionaries and implementers at the regional level who come from academia, business and government.
- An entrepreneurial culture: A technopolis is energized by startups and mid-size firms, not just large ones.
- The best technology research – that leads to new industries and home-grown tech companies.
- Globally competitive infrastructure – both "physical" as in roads, airports, the Internet, and city services; and "smart," as in talent, capital and know-how.

- A quality of life that attracts and keeps a broad range of talented people, including educators, artists, writers, musicians and poets as well as business people and entrepreneurs.
- Enlightened government with a regional and, increasingly, a global orientation.

As Austin becomes an increasingly important global technopolis in the 21st century, we have to ask ourselves some important questions:

- How can we better link creativity in the public and private sectors to speed innovation in the marketplace? By doing that, we can more quickly develop new and useful technologies.
- How can Austin train and educate the workforce needed for the 21st century, a workforce that includes all sectors of the area's population?
- How can we share the wealth? The average citizen in Silicon Valley – restaurant workers, educators, city employees, artists and police officers – can't afford to live in the heart of their thriving technopolis.
- How can Austin keep unbridled growth and greed from destroying the aspects of quality of life that gave birth to our technopolis?
- How will the distance-canceling power of the Internet impact our region – and the globe? No longer do all the technologists, entrepreneurs, business talent and venture capitalists have to be in the same city.

In 1623, Campanella offered a Utopian vision of "cities of light and wisdom." Is such a vision possible or even desirable for Austin? In the future, this column will look at challenges to, and the successes of, The Austin Model, as well as the characteristics of emerging, developing, and mature technopoleis worldwide.

7
Advantage Austin II

George Kozmetsky and Patricia A. Hayes

During the coming weeks, volunteers will call on more than 800 businesses to participate in Advantage Austin II, a four-year program sponsored by the Greater Austin Chamber of Commerce. While the business and civic reasons for participating are compelling, we offer additional support from the perspective of educators with a stake in this community.

We see Advantage Austin II as an investment in the future economic vitality of Austin. The program will help create jobs, diversify the economy, improve primary and secondary education, support small businesses, enhance Austin's national image, and provide overall economic leadership. It will help Austin continue its recovery from the 1980s downturn and become the kind of prosperous, forward-looking city in which universities – and indeed most people – want to reside.

This is not idle talk. Advantage Austin II follows three years of the first Advantage Austin program, which has produced an array of far-reaching results. Several of those results involve higher education and illustrate the impact on the greater Austin community.

For example, Advantage Austin funds permitted the chamber to be a charter sponsor of the Austin Technology Incubator, a project of the University of Texas Graduate School of Business, the City of Austin, and the Greater Austin Chamber of Commerce. The goal of Austin Technology Incubator is to help grow entrepreneurial companies which have the potential to become significant contributors to the employment base. In less than two years, the incubator has grown to house 17 companies.

Another example is the chamber's involvement in the recruitment of new employers, such as semiconductor industry suppliers. The fact that companies like Applied Materials are creating jobs and construction activity in Austin is a powerful statement about the appeal of Austin, the strength of our university research, and the chamber's Advantage Austin marketing program.

Advantage Austin has also led to the recruitment of the Dallas Cowboys training camp to St Edward's University. The presence of the Cowboys camp has brought regional attention to St Edward's and its programs. For Austin, the recruitment has brought an economic infusion, a lot of fun and excitement, and a new focus on sports as a targeted industry.

The announcement by PBS that Austin will be the site for the National Issues Convention in January 1992 is yet another product of the Advantage Austin program working with the University of Texas. For the university, it will be a first-hand opportunity for government and political science students to witness a historic change in the way television covers presidential campaigns.

For Austin, it will generate an estimated $10 million in economic impact and give us a historic role as a city. This event is expected to bring 1,000 journalists to Austin and generate significant media coverage as part of the Advantage Austin national public relations effort.

Once again, without the leadership of the business community, and the partnership with the University of Texas, this project would not have selected Austin.

With these successes of Advantage Austin, what does Advantage Austin II hold? Continued momentum – and new initiatives in job creation, small business assistance, national marketing, technology incubation, support for schools, and overall economic vitality.

Advantage Austin II is an action-oriented investment. It provides leadership to carry Austin toward excellence. Some communities are content with mediocrity. Not Austin, where we recognize that our future depends on educating our children, preparing our work force, and nurturing the companies that will provide jobs in the coming decade.

We are fortunate to have a business community that takes an enlightened, leadership role in economic issues. Advantage Austin merits the financial support of the business community at large, and we urge area businesses to consider a significant investment.

Part II
Portland

8
Portland Looks at International Benchmarks

Fred Phillips

Representatives of Oregon, Washington, Sweden, Taiwan, Canada, Washington D.C., Texas, North Carolina, and Hawaii gathered in Portland for two days of case studies and moderated group discussions to explore best practices for integrating technology commercialization, entrepreneurship, and economic development efforts for sustainable growth.

Topline findings

1. Metropolitan regions ("citistates") are replacing nations, states, counties, and municipalities as the loci of entrepreneurial economic development.

   - New intergovernmental and public–private initiatives will emerge to coordinate intra-regional development.
   - New "diplomatic" protocols will develop for managing relationships between metropolitan regions.

     CHALLENGE: If a distant region wants to establish ties *today* with the Portland metro area for economic, workforce, and intellectual exchange, what would the first step be? The second step? Third?

2. The point of a healthy entrepreneurial economy is political self-determination.

   - Sustainability means sustaining our social values as well as the physical environment.
   - Sustainable development is therefore self-defeating if it is coercive.

CHALLENGE: To wisely manage the forces of differentiation (e.g., the differing tax structures of Washington and Oregon, the multicultural workforce) and the forces of homogenization (e.g., free trade).

3. We derive economic advantage from our cultural uniqueness.

   - Our ways of urban planning and environmental protection socialize our residents, attract like-minded companies, and make "Made in Oregon" an appealing brand.
   - Environmental quality is critical for economic development. It attracts clean companies and reduces future remediation costs.

   CHALLENGE: Because of differing cultures, the role of government differs in techno-regions worldwide. This complicates our interactions with them and forces us to coordinate our public and private efforts.

4. A pre-eminent research university is not critical to Portland's success.[1]

   - Many local technology companies, both small and large, generate intellectual property and entrepreneurs.
   - Our universities can increase the entrepreneurial activity of the engineers we do have in Oregon and Washington universities, help corporate intrapreneurs, and network them with resources worldwide.

   CHALLENGE: The universities must leverage the Internet to coordinate resources locally and globally, and do this as well as private companies do. Public–private initiatives must also move at Internet speeds.

Entrepreneurial metro areas

Former Austin City Manager Dr Camille Barnett argued that cities are the center for entrepreneurship, and entrepreneurship can be fostered. Cities are not islands, but *citistates*, encompassing a metropolitan region, and entrepreneurial programs must take this into account. Her "five I's" for citistate entrepreneurial success are:

1. Images – create a visual image of public–private collaboration and systematic innovation to attract entrepreneurs, who "run in packs."

2. Incentives – encourage entrepreneurs through public/private development policies, tax incentives, incubators, and the like.
3. Ideas – experiment, share ideas, lead from within.
4. Industry – have constancy of purpose, follow through and become used to hard work as a way of life.
5. Indicators – benchmark the process and use results to shape public and private policies.

The resulting "civic entrepreneurs" are those that think outside the industry they are in, whether public or private, seek collaborations and address sustainability issues in economic development.

Four factors influence entrepreneurship and sustainable cities. They are: population growth, urbanization, a globalized economy and the decline of the nation state. Key issues for US cities in the future will be: a) disparity in incomes in our communities; b) urban sprawl, and c) governance, since the emerging governing "bodies" are global, regional and neighborhood, replacing city, state and country.

Summaries of case studies

Case Study #1, Hsinchu Science Based Industrial Park

Dr Alvin Tong, who had served as Deputy Director-General in the early years of the Hsinchu SBIP maintained that sustained top government leadership and commitment enabled the Park to develop and grow so quickly. Government's role in "cutting red tape" was as important as the five- year tax exemption provided to companies locating in the Park. Other important factors were the presence of two research universities, a national research institute and a technical high school within the Park, which not only gave the Park an instant "high tech" image, but provided trained workers and technologies. Later enhancements such as parks and recreational facilities enhanced the quality of life image.

The Park is now completely full, following a decade or more of development. Most of the companies started in the Park (86 percent of the revenue) are in computers and peripherals, 14 percent are in optoelectronics, and only 1 percent are in biotechnology. The vast majority (80–85 percent) of the companies are Taiwanese in origin, most of them entrepreneurial startups originally. This government driven model is considered ideal by several countries, which are trying to replicate it (e.g. China).

Case Study #2, Tri-Cities, Washington

Mr Mike Schwenk described the efforts of the Tri-Cities, Washington in transitioning their economy from federal government-based to private industry-based. He pointed out that, while many economic development groups emphasize the high-risk recruitment of companies to relocate to their areas, the real economic growth is through fostering existing companies and entrepreneurs who will start new companies.

In the case of the Tri-Cities, very few companies have relocated, but existing companies have benefited from public–private programs and more than fifty new companies have been started. As in other areas, the availability of a major research institution (Pacific Northwest National Laboratory); a university campus, Washington State University; the Tri-Cities Science and Technology Park; three high-tech incubators; and federal government funds, have all contributed to this growth. After a nucleating period of 3 to 4 years, they are now seeing major job growth. Recognizing the global nature of the high-tech industry, the Tri-Cities has also embarked on a set of "sister" relationships – sister city, S&T Park, University and high school – with Taiwan. This extensive networking is intended to foster exchange of ideas, people, technologies, and hopefully, companies in the future.

Case Study #3, Hjalmstad, Sweden

According to Dr Börje Årnedal, universities in Sweden are networked into an entrepreneurial consortium that links undergraduate engineers and scientists to the world of high-tech business. A university curriculum on New Product Development combines technical and business education, and the students are helped to form their own companies upon graduation; or they join existing companies with new product ideas. Technoparks and incubators have been established around the universities to accommodate these new startups. A venture capital network was formed to help finance them. This same university network also supplies technical assistance to Swedish companies, large and small. Over 1000 projects have been completed, creating 1200 new jobs, at a cost of $7000 per job. This is essentially a "home-grown" high tech economy.

Case Study #4, Vancouver, B.C.

Mr Anton Kuipers' focus with BC Trade (Vancouver, Canada) is linking high-tech firms with global markets in the US, Europe and Japan to accelerate global market penetration. Canadian high-tech companies are incubated and grown through a number of public and/or private programs. Amongst these, the most successful are:

- Advanced Systems Institute – an industry-driven commercialization "broker."
- National Research Council – centers of excellence across Canada in biotechnology, information technology, robotics and instruments, funded by the government.
- Industry Canada TPC Program – focus on aerospace, defense, biotechnology and environmental technologies.
- Innovation Center – incubating new industries (e.g., Fuel Cell Research Center) through public–private funding.
- Discovery Parks – developed by private industry, universities and developers.

Kuipers concluded that taking clusters of similar, small companies into foreign markets has the impact of a larger company, but a strong government role is required to identify and form the cluster, "train it," focus the marketing effort, and assist in making the connections.

Case Study # 5, Portland, Oregon

Mr Joe Cortright brought us back home to Portland with an analysis of the "Ecology of the Silicon Forest." Within the Portland Metropolitan area of 1.8 million residents, 50,000 businesses and a $60 billion/year economy, two "clusters" dominate – the high-tech cluster (70,000 jobs) and the traditional metals cluster (40,000 jobs). Creative Services and Nursery clusters are much smaller, evolving clusters.

The high-tech "Silicon Forest" of computers, electrical equipment, instruments, software, related electronics and machinery constitute 2200 firms, a $3.5 billion business and many high value jobs. Some 20,000 new jobs with an average salary above $50,000 have been created.

In analyzing this high-tech business, Cortright found it is based on strengths in semiconductor manufacture; SME/EDA equipment testing; printers; silicon wafers; computers; and display/imaging equipment. These descended from Tektronix and were later enhanced by HP and Intel influence. This is in contrast to other "Silicon areas" that have as their catalyst a major research university.

This private industry-driven economy notion is substantiated by the huge private R&D investment (which could be as high as $1.9 billion, compared to total state university R&D in Oregon of about $0.25 billion) and the number of patents, which is growing at twice the national average.

Therefore, according to Cortright, Silicon Forest's success is based on three factors:

- Knowledge creation in the companies
- Critical Mass/Clustering of the companies
- Cultural and Institutional Environment.

In other words, existing and new firms create and extend knowledge and a critical mass of such firms *plus* quality of life is needed for sustained growth.

Further findings from the conference are in the concluding section of Chapter 9.

Note

1. Hall (1998, p. 89): "Paradoxically, Florence gained intellectually from the fact that it had no university; the nearest university, at Bologna, was fifty miles (80 kilometres) away, so the city was intellectually isolated; thus it was both highly literate, and yet preserved from a scholastic straitjacket."

9
The Power of Combination: Three Unpopular Truths about Civic Entrepreneurship

Fred Phillips

In the 1980s – yes, that recently! – a University of Texas economics professor told students there are only three routes to wealth: sit on natural resources, buy undervalued stock, or exploit peasants. He never dreamt of mentioning "to create highly valued stock by innovation and entrepreneurship."[1] To think of such a thing still requires a rare mindset, one that is found with relative infrequency outside the United States and only regionally within this country.

Nor is it enough for just one person to think this way; that generally won't make him or her an entrepreneurial success. I would enjoy saying, "it takes a village to raise an entrepreneur," but even that doesn't suffice. To make an entrepreneurial company succeed requires focused social and technological support and a significant communications and transportation infrastructure. This can only happen in a sizeable city, and when institutions in the city reach out to surrounding hinterlands, a self-sustaining entrepreneurial region is made possible. Can in happen in Portland, Oregon?

The power of combination

In a 1992 *Harvard Business Review* article, Fumio Kodama claimed that when markets drive the R&D agenda, market data are translated into a product concept. The product concept in turn drives development projects that draw technologies from multiple sources. Moreover, Kodama continues, there is now such a smorgasbord of recent technological advances in the world's companies, industries, and regions that a company can introduce new products in this way for decades without resorting to further fundamental scientific research. He contrasts this process of technology fusion to that of developing new products by directing R&D effort at the linear progress of an individual technology. Kodama's thesis has wide implications:[2]

- *No single company can master all the technologies it needs to succeed in a competitive marketplace.* Today's business environment is necessarily rich in licensing, outsourcing, and all the other mechanisms of inter-firm technology transfer.
- *Technology scanning takes on greater importance.* Companies need to gather intelligence from broader channels than have been generally considered in the past – and from more than the obvious competitors. A company's "invisible competitors" are in a different industry and possess technology that could become a threat if turned to new markets. An example was the threat to disk drive companies from flash memory semiconductor makers.
- *Alliances are the order of the day.* Technology fusion grows out of long-term R&D ties with a variety of companies across many different industries.
- *Globalization is driven by the need to fuse technologies* and to assess diverse market needs, as well as (of course) by capital liberalization.
- *All this affects entrepreneurship.* Global networking is now an essential element of entrepreneurship. Entrepreneurs hoping to survive must be globally connected from day one if they are to find the right technologies, the right markets, the right management talent, the friendliest capital, the most helpful community support programs, and the best suppliers and alliance partners. Obviously, entrepreneurs need help to do this, and this help must come from the local community. This gives rise to the unwieldy but descriptive phrase "globally networked civic entrepreneurship."

Some years back, Craig Fields, then President of MCC, observed that we are living in the age of eight "multis": The new business environment is

- Multi-product
- Multi-country
- Multi-culture
- Multi-company
- Multi-industry
- Multi-technology
- Multi-career
- Multi-tasking.

We must, Fields said, recognize the multis and learn to tolerate them. But even more than that, we can and must combine the multis in a profitable way. This is the power of combination.

Using this power, though, can be like hiring a tiger to rid the town of mice; it makes us nervous if we don't do it, and even more nervous if we do. All creative strategies for dealing with growth dilemmas will be "unpopular ideas" in some quarters.

Three unpopular ideas

1. Beware of colonization. In 1980, the Finance Minister of Australia warned that if its manufacturing base continued to shrink relative to its exports of unprocessed natural resources, Australia would become a banana republic. This shocked and insulted Australians, whose self-image involved parity with European nations of the first world.

But history shows that regions, like Portland's, that are sparsely populated, that have good ports and abundant natural resources, and that under-invest in education ... get colonized. Colonization means little foreign direct investment comes in; value-added activities occur elsewhere; and only low-wage jobs remain. Most important, it means that the colonized lose their self-determination, if not their sovereignty, regaining it, if at all, only after blood has been shed.

2. There are limitations on the growth of new technopoleis. The spatial concentration of both wealthy individuals and successful startup companies, as in Silicon Valley and elsewhere, means that lock-in occurs. It becomes harder to build a viable high technology cluster in other places.

Other places attempt, through tax-abatement programs and the like, to selectively encourage certain kinds of companies to locate in their jurisdictions. However, international capital "liberalization" treaties like NAFTA, WTO and the currently under-negotiation Multilateral Agreement on Investments (MAI) largely prohibit the differential tax treatment of companies, even at the local level.

These forces mean there will be a reduced opportunity for Silicon Valley "wannabes" to catch up. The only counter-measure I can see (aside from some localities proclaiming themselves "MAI-free zones," which has already happened) is to expand research expenditures and formulate technopolis strategies around niche technologies that could become important in a number of application areas. Chances are improved if these applications include defense, and in the Northwest this might include aviation technologies, and defense applications of flat panel displays.

3. There is a role for government. Most of us do not believe in the government's ability to "pick winners." But government can constructively invest in:

- Funding high-cost, high-risk cooperative ventures, as does the US National Institute of Standards and Technology's Advanced Technology Program.
- Helping entrepreneurial companies traverse the "Valley of Death" between their first product idea and their first significant investment.
- Stewarding the public's interest in communication and transportation networks. Much high tech these days involves communications networks, and such networks always raise questions of universal service, spectrum allocation, monopolies, and so on.

Beyond investing in education and R&D, governments must work with industry and academe to create the entrepreneurial mindset and the entrepreneurial society that I described earlier. How can an entrepreneurial mind and an entrepreneurial society be created? There is no magic recipe, and many regions are struggling to find a locally practicable solution. But I believe the most important ingredient is *sharing*. Share expertise, share news, share successes and failures, share credit for successes, and share networks of acquaintances and colleagues. Share your vision and share your methods. This is the power of combination!

Let's go back, for a moment, to Australia. During the Second World War, Australians were terrified of being overrun by Asia. But by 1980, the majority of cars on Australian streets were Japanese. The Australian Minister's "banana republic" speech was widely reviled, but its message struck home. In the years 1980–99, Australia welcomed entrepreneurial immigrants, handled multi-ethnic democracy with some flair, cast aside the cartographic conceit of Australia as a separate continent, and engaged with Asia. Today, Australia is a stable democracy that attracts Asian stock investment, has developed technology and manufacturing exports, and (despite significant debt) is a leading economy in the Asian–Pacific rim. Australia can be a role model for Portland.

I'll conclude with a word picture of another island nation, from a novel by Stuart Kaminsky: "If a Cuban is at home when the rains come, he feels protected. It is like being in a castle with a great moat. No one will enter. It is a time for peace and security. All are equally trapped and protected by it. It is a time for coffee and love." Sounds like Portland! It is indeed a trap, and Portland must find the key, to be able to enter and exit at will.

The New Oregon century: globally networked entrepreneurs

Oregon Graduate Institute helped the Oregon Entrepreneurial Business Initiative, American Electronics Association, Software Association of Oregon, and other Portland entrepreneurship facilitators search for that key. We brought experts from the United States, Sweden, Canada, and Taiwan to share best practices for global networking and linking technology entrepreneurship to regional development. Their findings, discussed in Chapter 8, are repeated in a summary form below:

1. *Metropolitan regions ("citistates") are replacing nations, states, counties, and municipalities as the loci of entrepreneurial economic development.*
2. *The point of a sustainable entrepreneurial economy is political self-determination.*
3. *We derive economic advantage from our cultural uniqueness.*
4. *A pre-eminent research university is not critical to Portland's success, at this time.* (What seemed true in 1999 looks less certain in 2005. Tektronix has consolidated around a smaller set of strategic competences, and Intel's attention is on expansion opportunities overseas. This leaves Portland weaker in science, and steady in engineering innovation, though perhaps left behind the leading edge in some new technology areas. Oregon's universities are suffering their own cutbacks, but these are not necessarily due to the globalization that has taken the companies in new directions. Conclusion: A great university may have been dispensable in 1999, but one could very much wish for one now.)
5. *In this era of technological turmoil, entrepreneurs take the lion's share of the risks in bringing beneficial new products to market, and can be the most important factor in community job creation.* For this reason, Portland's university and private entrepreneurship facilitators focus not only on educating individual entrepreneurs, but on initiating university–industry–government partnerships for the mutual support of clean regional economic development and new business ventures.

These promises and challenges must shape our agenda in the coming years. And because other regions are thinking likewise, it is an agenda of considerable urgency.

Note

1. One hopes this professor's students took the "exploiting peasants" option as a historical note and not a serious action proposition.

10
Gaining on Us and Closing Fast

Fred Phillips

Ballplayer Satchel Paige said, "Don't look back – somebody might be gaining on you." The 4th International Conference on Technology Policy & Innovation in Curitiba, Brazil (August, 2000), suggested the opposite: We Portlanders had better look back – to remind ourselves that others are gaining on us.

Like Portland, Curitiba is known worldwide as a liveable city that excels at civic planning. Mayor Cassio Taniguchi now pushes, in addition to education for Curitiba's citizens, access for all to the Internet and computers. "We can't afford to lag behind," he said, "We cannot afford to miss an opportunity." His newest thrusts are integration of information (universal smart cards, for everything from bus fares to utility accounts), and measures to foster creative talent in the populace.

Mayor Kirk Watson of Austin, Texas, told the conference that wealth now flows from ideas. A company in the knowledge economy can access capital, knowledge, and labor electronically, from anywhere, 24/7. Referring to the inland cities of Austin and Curitiba, he noted, "You don't need a port when you can be a portal." Portland take note! Austin has nine sister cities with which it conducts cultural exchange. But Mayors Watson and Taniguchi have negotiated a "technopolis partner" relationship between Curitiba and Austin. This new kind of intercity relationship will connect growth-oriented technology companies with global opportunities and will allow cities to share strategies for attracting knowledge workers and companies.

We'd be mistaken to think Curitiba is the only new technopolis nipping at Portland's heels. There are 135 business incubators in Brazil alone, 40 percent of these in São Paulo state (Curitiba is in Paraná state). Not to mention the rest of Latin America, the Caribbean, Southeast Asia, India, and the Middle East! Norman Kaderlin of the IC^2 Institute described the technology commercialization workshops the Institute held in Bogotá and Medellín: "The Colombians don't just want to be taught. They don't just want to make deals. They want to transform their economy, with our help." Fear of the "digital divide," the highly publicized notion that new technologies will enrich those with access to information and marginalize those without it, drives less-developed regions even more desperately to technopolis efforts.

While dramatic things are happening in developing regions, the OECD nations are hardly standing still. Denmark is among the top ten nations in GDP per capita, despite what Bengt-Åke Lundvall of Aalborg University calls "a low-tech orientation." How did Denmark, a country comparable in population to Oregon, succeed economically? Denmark, says Lundvall, invests in education, educates its people, steeps them in international news, and teaches foreign languages. While Oregon loses its flights to Asia, Denmark builds a bridge (no metaphor here, but a real steel and concrete bridge) to Sweden. The ability to learn is the ability to create wealth, in high- or low-tech sectors, he says. "New-economy euphoria threatens to result in the neglect of competence building" in traditional industries, notes Lundvall, but Denmark has successfully dealt with this.

More recently in the Netherlands, the Maastricht Mayor's office polled the local institutions that are international in orientation, measured how much foreign exchange they generated, and were impressed enough to build a website touting Maastricht as an international city and encouraging interaction with and among these institutions. The site and the international initiative were kicked off with great celebration. When the microphone reached me, I noted the four steps to making a city internationable (a made-up-on-the-spot neologism for "comfortable being international and good at making foreign visitors and residents comfortable"):

1. *Measuring.* Know how many companies, agencies and institutions you have with more than x percent international activity. Know how many visits and export bucks they generate.
2. *Networking.* Have them talk to each other and generate synergies.
3. *Evangelizing.* Declare success when two random citizens, newly introduced, turn out to be committed to internationalization already, and try to convert each other.
4. *Cooperating in action.* Stop talking and start doing. No, make that "start helping each other do."

Governments everywhere are investing in infrastructure, especially Internet Protocol backbones. This is not the kind of industrial policy that has famously failed in the past; this kind helps everyone. It enables entrepreneurs in developed and developing regions alike to challenge US rivals on a level field.

Sparsely populated regions that export natural resources without enough value-added, even if they are located in the first world, slide toward banana-republic status. Portlanders Peter Bragdon and Rich Read have also sounded this alarm, using words like "colony" and "backwater" to describe a possible future Oregon. We have new evidence of the entrepreneurial energy and Internet savvy of regions that, prior to today, were flying under our radar. This makes the alarm more urgent. What needs to be done?

- Increase K-16, graduate, and lifetime educational opportunities for Oregonians, and make sure Oregonians take advantage of them.
- Encourage academic research excellence *and* effective commercialization of research.
- Extend Internet training and access to all segments of our population.
- Maintain our high quality of life. If knowledge workers can live anywhere, this is the *only* thing that will make them decide to live and spend their salaries here.
- Help entrepreneurs learn business skills and learn to network globally.
- Create an entrepreneur-friendly tax structure and social environment.
- Increase international news coverage and our knowledge of foreign cultures, languages, and markets.
- Make Oregon easy and pleasant for foreigners to visit.

In 2001, I moderated a panel on new business incubation at the Forestry Center. The event showed the enormous demand (340 people attended) that exists in Portland for measures like those I've listed above. It also showed that our various organizations (Software Association of Oregon, American Electronics Association, Oregon Entrepreneurs' Forum, Oregon Graduate Institute, Portland State University and others that sponsored the panel) can work together to make them happen. The Center for Entrepreneurial Growth held a conference last fall to benchmark our technopolis parameters against regions in Sweden, Taiwan, Canada, and elsewhere in the United States (Lundvall calls this "learning by comparing"). Portland economist Joe Cortright and PSU's Institute for Metropolitan Studies continue to collect these vital data. Other Portlanders are working to extend net access and entrepreneurial training to the state's underserved regions and populations. Still others are addressing the capital gains tax, the urban growth boundary, and local INS procedures. OGI, PSU, and Washington State University together comprise a world-class academic force in technology management. Oregon universities and firms are unexcelled in their computer science, circuit design, and semiconductor manufacture talent. All this is encouraging, but there's no room for complacency.

They're gaining on us, Portland. Like Mayor Taniguchi, we must proclaim, "We can't afford to lag behind. We cannot afford to miss an opportunity" – and then act accordingly.

11
Sometimes, Montana
Fred Phillips

As a Texan, I'm duty-bound to look for the lost town of Sometimes, Montana, and I hope that makes sense to you.

In 1995 I moved from Austin to Portland, Oregon, and while the laws of physics seem different there (Oregon is home to a part of the electromagnetic spectrum I hadn't known about before. It's called "green"), it's a lot like Austin in the important ways. In fact, the similarities can be eerie.

Austin hosts the South by Southwest music festival; Portland has one called North by Northwest. Portland has the Col-umbia river, Austin the Col-orado. Both towns use cuss words as pronunciation mnemonics for local place names: Austinites say Burnet, durnit, and Oregonians shout Willamette, dammit!

The towns compete in the business, art, and education arenas. Recently University of Texas Provost Mark Yudof and Portland State University President Judith Ramaley were finalists for the presidency of the University of Minnesota.[1] In music and technology, we seem to share the spoils. How bizarre to see the Oregon Public Broadcasting logo in super over the broadcast of Austin City Limits – and then hear a Portland singer performing from the UT soundstage.

Portland has Intel, Austin has AMD. Austin got Samsung, Oregon won Hyundai. Austin and Portland are home to hundreds of software companies, making up a significant part of their industrial strength, and in fact in the early '90s we modeled the Austin Software Council partly on the Software Association of Oregon (SAO). Austin has the edge in terms of number of software firms. Both regions tout semiconductor clusters, though Portland's seems more robust. In 1998, each 100,000 Austin residents generated 130 patents, for a total of 1440 (Rivera 2001); Portland was responsible for 948 patents, or 52 per 100,000 residents.

With apologies to National Public Radio's Ketzel Levine, who thinks the two words are "banana slug," the two words that sum up the Pacific Northwest experience for me are "interval wipers." Rain is the price we pay for green. (Our annual Rain Festival, the story goes, runs from January 1 to December 31.) It's easy to see why environmentalism is strong in Oregon. Easy to feel the pristine environment is worth fighting for; people who have fled more polluted locales see Oregon as a second chance. (If they see Oregon as a second garbage dump, the locals pretty quickly chase them back to where they came from.) More than any other American city, Portland believes in urban planning and sprawl control. Portlanders accept, more or less, that environmental preservation and economic development can co-exist. While there is a more active green construction movement in Austin, I still see more acrimony in Austin between "real estate rapers" and "effete tree huggers."

Both cities see technology entrepreneurship as the key to clean growth. Despite recent growing pains, I think Austin accepts this more wholeheartedly than Portland. Still, Portland has a harder uphill battle. In the 1960s, George Kozmetsky drew a mental line around Texas, New Mexico and the bordering states of Mexico – with their large population (30+ million), industries, national laboratories and enormous engineering schools – and said, "This is the place." In contrast, Oregon, the 9th largest US state in area, plus the parts of southern Washington that are in Portland's orbit, contain only a bit over three million people, one national lab, and a number of good, smaller universities with specialized, rather than across-the-board, research strengths.

I believe a strong-willed community can turn Portland's strengths in multimedia and semiconductor innovation, education, liveability, and access to Pacific Rim markets into a viable technopolis. Growth in venture-backed entrepreneurship has led to greater intercourse among the "sisters" of the west coast – San Francisco, Portland, Seattle and Vancouver, B.C. – and this may lead to regional strategies similar to Kozmetsky's plan for Texas.

Where some land appears in Lake Travis during low water, mapmakers have marked the charts "Sometimes Islands." You can't find a true Austinite who doesn't believe that this is the *name* of the islands – "We're gonna picnic on the Sometimes Islands." And in the Northwest ... well, what *is* the Northwest anyway? Geographers say the term applies to Oregon, Washington, Alaska, Idaho, and sometimes, Montana.

An Austinite to the bone, I'm still looking for a town named Sometimes, Montana.

Note

1. Yudof got it, and spent some years there before returning to Austin as Chancellor of the UT System.

12

Lack of Investment Puts Portland Behind

Fred Phillips

In recent editorials, *Portland Business Journal's* Craig Wessel and Portland Development Commission Don Mazziotti waxed enthusiastic about new efforts to boost economic development in our state. At about the same time, investor Ralph Shaw and reporter Ted Sickinger separately warned of less upbeat futures for Oregon. It's good to recognize that steps have been taken, but Ralph and Ted's view is the right one: Oregon needs a louder wake-up call. We must do much more, and do it much faster.

Picture a place with vast natural resources, a small population, a great port. With few viable indigenous business firms, and losing more of them every week. A plum of a place, just waiting to be exploited by a foreign, imperialistic invader. Is this some Caribbean or Central American banana republic? No. This place is Oregon, and Oregon is in danger.

Here is what we need to do.

1. Fix elementary education. A great university should *not* be our top priority. Successful economies as diverse as Japan and Malaysia grew by emphasizing primary education. Young Malaysians, like young Oregonians, can go elsewhere to college, and many will come back, with foreign investment in tow, *if* on their return they find a solid workforce with high school and associate degrees, and fine public schools for their own children. Pre-K and K-14 education must be Oregon's Job One, all others a distant second. Without this, we become ... Haiti.

2. Get multicultural. Sunday's *Oregonian* highlighted the mutual discomfort of Woodburn's Anglo and Latino communities. I've observed the same in Hillsboro. That is so 20th-century. To see the future, look at the rainbow of faces in any Intel facility.

We must reach out vigorously to our Mexican-American neighbors. If Oregonians don't see that it's simply the right thing to do, here's a selfish reason: Anglos are not having many children. The growing cohort of Mexican-American children will, during their working years, pay the Medicaid taxes that will care for us as we grow old. Let's ensure they, and other minority youngsters, enjoy productive working lives as valued members of Oregon society.

3. Start crosstalk. The several organizations engaging in development dialog need to talk to each other, via overlapping membership, to avoid fragmented effort. Further, they and we must look beyond Oregon's borders to craft a regional strategy that includes neighboring states and provinces. As Mazziotti notes, we must influence federal policies that affect our development. No single sector can make a difference; high-tech people must talk to creative services people, and they with arts and community activists, and all with the tourism sector, finding common ground and efficiencies in their development efforts. Finally, we must build and maintain global contacts that allow our entrepreneurs to find international customers and suppliers quickly. The world has become global, so to speak, while Oregon remains inward-looking. This has to change.

4. Get entrepreneur-friendly. Venture capitalists are notorious for the scorn they heap on business plans. In no other industry than venture capital do executives whine that customers are "wasting my time." Instead, these other industries educate customers on how best to use the industry's product. Portland has VCs that serve as judges in OGI's new venture competition and at other educational events. More of them need to engage in this outreach. Otherwise, it's no surprise that VCs are returning funds uninvested at a time when new technological developments are opening vast new business opportunities.

Most new Oregon companies have been spin-offs from large firms. As a result, local investors remain uncomfortable with garage start-ups and university spin-outs. Time to get over it, investors! Portland's hottest growth company, Tripwire, was a university spin-out.

Complex zoning, permitting, and licensing processes favor the large companies that can afford to navigate and lobby the bureaucracies, and work against small and new businesses that cannot afford it. Cut regulation back to what's really needed for consumer protection, and let small businesses run with it.

5. Get real about spreading the wealth. Modern industry clusters work only if they achieve critical mass. A limited state budget cannot create critical mass uniformly across Oregon. We have to pick and choose our industry and geographic targets, and – not to be too Reaganomic about it – make the resulting wealth trickle down to outlying areas. Sure, there's political pressure to spread opportunities equally to all Oregon counties. But Don Mazziotti said it well: "We're committed to Portland's economic success and ultimately the success of the region."

6. *Invest in ourselves.* Attracting companies via tax breaks too often leaves us holding the bag. Instead, invest in infrastructure. Attract companies by saying, "You will have the best workforce, roads, schools, air connections, industry associations, and wastewater treatment anywhere." If the company locates here and then fails, we still have the infrastructure. We can use it to attract or grow the next company.

7. *Toot our own horn.* Even Cleveland – without a fraction of Oregon's quality of life – has Drew Carey to yell, "Cleveland rocks!" Who is shouting "Portland rocks?" The time for quiet pride in Oregon is past. Each of us must become a madcap marketer. No out-of-state visitor should leave our offices without a gift bag full of Made in Oregon products, and a pile of brochures. Take your visitors fishing or skiing. See? Marketing can be fun.

And we must get more skillful at it. Have you noticed how hard it is to find a product made in Oregon outside the Made in Oregon store? Have you noticed what an unfocused muddle our new state tourism magazine is? Mazziotti mentioned the Regional Economic Development Partnership. Have you ever heard of it? Neither have I. How can it engage the public's imagination and energy if the public isn't aware of it?

This week's *Business Week* has a full-page ad touting the business climate in El Salvador! Anyone who still believes things are done right in the north and wrong in the south should try to recall the last time Oregon essayed any bold marketing at all.

8. *Break the pattern.* My hometown, Austin, didn't turn to high technology until the economic crisis of the 1980s. As Craig Wessel pointed out, no momentum developed in Portland until the current prolonged recession. These days, no region can afford to wait for a crisis. From Helsinki to Shanghai to São Paulo, other regions have got sophisticated about attracting the very same people, companies and technologies that Portland wants. Should we jump on the biotech bandwagon when its axles are already strained by hundreds of other cities? As Mazziotti implies, "proactive" must be the watchword. We must work doubly hard and smart to make up for having waited too long.

Why the urgency? First, other regions are investing far more than Oregon in their development strategies. Second, globalization now allows foreign cities and nations to compete with Oregon in ways that were unimaginable ten years ago. Third, new World Trade Organization treaties forbid, after a ten-year phase-out period, many of the incentive agreements localities now use for attracting companies. Fourth, the "lock-in" effect that characterizes most highly networked tech clusters means the chance to grow each such cluster comes only once.

If we don't initiate the kind of growth we'll like, we'll be forced to accept the kind we won't like. Fellow Oregonians, please follow these eight rules. We have a narrow window in which to build a new Oregon that Oregonians will still enjoy.

13

Twelve Hurdles to Starting an Executive MOT Program: How and Why to Overcome Them

Fred Phillips

Overview

Management of Technology (MOT) programs present unique problems of staffing, marketing, curriculum development and delivery, and fundraising. The IC^2 Institute, Oregon Graduate Institute, Portland State University, and Maastricht School of Management have faced most or all of these problems, and overcome them with a combination of innovative business models, industry outreach, and quality improvements. This chapter lists the problems these schools have faced in building MOT and allied programs, and how they dealt with them. It also addresses the important question of why, despite the obstacles, it is worthwhile to build and expand MOT offerings. While centered primarily on American experiences, I believe most of the discussion is globally applicable, and ask readers to excuse any parochialisms.

The global and societal context

In recent years, my US technology industry contacts have repeatedly told me that, of the four ingredients for successful new growth companies (money, technology, entrepreneurial energy, and management talent), it is seasoned management talent that is in shortest supply. My Asian contacts also feel their companies' lack of talented, knowledgeable management cadres. While they believe better management could not have prevented the post-IMF Asian financial meltdown, they hold that it could have lessened its impact on companies. Additionally, they see technology as the key to modernizing military, environmental and industrial processes of importance to their countries. All growth companies need to promote their management ranks from within, for reasons of morale and cost, and so must invest in training if their managers are to be ready for promotion. As my Asian colleagues add that they consider US management schools the best available, it is easy to see a future in which the best management schools – in the US, Europe, Asia and elsewhere – pool resources to offer executive degree and certificate programs to participants worldwide.

The academic context

A baccalaureate degree, formerly seen as the ticket to a comfortable life, is now merely the minimum qualification for competing for a professional job. This is especially true (Hernandez 1998) in regions like Oregon which have transitioned from a natural resource-based economy to one characterized by high-tech employment. Statistics indicate current and future growth in Master's level education for such jobs (Hernandez, 1998):

- In the US, Master's degrees conferred increased 23 percent from 1990 to 1995, while Bachelor's degrees increased only 10 percent. In 2005, almost half as many master's degrees were awarded in the US as bachelor's degrees.[1]
- US Bureau of Labor Statistics charted a 29 percent growth between 1994 and 2005 in jobs requiring a Master's, a faster rate than for any other degree.
- One out of five Bachelor's graduates are continuing their education within a year of graduating.
- More than 80 percent of top-achieving Oregon high school seniors expect to earn graduate degrees.
- Though MBA enrollments are down in the US in 2005, demand for MBA education is unabated in the emerging economies, including China.

As technology plays a more important role in the employment growth of nations and regions, students demand that university business departments offer more courses and degrees in management of technology (MOT).

Hurdles to overcome

Problems encountered in executive MOT programs can include:

Accommodating the busy schedules of working professionals: class schedules and distance learning

Students demand convenient course delivery, preferably to their desktops, yet crave personal interaction with their peers from other companies. Executive M.S. students work long hours for their employers, may travel often on business, and may have families with young children at home, while taking one or two courses each quarter toward their degrees. Such students naturally want their required courses to be offered at predictable times – preferably, predictable over a time span reaching to their graduation. They want flexibility as well, including a chance to retake a course their business travels caused them to miss (without unduly delaying graduation) and new, topical electives. In a rapidly growing program, a dynamically changing long term course schedule is a necessity.

While this presents ample challenges for on-campus course scheduling, distance learning options become a necessity also. Yet management faculty are troubled by the idea of distance instruction. Much management education cannot now be reduced to a bit stream. Facial expression, body language, and spatial placement aspects of communication are important for instruction in management areas like leadership and negotiation, and require personal contact.

Despite these considerations, there is a danger that bigger, richer schools (and with a few exceptions, these are schools located in agricultural or urban regions far from today's technology centers) can invest heavily in distance learning technology and drive newer schools out of the market. How can a start-up MOT program stay "in the game" in a time of investment-driven shake-out and consolidation?

Dealing with the philanthropic profiles of technology entrepreneurs

The wealth of technology entrepreneurs may be mostly on paper, and modest compared to traditional fortunes. Due to their youth, these entrepreneurs may still worry about financing the education of their children and putting aside money for family emergencies. They are unlikely to be thinking in terms of testamental bequests, and have not developed the skills and enthusiasms needed for philanthropy. Their entrepreneurial pride may make them believe all enterprises, including universities, should "kill their own dinner," and so while their companies are willing to pay as they go (that is, the tuition for their employees' degrees), they may be reluctant to fund endowments. Finally, technology industry is global, and these entrepreneurs live in a borderless world. Unlike traditional donors who have made money in the local community (from car dealerships, shoe stores, and the like) and wish to pay back to the community, technology entrepreneurs think globally, travel extensively, and may be hard-pressed to find time to connect, emotionally and financially, to their local communities.

Of course there are exceptions, and I have no wish to libel my many friends who are in this situation. But the problems I have just described are widely acknowledged.

Finding and motivating qualified faculty

Students with 10–15 years work experience demand a high reality level in the classroom. Their needs can be met only by mature faculty who have had technology industry careers (in addition to their academic qualification), or at least, very extensive industrial consulting experience. Such people can be hard to find.

Faculty with traditional business school experience can find the transition difficult. To take one business discipline as an example, most leading marketing professors have had their research funded by companies like Procter & Gamble. Experts on consumer marketing of brand-differentiated commodity food and home products, they cannot stand before the executive MOT class and credibly talk about business-to-business marketing of early life-cycle, fast-changing, complex technology products.

Because the field is fast-changing, the faculty's course preparation burden is high. The usual academic convention of 2 percent FTE (annual full-time equivalent) per quarter-credit is unrealistic. No MOT course is "in the can"; almost a full course prep is required every time the "same" course is repeated.

This presents a dilemma for production of multimedia and distance learning courses. The investment needed to script and cut a CD must be amortized over a large customer base before the course content becomes dated. The faculty must be incentivized to allow their lectures (on videotape, WWW, CD-ROM, or DVD) to be used repeatedly at distant sites, and the associated legal issues of intellectual property must be resolved.

Unsuitability of standard textbooks

The same considerations mean that the faculty must insert a great deal of original material into the class notes. Standard textbooks present principles for marketing disposable diapers, breakfast cereals, and other products MOT students regard as irrelevant to their work environment. Cases must be found (or written) that illustrate a broad range of management principles in the context of technology industry examples.

Dealing with the "two cultures" of engineering and management

Companies need a certain number of their engineers to transition into management. If this does not happen, the management ranks will have no technological competence. Engineers are often reluctant to make this transition, as their career advancement so far has been based on their cutting-edge technological skills, skills which they won't keep current if they become managers. In addition, there may already be tensions between engineering and management in the company, and making the transition can be seen as defecting to the enemy.

Accreditation issues for "Non-Standard" master's programs

A well-considered MOT program will have no difficulty meeting the requirements of its regional accrediting body. While MOT-oriented schools will eventually want to consider a bid for accreditation with AACSB (the national accrediting body for business schools that has now gone global), some potential issues have already appeared. Accustomed to accrediting MBA programs, AACSB accepted its first accreditation-candidate school offering a technology-focused Master's of Science (M.S.) in management only recently, and, it seems, will be designing the standards as the candidacy proceeds. In a technology-focused management M.S., it is likely that the best faculty will come from engineering backgrounds – perhaps combined with a career in industry and entrepreneurship. As traditional business schools have matured and gained influence, business school accreditors have begun to look at the percent of faculty with doctoral degrees from accredited business schools. As we have seen, these may not be the people best prepared to teach in an executive Master's in MOT. The question of adjunct faculty versus tenured faculty as teachers of entrepreneurship has been a divisive one at some schools. This may or may not turn out to be an accreditation issue for MOT degree programs.

Social perceptions of the role of technology companies in the local economy

A region's transformation from resource economy to high-tech economy (see IC^2 1990; Phillips, 1995) does not occur without social dislocations and political disputes. At best, a smooth transformation takes many years. At worst, bitter and more or less permanent differences divide the population into "traditionalist" and "modernist" factions. In that high-tech is spatially agglomerative, with producers and suppliers co-locating, certain areas of a city or state will experience an economic boom while others will not; perceptions of inequity in taxation and benefits become politically volatile. The MOT program will be identified with the modernist faction, and must navigate these sociopolitical waters.

Perceived value of advanced degrees in client companies and among prospective students

The key to career advancement in fast companies is skills – not necessarily a master's degree. Salaries are high for technical B.S. graduates, especially in software engineering and electrical engineering.

Graduate degrees are a status symbol at some tech companies (perhaps most notably, Hewlett-Packard), but even there, employees can get locked into a "6-month product cycle mentality" and feel unable to commit to a 2-year master's program or to formulate a longer-term career plan.

Difficulties of forecasting enrollments

Although it is becoming less so, the semiconductor industry is still cyclical. This, and unexpected events such as the Asian economic crisis, make executive MOT enrollments in Portland or Austin difficult to predict. Likewise, client companies' project cycles affect enrollment. As release dates loom, employees cannot spare time to attend classes. After the release, they enroll in droves! Unless each client company is unusually open about its project timelines and the MOT program can plan marketing accordingly, enrollments will be irregular and surprising.

Enrolled employees can be transferred on short notice to corporate locations outside the University's service area.

Technology company employees don't know (especially in regions with high employment mobility) whether in a year they will be working for a company with a tuition reimbursement policy. Acculturated to reimbursement as an entitlement, they are often not willing to think about paying tuition from their own pockets, especially at pricier private universities. This affects both their willingness to start the executive degree program, and their probability of attrition from the program.

Technology industry is global

Technology industry is global, and few universities have the resources to gather curriculum material from, and disseminate courses to, sister technology regions in distant locations.

The trap of the techno-MBA

An MOT program must build curriculum around the semiconductor, electronics, software, biotechnology, semiconductor equipment, aerospace, medical, and materials industries from which its students enroll, using cases and problems from all of them. I cannot overemphasize that the standard "techno-MBA" – in which the "techno-" means only "information systems" – cannot satisfy these students' needs.

Your university may not be located in a high-tech corridor

Geographic distance from a high-tech cluster naturally makes internships, access to good adjunct faculty and advisory board members, research data, guest speakers, and financial support difficult to procure – even though students still demand MOT courses.

Constructive strategies

MOT programs may respond, as have the role-model schools I've mentioned, with a varied marketing portfolio, innovative segmentation in terms of degree concentrations, a mix of distance-learning technologies, a quality adjunct faculty drawn from the resident faculty's worldwide contacts, alliances with other universities, a focus on customer service, a positioning of the curriculum that meets the approval and needs of local industry, plans for realizing revenue from the newly recognized need for lifelong learning, and focused, limited fundraising combined with private-sector partnerships for sourcing capital.

OGI's MST focuses on managing people and processes and building effective and competitive organizations in the specific contexts of technology and science. The MST M.S. program bridges the gap between traditional MBA and engineering-management programs. Each course in the program is designed to address management and business administration in the specific contexts of science, technology, engineering, and manufacturing. The M.S. program was begun at the request of local companies, and its curriculum was designed with the input of local high-tech industry. Ninety-five percent of MST M.S. students are employed full-time by these companies and enrolled at OGI part-time.

PSU's Technology & Engineering Management program has focused on serving foreign students as well as local working professionals, on dual downtown/suburban teaching locations, and on its Portland International Conferences on Management of Engineering and Technology, now the world's premier conference series on that topic. IC²'s Master of Science in commercialization of science and technology is a one-year, full-time program for those contemplating career changes. The MSSTC emphasizes technology-leader strategies and networking with technology-follower economies.

Maastricht School of Management's master's programs are an MBA and a Master of Management in international business, both focused on the needs of nations now modernizing and joining the global economy. Its technology and innovation management courses are taught in that context, emphasizing the problems of "technology follower" regions, also with a networking focus. MSM's MBA is a thesis program, thereby a little more research-oriented than an American MBA. MSM's "flying professor" model sends professors to teach in the 30 countries in which MSM maintains academic partnerships and local (some full-time, some part-time) MBA enrollments.

Both PSU and MSM have doctoral programs into which the master's programs feed.

Accommodating the busy schedules of working professionals: class schedules and distance learning

Weekend classes meet the needs of participants who travel for their companies or who must commute some distance to campus; weeknight classes are acceptable for those nearer and those who travel rarely. OGI offers on-campus weekend classes plus corporate on-site weeknight classes. Its administrators schedule classes heuristically, making heavy use of a student-tracking database that lets us know which matriculants will need which courses in order to graduate in a timely fashion. The students' heavy business travel schedule forces a menu approach to course registrations, in which certain core courses and a certain number of electives must be passed in the three years the average student requires to complete the program. At Maastricht School of Management's on-campus program, where students demand a one-year, full-time program, a cohort system works well: All students in the same "intake" take all courses together at fixed times. MsM's outreach MBA programs are a mix of full-time and part-time arrangements, but still hew to the cohort approach, allowing a student who misses too many class meetings to make it up by attending the respective course with the next intake.

Distance learning technology should not replace classroom offerings except for students who cannot attend a quality school in any other fashion. Many prospective students fall into this category for as many varied reasons. In Fall, 1998, OGI's first courses were offered that can be completed totally by distance learning at the student's home or workplace desktop. As we examined distance learning technologies and products, we found several relevant ways of characterizing their suitability for

MST's purposes:

- Open vs. password-protected
- Text/graphical/video/ live

- Windows vs. Mac
- POTS/ISDN/Tn
- One-to-one/one-to-many/ networked
- Licensed server software vs. third-party websites

- Synchronous vs. asynchronous
- Ephemeral vs. captured (threaded) content
- Downstream-only vs. two-way
- Learning-focused vs. general-purpose
- Client software vs. server-only

Each of these distinctions is relevant to decisions about distance learning.[2] OGI's distance learning initiatives were several, and involved both partnering and licensing mechanisms to hedge against technology risk. In particular, OGI and IC[2] partnered with Cenquest, Inc., of Portland to produce Master's degree courses on CD-ROM with Internet links (Yim 1998). We licensed the WebCT courseware suite and later experimented with Blackboard. We explored partnerships with another well-reputed US technological institute for extensive course sharing by distance learning. Each these options require minimal capital investment on the school's part, but open the door to significant increases in tuition income.

An advantage of the executive MOT format is that most students have their own computers, Internet access, and access to corporate libraries to supplement the school's library resources.

Philanthropic profiles of technology entrepreneurs

The MOT program director must map the policies of each constituent company (and its affiliated foundation) regarding tuition reimbursement, ad hoc donations of cash and equipment, contracts for degree and professional education, major endowments, and so on. Technology companies are the logical, but by no means the only possible, sources of funding for MOT programs.

Naturally, technology entrepreneurs should be represented on the MOT program advisory board. They can be mentored by more traditional philanthropists who are involved with the university. Some among the technology entrepreneurs will be leading the others in terms of philanthropic maturity, and these individuals should be given many opportunities to be visible to the others. The others should be subject to small "asks" that will show specific payoffs. Show them how the results of their donation will be relevant to their own companies' entrepreneurial focus. Example: With the support of Planar, Inc., OGI re-named its student entrepreneurship competition in honor of Planar's late president, Jim Hurd.

Finding and motivating qualified faculty

A critical success factor is a high-quality faculty who:

- Have experience and achievements in industrial management
- Have shown they can structure ideas for research or training
- Set high expectations for the students, and
- Have read widely about management ideas as they relate to technology enterprises.

Adjunct faculty (people working in industry or consulting who are hired as faculty on short-term contracts) are important for bringing diverse and topical ideas into the classroom, and should have the same characteristics. Adjuncts at MST were hired on the basis of personal referrals only. This requires that the program manager have good personal networks, but it is also achieved by leveraging the networks of current resident and adjunct faculty, the university's administrators and trustees, and the technology entrepreneurs on the advisory board.

It is worthwhile to fly adjunct instructors in from reasonable distances if they are the best people for the job. Cost can be mitigated by use of distance learning or by compressing the classroom contact hours into a shorter number of class meetings.

Extend considerations and privileges to adjunct faculty to the maximum extent allowed by university rules, and fight the rules if need be. Generally, adjuncts participate because of their enthusiasm, not for the small amount of money you can pay them. They constitute a secondary advisory board, and must be treated as valued insiders. If their courses are to be produced for distance learning, ensure they participate in a royalty stream.

The unsuitability of standard textbooks

Scan case catalogs for pertinent cases. Write original material based on the company experiences of your faculty, students, guest speakers, and advisors. Host conferences on topics of special interest (see, e.g., Phillips and Drake 1999), and use the conference papers as class readings.

The "Two Cultures" of engineering and management

If hard-core engineers regard becoming a manager as defecting to the Dark Side, help them distinguish "acts of management" (which they commit every day, and which can always benefit from improvement) from "being a manager." Focus class discussion on issues of communication, motivation, negotiation, and change agency.

Many distinctions between tech and non-tech industries are disappearing. High-tech penetrates commodity distribution, food chemistry and packaging, oil exploration, banking, lumber milling, and myriad other aspects of old-line industries. Conversely, mature-life-cycle marketing penetrates information technology industries, viz. the hiring of Lou Gerstner as president of IBM. MOT students learn to bridge the culture gap when these considerations are raised in class.

Students from traditional industries may be in the Master's program because they feel their careers are at dead end. Students from high-tech engineering, in contrast, are looking for an extra edge in an industry that is growing explosively. The latter, accustomed to continual training on leading-edge techniques, convey this orientation to lifelong learning to their fellow students, opening the door to educational "reunions" of alumni and other options for the university. The flip side of this is that high-tech students, accustomed to relatively undemanding corporate training classes, must re-adjust to rigorous university work.

For some decades, society has been changing rapidly, resulting in a reduced roles for family, religion, and other traditional transmitters of values. Furthermore, in fast-growth, high-tech companies, cultural values are still "under construction." MOT students, especially younger ones, are trying to formulate values for their lives and find meaning in their work. They seem to appreciate class content that aids this process; MOT programs can serve by educating "the whole person."

Accreditation for "Non-Standard" master's programs

As the percentage of degree courses offered via distance learning increases, accreditors must be kept informed. As it is not known what operating statistics on an MOT program's performance should be recorded, the program manager should try to exercise foresight, and err on the side of tracking everything. Watch AACSB's website (or that of the organization that is appropriate for your MOT program's affiliation), and attend its conferences.

Social perceptions of the role of technology companies in the local economy

Highlight the experiences of other regions that have resolved tensions between traditional and high technology businesses. Speak at local functions and write op-ed material; be a highly audible voice of moderation, advocating community unity. High-tech may be the only local source of well-paid jobs for the sons and daughters of loggers and ranchers. Technology companies therefore keep local families together, and this fact can be gently leveraged.

Perceived value of advanced degrees in client companies and among prospective students

Despite the statistics cited earlier, MOT program managers must understand the motives of their end-customer segments, not all of whom are highly motivated to take a Master's degree. Talk with employees and managers from as wide a range of companies as possible.

Offer specialized degree concentrations, perhaps in cooperation with other departments at your institution, that help undecided candidates see the relevance of the Master's degree to their work. MST's concentrations have included Managing the Technology Company; Managing in the Software Industries; Computational Finance; and Environmental Systems Management.

Ensure that classes are truly useful, and publicize students' and alums' testimonials about their value. Highlight the career successes of alumni.

Difficulties of forecasting enrollments

Get to know the top managers of "major account" companies. They may share information about their project schedules and the likelihood of their people enrolling. Respect the confidentiality of this information. Ideally, a full-time marketing manager at the university can keep a database and make regular calls on these major account companies.

Broaden your customer base by considering the admission of full-time and foreign students, and distance-learning enrollments.

Technology industry is global

Network! Share material unselfishly with distant colleagues. Attend conferences. Apply for National Science Foundation support (or support from your country's corresponding agency) for faculty exchanges. Use the Internet to conduct joint class exercises with classes at foreign MOT schools.

There are many avenues for dealing with globalism. The challenge is to commit to them and act on them.

The trap of the techno-MBA

High-tech is more than corporate information systems! Biotech and new materials, to name two examples, will change business in the next decades as much as computers have in past years. MOT graduates must be conversant with these possibilities.

I have suggested using material from the company experiences of your faculty, students, guest speakers, and advisors. Use live cases from local technology incubator companies. Get out of your office and meet people from a wide range of advanced industries. If industry associations don't exist to bring people together for networking, then start one – as MST has done for the Flat Panel Display industry.

Your university may not be located in a high-tech corridor

Many of the suggestions under "Technology Industry is Global" apply here also. Use videoconferencing to bring guest speakers to the classroom. Take advantage of programs that offer short-term university exchanges to allow experienced faculty to spend some time in other techno-regions gathering data and making contacts in local industry.

Why it is worthwhile

In the US, all economic sectors that can be considered "high technology" comprise at most six percent of the Gross National Product. The high-tech market is a tiny fraction of the nation's output, especially compared to, say, the food industry. (As one wag noted, "Few people compute, but everybody eats.") However, technology is the fastest growing US sector. New growth companies are most likely to be technology-based, because the innovative nature of their products or processes opens new markets. These companies, then, will provide the lion's share of new, high-paying jobs in the future. While it is not the direct responsibility of the university to create millionaires, being involved with companies and executives undergoing rich initial public offerings is exciting for students and faculty, and in the long run will result in endowments to the academy. Moreover, again due to their inherent innovativeness, technology firms change the way we live, learn, and work. To many of us, this is far more stimulating and challenging than, say, merchandising a new flavor of soda or breakfast cereal. Thus, MOT programs are gaining favor (Tobias 1997) as an alternative to the MBA.

The social and economic contributions of MOT programs are significant. This makes them easy to justify in terms of a science and technology university's mission. In addition, the students' motivation and intelligence make executive MOT degree programs highly rewarding and challenging endeavors for faculty. The fast-moving industries from which the students are drawn make for a stimulating environment. The students and their companies are a rich source of research data and of new research problems. In contrast to MBA students who may be concerned mainly with making contacts and landing the "best" job offers, executive MOT students know that in technology industries the saying "It's not what you know, it's who you know" is not true; what is important is what you know *and* who you know. Faculty find this dedication to knowledge very rewarding. Technology management is a discipline where students understand that brainpower and knowledge are the paths to advancement, and so it is a pleasure to teach them. Thus, building an MOT program is a worthwhile endeavor regardless of the significant problems involved.

Notes

1. National Center for Education statistics, http://nces.ed.gov/das/library/tables_listings/2002156.asp#
2. The details are beyond the scope of this book, but appear in Phillips (1997).

14

Do We Know How to Play This Game? Some Thoughts on Regional Leadership

Ralph R. Shaw

> "If you are successful you will win false friends and true enemies. Succeed anyway.
> The good you do will be forgotten tomorrow. Do good anyway."
>
> — *Kent M. Keith*

Good evening, ladies and gentlemen. Does anyone here know how to play this game?

Our political candidates debate the issues as they see them, with conclusions and recommendations designed not to solve problems but, rather, to avoid offending any constituency. Their "Casper Milquetoast, talk a lot and say nothing," approach is a forerunner for political careers that will likely be more of the same – trying to make an omelet without breaking any eggs.

Having watched the failure of economic development policies focusing on dotcoms and telecommunication hotels, our economic development planners are now succumbing to the irresistible, lemming-like, urge of looking to biotechnology as our long-term economic savior. This, in spite of the huge capital requirements incumbent in achieving success in that highly risky business, and the absence of any commercial evidence that our state has something unique to offer. Moreover, as the Council on Competitiveness concluded, the overall impact of success in a biotechnology cluster on a regional economy is usually relatively small. (For greater insight into this subject, I recommend you obtain a copy of Joseph Cortright's study for the Brookings Institute (Cortright and Mayer 2001). Mr Cortright of Impresa Inc. in Portland is probably the finest economic/market analyst in the West Coast and as good as they come anywhere in the United States.)

Meanwhile, we proudly claim education is our most important product, and then proceed to reduce the budgets of our educational institutions.

Does anyone here know how to play this game?

For starters, let's take a look at the current scene.

The State of Oregon's Department of Administrative Services' Office of Economic Analysis has laid the depressing facts in front of us. Its March, 2002, economic forecast said, "Oregon is in a recession. The fourth quarter initial estimate of job growth was a dismal negative 2.1 percent annual rate. This continues the job loss of the third quarter, which saw a decline of 3.6 percent at an annual rate. Oregon has lost jobs since the first quarter of 2001." At the end of January, Oregon's 8.0 percent unemployment rate led the nation.

The pain will continue. The OEA forecasts employment will fall 0.7 percent in 2002. It expects manufacturing to slow in the year with an annual decline of 4.3 percent. The lumber and wood products sector is projected to be down 0.7 percent and the electrical machinery sector that contains semiconductors should decline 5.7 percent. Construction will continue to lose jobs in 2002. The OEA estimates job losses in this area will be 7.7 percent. In addition, trade jobs will decline 0.7 percent.

In all, Oregon ranks number 50 of all states in non-farm job growth from December 2000 to December 2001.

Not quite what our leaders led us to believe a few years ago as they celebrated the success in attracting semiconductor-related companies expanding out of Northern California, Japan and South Korea.

Actually, the longer-term outlook for the semiconductor industry continues to be bright. But, the sharp recession of the industry, particularly in this region, in 2000 and 2001 begs a question. "Is Portland's metropolitan area a center of technology innovation, or is it in many respects little different than the manufacturing and assembly sites the electronics companies have opened in Malaysia, Singapore, China and the Philippines?"

Before you allow defensiveness to color your answer, think of where the Portland area's Epson and Hewlett Packard printer and InFocus projector plants have gone. Then look at those semiconductor companies that have decided to close their fabrication facilities in the United States while contracting with firms in Taiwan, Singapore and elsewhere to supply the packaged chips. For these firms, there is a better return on capital focusing on design and development of new products, usually in a center of innovation – namely, Silicon Valley. So, if your answer is "maybe," or "yes," then Oregon's past advantages will be short-lived and always vulnerable to lower cost facilities outside the region or the United States.

(The latest in semiconductor manufacturing technology may be considered the 300 mm fab. Currently, the industry has only one 300 mm fab in full production. Nine more are ramping up production, three are accepting equipment, 14 are in construction and 13 additional sites are planned. Noteworthy for those concerned about the diminishing American position in this area is that many of these new facilities are in Asia, resulting from national strategic decisions.)

Does anyone here know how to play this game?

I suggest that Oregon's "unique quality of life" is also subject to competition and deterioration. For example, the other day I came across the following promotional release:

> The state is rich in natural resources. It has a strong resource base of highly educated people, backed by an extensive educational infrastructure comprising world-renowned schools, colleges, and institutes of higher learning, and research and development centers. Its labor force is highly skilled, disciplined and hardworking. And, above all, it has a far-sighted, development oriented, investor-friendly government. A government that firmly believes in, and actively encourages, public–private partnerships. A major attraction of the State is its excellent living conditions, which brings talented professionals from all over the country and overseas to live and work here. ... Beach resorts, holiday homes and clubs cater to diverse recreational needs. Facilities for sports like golf, tennis ... and swimming abound. Its main city is known for its ... cyber cafes [and] restaurants. ... The entire State offers a wide range of cultural offerings ... theatre, dance and music. The State boasts of some excellent medical facilities. Well-equipped hospitals, nursing homes, as well as national level medical institutes offer a wide range of medical services.

Moreover, the United Nations' Human Development Report-2000 recognizes the State's largest city as the fourth leading global hub of technological innovation, with San Francisco, Austin and Taiwan's capital, Taipei, being ahead.

As you are sitting stalled in traffic heading out to Hillsboro or Wilsonville or downtown to Portland, listening to the news reports about cutting school hours from a schedule that already is one of the shortest in the United States, or reductions in the budget for higher education, you just might want to learn a little more about India's Karnataka State and its capital, Bangalore.

If you are comfortably entrenched in Portland it is unlikely that you will spend even a minute contemplating a move to India. But, if you are a developer of computer software, you had better consider what Bangalore has to offer, or be prepared to have your domestic costs make your products non-competitive. Texas Instruments and Intel certainly have. Or, if you are a partner in a law firm, you might think about having your legal research and generic drafting done by highly trained, English-speaking law clerks who charge a fraction of what you pay your first-year lawyers who just graduated from law school. Indeed, that is what one of Texas' largest legal firms is doing today.

And India is not alone in recognizing it must "industrialize or perish." Vietnam has announced it will have more than 50,000 highly trained software engineers in three years, each earning 90 percent less than the average American software engineer (and 40–60 percent less than the average Indian programmer).

It is time for concerned Oregonians to stop daydreaming about the advantages of our "quality of life" making us wealthy forever and start reading the tea leaves. Already one of Oregon's important advantages has largely been priced away. I am referring to low-cost electricity and competitive natural gas prices. Unfortunate decisions by the Bonneville Power Administration and other utilities during the illusory period of long-term supply shortages have forced our energy prices to rise at the same time they are falling elsewhere in the nation. Resultantly, our non-ferrous metals producers and their employees have been decimated. Although many believe this to be a short-term interruption of operations for these high wage companies, Kaiser Aluminum's bankruptcy may be a harbinger of things to come. Keep in mind that smelters and factories somewhere else are now filling the demand for aluminum and they may not be so easy to displace, even if energy prices in our region go back down.

Losing jobs and suffering at home from the winter cold because your electric bills have gone up more than 40 percent doesn't do much for one's quality of life. And neither does persistent hunger.

In our state, where the elected officials proudly proclaim their stewardship of their constituents' quality of life, there resides the highest percentage of any state of households where one or more household members were hungry at least some time during the year due to inadequate resources for food. The US Department of Agriculture's Prevalence of Food Insecurity and Hunger, by State, 1996–1998 calculated that Oregon is a full 16 percent above the second state in ranking of those who are "food insecure with hunger" and 66 percent above the nation's average. "Quality of life" – for who?

In its *Profiles of Poverty and Hunger in Oregon 2000*, the Oregon Food Bank said, "Every week, thousands of Oregon and Clark County, Washington residents have difficulty getting enough food to eat. ... In fiscal year 1999/00, nearly 515,000 people received an emergency food box and nearly 2,900,000 meals were served by Oregon Food Bank Network member programs and sites. ... Approximately one in seven people in the state received food assistance through this network."

Does anyone here know how to play this game?

Being unemployable at a living wage is the result of the failure of our schools.

I suggest we demand our leaders stop paying lip service to supporting education and start fixing a system that leaves its students wondering why they are forced to take courses that have no immediate or longer-term meaning to them other than they are "required" in order to graduate. Perhaps that is why 33 percent of Oregon secondary school students fail to graduate (compared with 26 percent nationwide) putting Oregon in the bottom 20 percent of all states, according to a study of the Class of 1998, published by the Manhattan Institute for Policy Research.

Let me translate the meaning of these numbers for you. How profitable do you feel your real estate investments will be if the vacancy rate was 33 percent? In fact, how many financial institutions out there will finance your project if you forecast it would be 67 percent occupied at maturity?

Then think how much you will have to raise the rents for those occupying the remaining 67 percent of the space available to cover the costs of maintaining the empty offices and storefronts. That, essentially, is what working Oregonians will be asked to do for the high school dropouts who will earn a median income of $15,000 a year, and not be able to afford habitable living conditions, medical care and education for their children.

Does anyone here know how to play this game?

Perhaps it is time to ask, "if our failure in public education is due to large class sizes or budgetary concerns, why does the State rank among the highest in the Scholastic Aptitude Tests (SATs)?" Acknowledging that those who choose to take the exam are likely to be among our educational elite, isn't that also likely to be true in the other states? Furthermore, aren't these "successful" students going to the same schools as our "unsuccessful" students?

Maybe, just maybe, our teachers are pretty good after all. Maybe, just maybe, it is the curriculum's failure to inform the kids why they are asked to study geometry and algebra, ancient history and foreign languages that leads to their disinterest in spending their time in these pursuits. Could it be that Oregon's employers might provide graphic illustrations of the application of these disciplines through internships and site visits? I believe it is worth a try.

Before I leave education, I'd like to toss another idea into the maelstrom. As you are probably aware, some of our leading technology-based citizens are working hard to get the Legislature to appropriate several hundred million dollars to establish a "world-class" technology-based university. Although it would be wonderful if they were to succeed, I suspect the fiscal hurdles may be insurmountable, particularly in light of the almost $1 billion budget deficit the State is facing in the next biennium. Additionally, the political climate may not be accepting of such expenditure as might be inferred from the cold reception Richard and Nancy Wendt received when they offered $100 million to the Oregon Institute of Technology, if that school was to become a private college. Yet, few people disagree with the widely held desire for an educational center of excellence in Oregon.

So, here is my idea. Let us take a page from the consortium of five colleges located in Claremont, California. A student enrolled at Scripps College For Women, for example, can take courses at Harvey Mudd, one of the world's finest engineering schools despite its small size, Pomona, Pitzer or Claremont McKenna colleges. A similar successful model can be found in Northampton, Massachusetts. The participating institutions there include Amherst, Smith, Mt. Holyoke and Hampshire colleges and the University of Massachusetts at Amherst. Why not try to accomplish this in Portland with Lewis & Clark, Portland State University, the University of Portland, Reed College and the Northwest College of Art?

Well, let's go back to Portland's reality.

Another step on Portland's slippery slope towards mediocrity is the continuing loss of our larger corporate headquarters to other communities. The recent acquisition of Willamette Industries by Tacoma-based Weyerhaeuser furthered the management brain drain that has stifled entrepreneurial innovation and community leadership in our state and region. It is the competitive spirit that comes with jousting against the best managements in the world that brightens one's imagination and trains one to take positive actions. Branch managers don't have that competitive opportunity or, if they do, they are promoted to headquarters' positions, leaving their former communities with very few examples of "real winners." Indeed, as *Newsweek* magazine concluded in its November 1998 report on the cities that have emerged as high-tech hubs, "A combination of Vegas-style 'win big' gaming mentality and techno-wizard creativity is the mind set in the hottest tech cities. Places with this unique and dynamic attitude are soaring to new high-tech heights." Let me add, if you, individually, don't have the initiative to soar you will always remain on the ground. The same message pertains to Oregon.

Does anyone here know how to play this game?

If these unsettling thoughts are the nucleus of Oregon's resourcefulness how will we ever make any meaningful progress? Let me turn to a study sponsored by the Council on Competitiveness and led by the highly respected Harvard professor, Michael Porter.

Its recently published, "Clusters of Innovation: Regional Foundations of US Competitiveness," presents the conclusion that, while the American economy depends on national policies and national investment choices, innovation starts at home. The Council's report is clear that "in healthy regions, competitiveness and innovation are concentrated in clusters, or interrelated industries in which the region specializes. ... [A] region's ability to produce high-value products and services that support high wage jobs depends on the creation and strengthening of these regional hubs of competitiveness and innovation." Furthermore, "the prosperity of a region depends on the productivity of all its industries."

As Russell Gold wrote in the *Wall Street Journal* in June 2001, "Everybody wants clusters these days. The problem is how to get them."

To help find the answer, I turned to William Hoffman, a unique combination of academic, social and industry entrepreneur, who has played a major part in developing Minneapolis' highly successful role in the worldwide effort to enhance our knowledge of biomedicine and bioscience. The Communications Coordinator of the Biomedical Engineering Institute of the University of Minnesota, Mr Hoffman created MBBNet, the largest regional university–industry collaborative network in the world, connecting more than 950 regional health-oriented organizations and providing medical and scientific information to more than 16,000 people around the world each month. By networking the Minneapolis community of health innovators and integrating them into the global community, he subtly changed global cooperation, regional competitiveness, and the high-wage base in the Twin Cities. He is credited with enabling over $700 million of new investment in the region.

Through Mr Hoffman's writings I became acquainted with British economist Paul Ormerod, author of *Butterfly Economics: A New General Theory of Social and Economic Behavior* (1999). Introducing Mr Ormerod's book, Mr Hoffman said, "Conventional economics refuses to consider the influence the behavior of an individual has on other individuals.

Ants, for example, leave chemical secretions in their wake. These secretions, called pheromones, influence the decisions of other ants in pursuing a food source."

Mr Ormerod further suggested, "So an ant emerging from the nest for the first time would be influenced in its decision by the trails of the ants it encounters on its journey. In economic terms this means the behavior of agents is influenced directly by the behavior of others. ... The signals left by the creatures mean that the random choices of the first few ants to leave the nest could exercise a decisive influence on the behavior of the whole colony."

It is a system in which positive feedback predominates. "It predicts that, once a few more ants, for whatever reason, start to visit one of the sites rather than the other there will be a strong tendency for that site to become the favored destination for more and more ants."

Mr Hoffman then suggests, "substitute 'cluster' for 'colony' and 'people' for 'ants' and you have a plausible explanation for the regional basis of innovation. A change in behavior can occur, of course, even a dramatic one [the theoretical 'butterfly effect' in which the air turbulence from a butterfly's wings sets off a dynamic that later yields a hurricane]. But the underlying conditions must change first. In clusters that means the condition of economic opportunity."

Stephen Johnson, author of *Emergence: The Connected Lives of Ants, Brains, Cities and Software* (2001), was interviewed by the online magazine *Salon.com* in November last year. Asked about the connection between ants, cities, brains and software, Johnson recommended we look at the ant colony,

> where you have this system of 10,000 ants, none of which are actually in charge but somehow they manage to do these very complex engineering tasks and social organization and resource management things that are mesmerizing feats.
>
> They look like they should be planned from above, but in fact they are entirely organized by local rules and local interactions. The catchphrase is that the whole is sometimes smarter than the sum of its parts. And when you look at something like an ant colony, the question that you ask is who makes this happen? Who makes this collective intelligence happen? And the answer is everybody and nobody at the same time.

Mr Hoffman concluded, "So it is with regional innovation centers like Silicon Valley."

Paul Krugman, an MIT economist has similar thoughts about the application of conscious design and concerted effort to create innovation. In his essay, "Some Chaotic Thoughts on Regional Dynamics,"[1] Professor Krugman commented, "I think Henry Ford once said that history is just one damn thing after another. Maybe not, but explanations of economic location are almost always historical, and the history does tend to have a 'one damn thing after another' character. If you try to explain why a particular region is home to a particular industry, you usually end up explaining it largely by describing the sequence of events that caused the industry to be there."

The sequence involves the ability of producers to share specialized providers of inputs, the advantages to both employers and workers of a thick labor market, and localized spillovers of knowledge. Professor Krugman says they apply just as well to Boston's complex of world-class hospitals as they did to the Sheffield cutlery district that developed in England starting 700 years ago. "Now as then," he says, "such localized externalities provide a virtuous circle that tends to keep an industrial cluster locked in place once established."

How do such clusters get established in the first place? he asked. "You might think that the process is largely random: an accidental event, or a remarkable individual, creates the seed around which an industry grows." Two Federal Reserve Bank of Boston economists, Lynn Browne and Steven Sass suggest, however, that the process is …

not so much random as it is chaotic. Examining the New England economic base, Browne and Sass traced the evolution of the mutual fund industry and the resulting ability of metropolitan Boston to benefit disproportionately from the ten-year stock market boom of the last decade, to the financing needs of high-technology startups that built up a special sort of financial competence in the area. They went further back, recognizing that the high-technology industries, equally clearly, did not emerge by accident. Instead, they were there largely as a legacy of World War II and Cold War research. And this research was concentrated in Cambridge because of the presence of universities, which was ultimately the product of the need of Puritans for someplace to train preachers. At each stage, there was a clear reason for what happened; but nobody could possibly have predicted the sequence. (Krugman)

Can we apply New England's history to Oregon?

Would Nike have emerged here if Phil Knight had not attended the University of Oregon? Would adidas' US headquarters be here if

Nike had not been established in the Portland suburbs? If not, would a well thought out economic development program have conceived of the athletic footwear and apparel industries as attractive for support? Your guess is as good as mine.

Oregon's emergence as a leader in displays and electronics test and measurement equipment is also the result of an unplanned series of events.

Marshall Lee, in his book *A Passion for Quality: The First Fifty-Five Years of Electro Scientific Industries 1944–1999*, detailed the serendipity that led to the formation of Oregon's electronics industry. Mr Lee wrote,

> Even during the Depression, the diversified economy of Portland provided many of her citizens with a comfortable, middle-class standard of living. ... Indeed, in 1935, Portland ranked second, behind Long Beach, California, in "spendable family income," with an average of $3,382 per household. Not surprisingly, those who could afford it indulged in the purchase of the nation's newest entertainment technology: a radio. From 1937 on, those who could afford a radio might well have gone to the shop of a young businessman ... whose store was on Portland's east side, at 57th and Foster Rd. Here, in "the House that Jack Built," Jack Murdock sold appliances and radios: GEs, Philcos, RCAs and Stromberg-Carlsons. And, if your radio needed fixing, in the back of Murdock's shop a young man, Howard Vollum [Murdock and Vollum later co-founded Tektronix], operated a repair shop.

Coincidentally, Mr Lee noted,

> Since the turn of the century the United States Forest Service (USFS) had maintained an active interest in wireless communication. Even before World War I, the USFS attempted to link its vast network of ranger stations, camps and fire lookout towers by means of telegraph lines. In the Pacific Northwest, Region 6, the Forest Service Radio Lab was ... located in Vancouver, Washington. There, under the direction of Harold Lawson, the Lab designed the rugged, portable, battery-operated radios the USFS needed in the field.
>
> Harold Lawson is the grandfather of high technology in the Pacific Northwest. Lawson was a self-taught radio expert . . . He worked in the woods, started a radio station at Oregon Agricultural College, and eventually joined the Forest Service. His knowledge of radio soon brought him to the Region 6 USFS Radio Lab. As its director, by the

mid-Thirties he led a small team of engineers, among them Logan Belleville who with Vollum and Murdock would become Tektronix' founders. With the outbreak of the Second World War, Lawson's work at the Forest Service Developmental Lab took on new urgency. During the war, [Harold Lawson's] job was complicated by the Air Raid Warning Service, which became a responsibility of the Forest Service. Suitable communications equipment was not available for Air Raid Warning purposes and, even after the Laboratory had developed prototype equipment, there was no place for such a civilian agency to let contracts. Mr Lawson took the bull by the horns, turned the laboratory facilities into a manufacturing plant, hired a work force, and with only civilian priorities, began the manufacture of the necessary equipment. Thus it was that the unlikely spot of Portland, Oregon, whose infrastructure and infant industries had nothing to do with electronics, developed into one of the nation's leading centers for the development of practical, rugged, portable field radio equipment.

From their inauspicious starts, Tektronix and Electro Scientific Industries (which evolved from Brown Electronics) became world-class companies, hiring some of the finest engineers to graduate from many of the best engineering schools in the nation. By the end of 1979, Tektronix was a dominant employer in Oregon with more than 20,000 well-paid workers. Shortly thereafter, however, key patents expired and the high profitability of Tektronix withered. Budgets were cut and new projects deferred. Increasingly, the company encouraged its more entrepreneurial engineers to consider opening up their own companies and they did so. These spin-offs include, Integrated Measurement Systems, InFocus Systems, Magni Systems, Lattice Semiconductor, Planar Systems, TriQuint Semiconductor, Mentor Graphics, Cascade Microtech, and Laughlin Wilt. Thus began the second wave of entrepreneurial high tech activity in Oregon.

At the same time, Intel, which had built semiconductor fabrication facilities in Washington County based upon its position in DRAMs, also faced difficult times in the Eighties as memory chip prices fell sharply. There, too, the most entrepreneurial of the engineers left and companies such as Sequent Computer Systems, RadiSys and Protocol Systems emerged.

With Tektronix' number of employees now well below 5,000, the number of spin-offs emanating from that company has essentially disappeared. Intel's success in microprocessors has given it the currency to persuade its employees to stay at the company, rather than take the risk of starting a new firm. Moreover, it would be tough to find more than a few startup companies that have emerged from the facilities of the established electronics companies that rushed en masse to Oregon in the Nineties. Thus, the entrepreneurial spirit that characterized the 1980s and early-1990s is at best quiescent. (Keep in mind that, unlike at Tektronix and Intel, the new branches of the established electronics companies brought few skilled marketing vice-presidents, product management heads or research and development experts to Oregon. Instead, people with manufacturing skills and little entrepreneurial experience largely manage these plants.)

Does anyone here know how to play this game?

Is this important? Should we be concerned at the substantial secular slowdown in new entrepreneurial startups? Allow me to return to "Clusters of Innovation," the Council on Competitiveness' report. In its Findings and Implications section, the Council made it clear that above-average economic performance measures are not enough to ensure regional prosperity. Rather, maintaining, much less increasing, a region's standard of living requires the steady growth of productivity, which in turn requires innovation.

Its study provides ample evidence that research alone, e.g., at Oregon Health & Science University, will not assure growing wealth. Rather, it is the relative effectiveness of commercialization that greatly affects the economic impact of research. Commercialization, according to the Council's report, is a difficult but important ingredient for generating entrepreneurship. Some regions have high levels of R&D investments and numerous specialized research centers, but still lag in terms of innovation output because knowledge is not effectively or rapidly transferred to companies. Keep that in mind when you are asked to set aside scarce [State] Lottery dollars for supporting the virtually non-existent technology transfer programs at Oregon's universities.

As well intentioned as they may be, I don't feel our government economic development efforts will be successful without strong, committed private participation. Successful economic development demands thorough due diligence effort on an experienced, knowledgeable, realistic basis. Clusters of Innovation ... revealed that it requires strong leadership committed to regional economic development, to bringing together our companies, knowledge centers, governments and collaborative institutions to ensure they contribute to their full potential.

Current statistics make it clear that Oregonians cannot wait until its top elected officials learn how to play this game. In fact, if we are to solve our expanding fundamental problems, they need to recognize that leading this State is not a game after all.

Or, those tragic numbers of unemployed workers, uneducated students and hungry citizens will continue to grow.

Thank you.

Note

1. http://www.wws.princeton.edu/~pkrugman/temin.html   or   http://web.mit.edu/krugman/www/temin.html

15
Bring Back Oregon's Common Sense of Purpose

Chet Orloff

Once upon a time, Oregonians spoke the same language.

Indeed, we were nearly bilingual: We spoke not only with the honest conviction of self-reliant individuals, but simultaneously conversed in the dialect of the common good. Words such as community and friendship and culture actually meant what we like to think they do.

After listening to six months of raw and undigested politispeak, it's a wonder we're still speaking at all, much less to one another.

By their very nature, campaigns divide the candidates. Yet we voters have let the candidates divide us. The infighting among the candidates and, consequently, among us these past months has been corrosive. Always rough and tumble, Oregon politics long maintained a civil tradition. Lately and sadly, we've been lashed by most uncivil tongues. Recent politics has been bereft of the humor, surprise, wit, brilliance and respite that once made it as entertaining as it was educational.

Increasingly, the language we hear is financial, through which we've been offered the supposed best "deals" for our tax dollars – and hence, for our children, our land and our government – as if all that matters to us is our money. Rather than regarded as the communicators and conservators we have proudly been, we are now treated like consumers or, worse, mere commodities.

Before this chatter about the goods, there was once more talk of the common good. They weren't halcyon days – there never were such in Oregon's past. But, once, Oregonians made the time to speak with words grounded in a deep sense of place. And they spoke well about the kind of place they were creating, the kind of identity they were trying to establish. Many among them knew it was a long process they were engaged in, not the completion of a finished product. Without quite using the words, they spoke a great deal about the common good. Unbridled individualism was not part of the larger vocabulary.

The common good is one of those big, formidable ideas. To some, it threatens coercion or smacks of vacuity. To others, it's just another paunchy sentiment from the 50-somethings. To a few, however, it has long been a noble vision, never to be fully realized, but always to be strived toward, cynicism be damned.

How do we take such a big idea and instill it in small, everyday practices? Well, we can begin by looking at how Oregonians did it before.

Once, new Oregonians with vastly differing perspectives and backgrounds were able to organize an entire government, even taxing themselves in the bargain. Recognizing the value of the common good, another generation dug deep in its collective pocket and built an education system envied by neighboring states. Later generations understood plainly the value of making our beaches common property, comprehended clearly the value of preserving Oregon's lands and, notwithstanding the occasionally errant blowhard, elected legislators who not only communicated well but actually wanted to get things done in a bipartisan and timely way.

Previous Oregonians certainly tripped on their tongues and spoke out of both sides of their mouths. But they could speak a language, even as recently as 1990, that carried the idea of the common good a step closer to reality. Then, we seemed to go deaf and dumb.

We can't go back in time, but we can learn to speak an older language, with its own, rich vocabulary. We would need to become conversant with the actual usage of such terms as historicity and identity, mutuality and reciprocity, participation and integration. Hard work, and it would take discipline.

The premise of such a language is that we stand by words, trusting them and those who speak them. It is, perhaps, a visionary idea: that political and civic life for the common good depends on, even demands, a degree of trust and respect.

And learning an old language would, after all, take practice – what language doesn't? – practice in finding and agreeing on the shared standards of what is good and objective. While we've been schooled differently – to think urban/rural, upstate/downstate, eastside/westside – we can break old habits and yet learn anew. It's been done before in Oregon history, when there was hope and discipline; it can be done again.

16

Please, Portland, Don't Pearlize Joe's Garage

Pierre Ouellette

In a widely known song by the late Frank Zappa, he sang the praises of a place called Joe's Garage. Here, Joe and his band crammed in next to an old Dodge and blissfully banged out primitive rock n' roll for hours on end. The garage was cheap, crummy and minimal but had one glorious virtue: It was utterly uncritical of the musical explorations going on within it. And, ultimately, it produced Zappa, considered by many to be one of the great musical geniuses of our era.

A sizable chunk of central Portland once had swarms of Joe's Garages, places where artists of every stripe could operate outside the bounds of critical convention and roam along the far limits of artistic possibility. Today, we call this area the Pearl District, and you will still find art here – but not the kind produced in Joe's Garage. Instead you'll encounter a social phenomenon called the New Bohemianism, where highly educated, affluent people gather to embrace the simple virtues of the artist's life, and thus renounce the crass materialism that made them affluent in the first place. Not surprisingly, they have lifted the economic tide in the Pearl District to a level where those operating on the creative fringe are almost completely excluded.

In response, the artistic refugees have retreated across the river to what is called the Central Eastside Industrial District, which hugs the river under the main bridges into downtown. Here they coexist with their creative siblings in the commercial arts, such as fledgling design firms, photographers and start-up ad agencies. Often the two groups blur into a special kind of symbiosis: The radical fringe throws raw creative fuel to the commercial people, who reciprocate with paying gigs for the fringe dwellers. None of this would be possible without a bountiful supply of Joe's Garages, which this district has in abundance, in the form of primitive space within aging warehouses and other such structures in their industrial twilight.

But wait. Land in the central city is finite, and the gaze of Progress is gradually shifting from the Pearl over to the east bank. Talk of "development" and "flex space" is in the air. To be fair, many such schemes will probably be dedicated to preserving the district's "creative ambience." However, just as tree farms will never replace the majesty of old-growth forests, a refurbished industrial eastside will never preserve the fragile artistic ecosystem that exists there today.

Why? Because development costs money, which translates into higher rents. The commercial artists here may be able survive higher costs, but not those who operate in Joe's Garage. As the New Bohemian tide washes over the near eastside, it will drown the last spawning ground for progressive, experimental art in the central city of Portland.

So who should care? Everyone. The radical fringe in the arts is like research and development in corporations. It doesn't make any money, but it's critical to the organization's survival over the long haul. What's strange and alien today becomes acceptable and valued tomorrow. A place that turns its back on this fact is committing a slow-motion form of cultural suicide.

However, while the community may give up, the artists out on the edge will not. They are driven by an internal fire that's oblivious to zoning laws, development policies and master plans. They will simply pack up and move elsewhere in their search for Joe's Garage. And that will be a great loss to this fine city of ours.

Part III
And Beyond

17
Sustaining a Technopolis Initiative

Fred Phillips

Many regions have attempted to emulate Silicon Valley's success in economic growth stimulated by technology entrepreneurship. Some of these efforts have shown good results, some are ongoing and remain promising, and others have been short-lived. This chapter will present cases and advance hypotheses about the sustainability/persistence of regional technology entrepreneurship development initiatives. Where other chapters explored the critical success factors for aspiring techno-regions, the present chapter focuses on the initiative process itself, and the mechanisms that launch it and sustain it.

Regional technology economies and regional technology initiatives

This book's introduction characterized successful technopolis regions as having a robust local value chain, critical masses of companies in selected clusters, and a relatively compact geography. Technopolis regions grow by attracting new companies; nurturing existing local firms; encouraging entrepreneurship; providing a supportive context for research, technology entrepreneurship, and business; and networking energetically, both internally and externally.

Large companies can provide the technologies, management talent, financing, and ambitious entrepreneurs that are the essential ingredients for a vibrant new venture community. Large and medium companies are often the natural customers of start-ups. For these reasons, a regional strategy focusing solely on high-technology start-ups would have little chance of success; a balanced strategy is needed, reaching out to start-ups, SMEs and large companies alike. Nonetheless, a region that hosts university entrepreneurship programs, supports public–private new business incubators, and respects (or even makes folk heroes of) entrepreneurs is more likely to achieve a self-sustaining entrepreneurial culture as a healthy part of its technopolis.

In addition, the introduction implied that technopolis development can only flow from a community that displays a smart combination of all or most of the factors listed in Table 17.1.

In Silicon Valley, California, and in Boston, Massachusetts, a combination of top universities, local investors, trend-setting cultures, and pioneering entrepreneurs caused those regions to experience take-off almost spontaneously. Other regions, hoping to imitate the successes of these US coastal areas, have established a variety of government programs and civic initiatives to facilitate hoped-for take-offs. Some of these initiatives prove transitory, wasting time and money. Others persist as "seed crystals" for multiple waves of new ventures based on multiple new technologies. This chapter takes the view that in all but the most blessed regions, sustained intiatives are a necessary condition for ultimate regional success. It lists and discusses the factors that enable sustained initiatives.

It is hard to distinguish the critical success factors (CSFs) of the technopolis (Table 17.1) itself from the CSFs of the initiative organizations. For example, the technopolis initiative must have visionary and persistent leadership, just as the community at large must. It is clear, moreover, that some community CSFs are more easily achieved when the initiative organization pushes the community in that direction; a mayor and a chamber of commerce will, for example, do a better job of marketing the region when the initiative organization has educated these persons on the best practices of civic marketing.

That is, on some dimensions the regional and initiative CSFs are identical, and on some other dimensions the initiative is the proximate cause of the regional CSFs – the "factor behind the factor." In the latter

Table 17.1   Technopolis success factors

- Embracing change.
- Social capital, especially with cross-sectoral links.
- Cluster strategies that target specific company groups for collocation.
- Visionary and persistent leadership.
- The will to action.
- Action.
- Constant selling.
- Self-investment in infrastructure.
- Outreach and networking.

case, the initiative cannot survive without performing that service effectively. However, later sections of this chapter will identify still other CSFs for sustained initiatives that are less directly parallel to the overall regional CSFs.

One striking example of the latter, worth mentioning at this point, arose in Austin, Texas. By the late 1990s, several local initiatives had shown excellent results. Start-up and established companies in software, equipment for oil exploration and semiconductor manufacturing, and computers were flourishing. A number of these initiatives' movers and shakers had done well financially; they were tempted to say, "I've got mine, buddy, good luck with yours." There was, in fact, less public sentiment in favor of continued civic initiatives for entrepreneurship. Good had proven to be the enemy of better; people were content. The present author was not inclined to fight an uphill battle to continue the initiatives. Another civic leader, however, argued against resting on our laurels, insisting the public–private cooperative initiatives were needed "now more than ever." Of course, the Internet bubble burst shortly after that, proving him right. Another impressive Austin leader now says, "Every morning I ask myself, what I can do today to make Austin the best place in the world to live."[1] Through the efforts of these gentlemen and others, Austin launched new initiatives for clean energy and for the computer gaming industry. The gaming initiative is flourishing today, and several energy companies have been launched.

Though history may endow a region with many of the characteristics of Table 17.1, nearly all the items in the Table are learned behaviors.[2] They may be learned regardless of the region's history, geography, or natural endowments. Regions hoping to reproduce the Silicon Valley phenomenon should take encouragement from this. However, when the characteristic behaviors require culture change, one must count on generational turnover as the most reliable method of effecting it, and look at a 25-year planning horizon. The bad news, for those who are in a hurry to build a technopolis, is that all the items in Table 17.1, except the cluster strategy, require long-term culture change if they are not already prevalent in the region.

Organization and thrust of the chapter

Most publications analyzing regional technology development mix technopolis CSFs with process (initiative) CSFs. This chapter distinguishes CSFs for the region from CSFs for the initiative process, and focuses on latter, which are farther up the causal chain. However, if we accept (as I argue below) that technopolis formation takes a long time, then a sustainable process becomes a factor behind the factor.

What makes a sustainable and sustained process? Certainly there are some uncontrollable factors behind the factors, having to do with the region's history, culture and geography. This chapter looks only at controllable factors in the initiative process – organization, leadership, finance, and strategy – and argues that these comprise most of the pertinent CSFs.

The following sections contrast technology entrepreneurship initiatives with cluster initiatives, and discuss the time scale and life cycle of technology entrepreneurship initiatives. Both kinds of initiatives are often studied by a mix of survey and case methodology. The present chapter's mix of case and ethnological methods (the latter perhaps biased by the author's insider status) complements earlier efforts.

The chapter concludes with an annotated list of critical success factors for sustained and sustainable regional initiatives for technology entrepreneurship ("RITEs").

Time scale of technopolis

In this section I will argue that the transformation of a region by means of technology entrepreneurship is a long-term process, and that it is not unusual for a *crisis* to catalyze a region's entrepreneurial economy. One implication of this argument is that a long-lived regional initiative may be *necessary*, if only to ensure that the initiative organization is there to catch the crisis (whenever it may happen) and bend it to constructive ends. A secondary implication is that the currently prevalent models for incubator consulting and technopolis consulting are flawed, doing more harm than good to the region that hires such consultants.

There are no overnight successes. The technological renaissance of Austin, Texas, took 25 years – and by some yardsticks, much longer. See Table 17.2.

In 2005 the Austin Technology Incubator claimed a cumulative 65 "graduate" companies including four that have gone public on Nasdaq and 13 that have been acquired; more than 2,850 jobs created; more than $600M in venture capital secured; and approximately $833 annual per capita contribution to Austin-area GDP. Dell Corporation, of course, has grown to enormous size and is one of the most admired firms in the world.

Table 17.2 Timeline of the Austin technopolis

1955	Professor Frank McBee founds military electronics contractor Tracor Inc., the University of Texas' first major spin-out company and later Austin's first home-grown company to be listed on the New York Stock Exchange. Over subsequent decades, Tracor employees spin out at least twenty more companies.
1967	Attracted by Texas' industrial potential, the large engineering schools at UT and at Monterrey and the national laboratories in neighboring New Mexico, technology entrepreneur George Kozmetsky[a] becomes Dean of the University of Texas' School of Business.
1967	IBM comes to Austin.
1969	Texas Instruments comes to Austin.
1974	Motorola comes to Austin.
1976	National Instruments founded. Kozmetsky founds IC² Institute. The Institute proves key to the transformation of the Austin region into what *Business Week* magazine calls a "technology hot spot," that is, a fast-growing regional economy that clearly owes its growth to both start-up and established technology companies.
1980	Schlumberger comes to Austin.
1981	Kozmetsky resigns Deanship; moves IC² out of UT B-school, staying on as Institute Director.
1982	The microelectronics consortium MCC chooses Austin location.
1983	Stephen Szygenda founds the Rubicon incubator.
1984	3M locates in Austin.
1985	Dell Computer founded in Austin.
1987	IC² publishes book on public-private alliances for economic development. *US News & World Report* lauds the IC² Institute for "the world's most advanced research on the commercialization of new technologies."
1988	The semiconductor manufacturing consortium SEMATECH locates in Austin.
1989	Walter Bissex founds Technology Advisors Group, educating more service professionals and investors about high technology. Walt Rostow and Elspeth Rostow found The Austin Project, one of many exemplary civic entrepreneurship efforts in the region.
1989	IC² founds the Austin Technology Incubator (ATI).
1990	Texas Capital Network (now The Capital Network) founded and located at ATI.
1991	Economist Angelos Angelou announces software has become Austin's largest sector (measured by number of companies).
1992	Austin Software Council formed. ATI wins NBIA Incubator of the Year award.
1993	Kozmetsky awarded National Medal of Technology by President Clinton.
1994	Everett Rogers and David Gibson publish history of MCC and the Austin Technopolis.
1995	Kozmetsky steps down as Director of IC² Institute.
1996	Susan Engelking of Staats Falkenberg Partners presents invited paper on "Austin's Opportunity Economy" to the New York Academy of Science.

[a] Kozmetsky, a founding faculty member of the innovative Graduate School of Industrial Administration at Carnegie Tech (later Carnegie-Mellon University), left academe to work for Howard Hughes and later to found the very successful Teledyne Corp. In Austin he became (after McBee) the city's second godfather of entrepreneurship, encouraging and investing in many new ventures. Kozmetsky mentored Michael Dell and served on Dell's board of directors.

Kozmetsky offered a Dean's Scholarship to the present author, who arrived in Austin in 1969 and lived there until 1995, in that time playing several roles in Austin's technology renaissance under Kozmetsky's mentorship.

There are a number of things worth noting about these successes:

- Their foundations had been laid 50 years earlier – or perhaps more than 100 years earlier at the founding of the University of Texas at Austin.
- Texans founded UT (the university was authorized in 1839 but did not commence classes until 1883) desiring a "university of the first class." They were motivated by Texas pride, the desire to preserve culture in a frontier region, and a perception that wealth would flow, somehow, from knowledge. (Likewise, Stanford University, the seed crystal for the Silicon Valley technology entrepreneurship phenomenon, was founded in order to keep wealthy, conservative California youth out of the clutches of Harvard liberals.) There was in that day every reason to believe the benefits would flow statewide rather than concentrate in Austin, and for many decades that was indeed the case.
- Austin's educational infrastructure and its entrepreneurial activity (the latter enjoying an unremarkable growth rate) existed for decades before "take-off" (a self-sustaining, fast-growth phase) occurred.
- Though George Kozmetsky (see Table 17.2) had preached technology entrepreneurship for decades, it was not until the prices oil, cattle, and real estate – the traditional sources of Texas wealth – all declined precipitously and simultaneously in the 1980s that wealthy Texans decided to heed his sermon and invest in high tech.

Mukherjee (2005) shows how the same pattern of government investment, slow infrastructure and entrepreneurial development, followed by a crisis-generated opportunity (the Y2K problem) spurred Bangalore's growth in the 21st century. See Table 17.3. Mukherjee adds, "The 'sudden' buzz in Bangalore is actually just a new chapter in a 100-year-old saga. No amount of planning could have telescoped the process into 10 years."

One reason for this is that the crises could not have been foreseen. Indeed, crises are not part of conventional cluster theory, which instead emphasizes a critical mass of suppliers and competitors. Critical mass was important for Austin and Bangalore, but it was not the whole story. One might infer that a RITE must be sustained just in order to ensure that it is extant and ready to act when a crisis arises. A more constructive inference is that the community must be responsive when one of its elements (perhaps a member of the formal initiative) identifies a crisis somewhere in the world; the region must be ready to mobilize diverse

Table 17.3 Bangalore timeline

1911	India's British rulers invited Nobel-laureate chemist William Ramsay to help select a site for a science school. Ramsay chose Bangalore.
1950s and 1960s	Independent India's first Prime Minister Jawaharlal Nehru set up state-owned engineering companies near Bangalore to fulfill his vision of rapid industrialization. He selected Bangalore because of the talent available at the Indian Institute of Science, the school set up by Ramsay. Non-state companies like Motor Industries Co., a subsidiary of Germany's Robert Bosch Gmbh, moved to Bangalore to supply parts.
1977	A socialist Indian government asked International Business Machines Corp. to leave the country after it refused to dilute its stake to 40 percent. IBM's departure became an opportunity for entrepreneurs like Azim Premji, who was then running a Bangalore-based vegetable-oil business started by his father. Premji hired engineers and built his first minicomputer.
1981	N.R. Narayana Murthy, an engineer who wanted to become a communist politician, changed his mind and set up Infosys Technologies Ltd. with $250 in Pune in western India. He moved the company to his hometown Bangalore in 1983 after Motor Industries gave him his first order.
1996	Global companies panicked that the year 2000 date change would crash computers. Premji's Wipro Ltd. and Murthy's Infosys rewrote millions of lines of code for customers worldwide. Bangalore's software industry, which employed only 947 people in 1991, expanded rapidly.
2005	Companies like IBM and Accenture Ltd. are hiring in Bangalore to cut costs. Meanwhile, Bangalore's home-grown software makers are competing for consulting contracts outside India that were once the domain of US and European technology companies.

Source: Mukherjee (2005), used with permission.

community elements to make an opportunity out of the crisis.[3] The community as a whole, in other words, must be entrepreneurial.

A crisis in food production, accompanied by sharp increase in population, caused the launch of Greece's trade with Sicily, and thence the "rocketing" Greek economy of the sixth through fourth century (Hall, 1998, p. 49).

Three anecdotes, of course, do not prove that crisis is a needed ingredient. However, two of the cases that follow (Portland, Oregon and Palma de Mallorca) are instances of "no crisis, no entrepreneurial transformation."

Even Washington, D.C. (our third case), with its amazing collection of technology companies already attracted to the US federal money faucet, experienced a new burst of activity in security-related technologies subsequent to the 9/11 tragedy. We can be comfortable agreeing with Mitroff and Linstone (1995), who declare, "Crisis may be the best, if not the only, teacher of how to create an economy that is better matched to the needs of today's world."

These concepts allow us to pinpoint the serious flaws in the current service offerings of cluster consultants:

1. Sticking to the mechanical metaphor of cluster theory,[4] the consultants impose a mechanical "solution" that ignores the constraints and opportunities implied by the region's history.
2. If the consultants are sufficiently sensitive to absorb some local history, their short-term assignment allows them only to make recommendations based on historical trends and current conditions. The question of how the community responds to crisis is not on their plate.
3. The short-term nature of the engagement, perhaps a consequence of the initiative's budget but also due to a flawed consulting service design, means the consultant is not an ongoing network facilitator/ partner for the client region, and cannot help with the long-term culture change issues that the region almost certainly must face.

As a result, highly publicized but unused consulting reports give the technopolis or cluster initiative a poor image in the region. Alternatively, the RITE can point at the unrealistic consulting report as an excuse for the initiative's lack of action and results.

I have gone to some lengths to establish that it takes a long time to create entrepreneurial take-off in a region. This is because many of the sustainability factors for RITEs flow consequentially from this fact. For example (and rather obviously), an initiative launched on the basis of a 1-year or 3-year government grant cannot persist beyond that horizon unless it diversifies its funding sources.

Technology entrepreneurship initiatives versus cluster initiatives

A cluster initiative – focused on a single cluster – is different from a RITE. Succinctly, the differences are: Clusters may not involve advanced technology at all; clusters may focus exclusively on large firms; the collocation focus of cluster theory is mechanical and does not encompass the social and multi-dimensional characteristics of RITEs; and a focus on the cluster industry precludes the cross-sectoral cooperation that RITEs value, e.g., the connection of high-tech with local arts and tourism industries. RITEs and cluster initiatives do share an emphasis on internal and external networking, on learning, and on exchange of information and skills. This section will expand on these similarities and differences, and comment on the initiative's relationship with governments.

Earlier, we identified Porter's (1998) cluster concept as a generalization of technopolis to non-tech industries. Both technopoleis and other clusters require concentrations of customers, suppliers, and infrastructure. Technopoleis have special needs in this regard, with more emphasis on higher education, research, and formal knowledge. High tech industries seem to benefit much more from localization economies than do non-tech clusters. In addition, technopoleis usually involve public–private partnerships that work to build a local presence in several industries rather than just one cluster.

Nonetheless, cluster initiatives (CIs) and RITEs have many common concerns and features. Sölvell's studies (Sölvell, Lindqvist *et al.*, 2003) show that cluster initiatives:

- Are "concerted initiatives."
- "Are now appearing in less developed regions of advanced economies, as well as in developing economies."
- Involve companies, government, and research and financial institutions working together, each with their own specific roles, facilitated by initiative organizations.
- Involve internal and international competition; "specialised, local suppliers; advanced training and scientific infrastructure; highly developed social capital; and advanced institutions for collaboration" and support of initiatives.
- "There is usually an explicitly shared vision for the CI and often much effort and time is spent on sharing the framework with the involved parties."

Of the 239 CIs surveyed by (Sölvell, Lindqvist *et al.* 2003), "32 percent were initiated by government, 27 percent by industry and 35 percent by both jointly. Financing comes mainly from government (54 percent), while industry finances 18 percent, and in 25 percent the costs are shared." The CIs were involved in promoting an average of 2.5 industry clusters, and most respondents reported dealing with some technology industries, including Information Technology, Medical Devices, Production Technology, Communications Equipment, Biopharmaceuticals, Automotive, or Analytical Instrumentation/Control Equipment.

Why do CIs fail? According to Sölvell *et al.*, failure is strongly related to:

- Absence of an explicitly formulated vision for the CI and quantified targets
- Initiative framework not adapted to the cluster's own strengths
- No office or an insufficient budget for significant projects
- Limiting the membership scope
- Isolated firms and lack of competition
- Lack of advanced suppliers
- Basic human capital
- Lack of trust and networks
- Few supporting institutions
- Weak frameworks
- Facilitator not having a strong network
- No involvement of influential local decision makers
- Lack of consensus or difficulties in achieving consensus
- No brand-building objective.

Sölvell *et al.* (2003) assert that the objective most strongly related to failed CIs is brand building, and that CIs should focus available resources on the most promising clusters (a seemingly obvious point, but one that our Portland, Oregon case, below, proves must be repeated), organize activities to reflect the cluster's specific context, and monitor achievements. All these are valuable guidelines for RITEs as well. Sölvell *et al.*, conclude with a statement also very much in line with the RITE thrust: "Cluster initiatives alone, even if pursued on a broad level, are no substitute for a thorough assessment of crosscutting microeconomic policy issues, such as general education, the marketing of a region, or infrastructure issues."

We will see that RITE success factors show marked agreement with Sölvell *et al.*'s CI success factors, with some exceptions:

- Sölvell *et al.* find that a dedicated facilitator is essential to CIs. RITEs, in contrast, need a *godfather* or *godmother* (see the sections below), people with much more social status, connectivity and clout than even experienced professional facilitators can bring to bear.
- Where Sölvell *et al.* assert that CI practitioners need to set clear objectives, they also find that most of their respondents do not, in fact, do

this. In RITEs, particularly those that are not government-directed, clear objectives are not helpful. Chapter 4 of *The Technopolis Columns* followed Kozmetsky in advocating "fuzzy objectives" for RITEs.

* Sölvell *et al.* find variation in CI successes across the globe because "the trust companies have in government initiatives varies considerably from country to country." Having been involved in many RITEs, my colleagues and I have come to believe, first, that it does not matter whether governments initiate the RITE organization; what is more important is the evolution of the network – the patterns of communication and influence that emerge once it becomes clear who is having the good ideas and who is taking the most effective action. Second, we believe that the fact of government funding is less important than the diversification and longevity of the RITE's funding.

To expand on the last bullet point, there are gradations of government involvement in launching an initiative. The government may launch an internal agency action, or issue a request for proposals. The RFP may be very restrictive, or allow proposers great latitude in fulfilling program goals. Members of the RITE network may win several government tenders, ostensibly (that is, from the government's point of view) related to one another only in a tangential way or not at all, but bent to a common purpose within the RITE. Finally, total government funding as a fraction of the RITE budget may be quite small. However, even a nominal amount of government funding creates "moral buy-in" on the government's part. It enables the RITE to give credit to government officials (deserved or not!) for the initiative's successes, and to use the resulting goodwill as a lever to gain the cooperation of other agencies of the government. This was the case in Austin, where the City of Austin could give only $25,000 each year in support of the Austin Technology Incubator. The City's contribution, however, created stronger links among elements of the community, and thus a stronger incubator.

Technopolis is a phenomenon of metropolitan regions, and often (in the US) these regions more or less coincide with Congressional districts. As state legislatures struggle to dole smaller state appropriations equitably to all areas of their states, not much state money is available for any state's technopolis, at least relative to the large amounts needed to seed a critical mass of industrial activity. For these reasons, local city governments and the national government (through the district's Congressperson) are more forthcoming sources of RITE funding than the states.

Finally, whether the community displays trust in government or not, the initiatives of any elected official are at risk when that official reaches his/her term limit or fails to be re-elected.

Cases[5]

1. Portland, Oregon

The city of Portland is home to half of Oregon's three million inhabitants. Historically isolated in their corner of the US Pacific Northwest, Portlanders are of two minds about acknowledging Oregon's new proximity to the world, even as this proximity is inevitably brought about by "jets and nets." Their ambivalence about change has caused Portland to lag behind in technopolis development, as locals continue to debate the "best" strategy for a biotechnology initiative that at this point can only be too little, too late. Portlanders' desire to continue (against all reasonable prospects) to be left alone by the rest of the world causes them to look inward, neglecting the external monitoring and networking that are essential for tech-based growth.

Portland does have tech-based industry strengths in software, medical devices, electronics, and the building of large trucks and railway cars. Harrington (2000) reports that in 2000, Portland's two thousand technology companies employed 70,000 workers, and a majority of these were engineers, managers, designers or other professionals. Nearly all the region's semiconductor firms design and manufacture their own products, and the Portland area generates over half of Intel's US patents.

The electronics and transportation strengths are a result of US federal government investment in decades past (in radio communication for forest stations, and war materiel, respectively), and in an accident of location: Silicon Valley executives with summer homes in neighboring Oregon saw the Portland area as a familiar and easy plant expansion location when California wages became excessive.

Now, however, Oregonians say they prefer small government – even while trying to squeeze their government for additional entrepreneurship and corporate location incentives – and have forgotten government's role in early developments that still generate the lion's share of jobs in the state. Denizens of Silicon Valley, 750 miles away, regard laid-back Oregon as a place for low-energy people who don't have entrepreneurial fire in their bellies – a place to retire and go fishing. In fact, Oregonians are devoted to the outdoor lifestyle made possible by their spectacular natural environment. Skiing, mountain climbing, windsurfing, hunting, and running are enjoyed by many.

The Portland area enjoys a fairly energetic software entrepreneurship scene, especially in open-source and cybersecurity. However, promising homegrown start-ups tend to be purchased by out-of-state concerns, and the state loses these firms as fast as it can start them. Ironically, the thirteen thousand Intel employees in Oregon include two thousand who are involved solely with software, making Intel the biggest software employer in the state.

Portlanders are social and enjoy talking with one another. In fact, one might say the level of inward social capital is quite high. Any number of technopolis initiatives arise each year. The members enjoy meeting and talking. Nothing is done. The reward is that the participants get to meet and talk again the following year. In 2005, the Oregon Business Plan initiative (OregonBusinessPlan.org 2005) proudly sponsored a state senate bill to change the name of the Oregon Council on Knowledge & Economic Development to the Oregon Innovation Council! That's progress, Oregon-style. Unemployment remains high, even as the cost of living locally rises.

Is Portland in denial, showing the false optimism of the proverbial frog in the slowly heating pan of water? Noting the absence of a catalyzing crisis, one local leader noted, "Things are bad in Oregon, but not yet bad enough."

While high tech executives and government officials spar over tiny amounts of resources that might be devoted to software and biotech development, four de facto clusters are quietly flourishing, driven by Oregon's highly educated and outdoorsy populace:

- Outdoor clothing and gear (Columbia Sportswear and others)
- Knives and small tools (Leatherman and others)
- Running shoes and athletic wear (Nike and others)
- Education-related businesses (CollegeNet and others[6]).

Of these, only the education cluster is backed by a structured initiative, and it remains informal. However, all four are growing in employment. One may conjecture that other regions will also find their solutions in these "cultural survival technologies," that is, innovative products that:

- Are inspired by unusual, unique, or extreme local conditions;
- Find wide usage locally;
- May or may not utilize high technology in the product or manufacturing process; and

- Appeal to export markets because they prove beneficial in a wider range of environments and usage situations than they were designed for.

Portland has an excellent medical university (Oregon Health & Science University), but no premier university for the physical sciences and engineering. Mayer (2002) argues that Tektronix Corporation, with its high velocity of patent generation and a reputation of decades' standing as a playground for scientists, served as a surrogate science university for Portland, and that Intel was the city's engineering school. "Tek" is now decimated, leaving Portland without the upstream scientific creativity and innovation that a more stable university environment might have provided.

In any case, technology alone does not a technopolis make. Referring to Portland's social innovations under Mayor Neil Goldschmidt in the 1970s, Abbott (2002) complains that no one has had a socially creative idea in Oregon for 25 years. As a result, Portland is doing not quite as well as Campinas, Brazil (Druckerman 2000), despite a similar profile. Campinas' major funding for its universities and ambitious plans for indigenous growth in the 1970s gave way to today's under-funded university research and economic development initiatives based on luring FDI that "siphons profits out of the country." However, according to Druckerman, Campinas can still brag of being "easily South America's most important technology manufacturing center."

2. ParcBIT and Balearic Economic Development[7]

The Balearic Islands are a province of Spain in the Mediterranean Sea. The provincial capital, Palma de Mallorca, used a grant from the European Community to pursue a self-investment strategy, namely an attractive facility for Internet-based businesses and teleworkers. ParcBIT is intended to help trigger a diversification of Mallorca's economy away from its dominant reliance on agriculture and traditional tourism. Its name, Park for Balearic Innovation and Technology, implies the islands' diversification will rely on new, different, and perhaps unforeseen directions, though probably these directions will involve new technologies.

Impending threats to traditional tourism, such as shorter vacations – especially for two-career families in which both spouses cannot take two weeks' holiday at the same time – spurred this drive toward diversification, and attracted the EU grant for designing ParcBIT.[8]

ParcBIT was intended to attract teleworkers, entrepreneurs, and business conferences, and possibly the families of the persons making the vacation destination decision. ParcBIT aims to attract short-term visitors, vacation home owners (continual medium-term visitors), and permanent residents. All these will choose Mallorca because of the island's traditional attractions as well as the amenities provided by the innovation park.

The Balearics: Combining Tourism and Technology Development. There are only three ways to increase tourism revenue: Bring more people; get them to stay longer; and get them to spend more money per day. ParcBIT will attract people who will stay longer than charter-flight tourists, and who will spend more money in the Balearics. These will be individual teleworkers, sales teams, telework task groups (called "skunk works" in the US), and conventions, meetings, and management retreats. Eventually, ParcBIT will attract not just company delegations, but companies – start-ups, spin-offs, new and relocating divisions, relocating small and mid-size companies, and their vendors.

Mallorca has the potential for attracting the desired traffic. Its advantages include a perfect climate with clean air, good air transport service, and some strong university departments. The university, IUB, now has new school of hospitality and hotel administration that can be an effective partner in technology based tourism.

There is a proud heritage of artistic and literary achievement, and celebrity artists and performers vacation in the islands. English, Spanish and German are widely spoken. The clustering of British, German, and Scandinavian expatriates makes an interesting diversity that holds the visitor's interest. The Ministry of Finance and Economy seems skilled and energetic in dealing with the province's challenges, which include a water shortage, a government tradition of centralized decision making, and pockets of conservative sentiment in the business community.

The ParcBIT Masterplan International Ideas Competition. The Ministry's judging criteria were:

- Sensitivity to ParcBIT goals and requirements (that is, meets requirements).
- Innovative contributions to concept and objectives (that is, goes beyond requirements).
- Conceptualization of vision.
- Balance and interspersion of use.
- Ecological design solutions.
- Interest of building typologies.
- Technical interest.
- Integration with landscape.
- Use of resources.

- Infrastructure design.
- Architecture of buildings.
- Technical feasibility.
- Financial viability.
- Understandability to the general public.

Naturally, different competing entries displayed different emphases. None, though, seemed to attempt seriously to address all the published criteria. In particular, there was no state of the art discussion of intelligent buildings. Nor was there discussion of the many European cultures that will be represented at ParcBIT, and how to accommodate the various lifestyle preferences they will bring. Strikingly for an innovation park competition, some teams seemed biased against technological change. One sympathizes with the desire to preserve the best of one's culture, but preservation of the past can coexist with embracing the future.

The architectural competition made one fact surprisingly clear: that certain types of human behavior, e.g., innovativeness, can be "engineered in" in an enterprise not just by organizational or motivational means, but also by the physical design of working space.

What happened to Palma's initiative? The EU grant expired, and the Minister driving the initiative was not re-elected. With no further funding available, no influential godfather on the scene, and in the face of culturally conservative opposition, the initiative appears to have lost momentum.

3. Mason Enterprise Center

This case is based on an interview with Dr Roger Stough, Director of the Mason Enterprise Center. In his capacity as Director, Dr Stough reports to the Provost and President of George Mason University.

MEC runs a number of incubators, the number depending on how virtual incubators and incubators run on contract are counted. One of the incubators is a physical one occupying two floors (4,000–6,000 sq.ft) and designed to shelter sixteen companies (of any kind).

Another is an "incubator without walls," or "Technology Resource Alliance" that works with 30 companies/year. These companies are pre--launch or immediately post-launch, technical companies only. They enter the resource alliance by application, and only the best are accepted.

MEC also runs three federal telework centers (cubicles with internet access, videoconferencing, computer training room). These are scattered across northern Virginia, but all are in the general radius of Washington, D.C.

In addition, MEC manages an international incubator for Arlington County, for foreign companies wanting to do business in the US.

MEC holds contracts for four Small Business Development Centers (SBDCs). The SBDCs emphasize mentor/protege programs. In contrast to the competitive Technology Resource Alliance, the mentoring program accepts anyone wishing to start a business. A $1,000 small business loan (microloan) program is also administered. These are funded by separate federal programs, mostly intended for non-technology businesses. After completing the basic mentoring program, companies contract with the SBDC for additional services.

MEC operates a "Grubstake Program" that resembles venture fairs for angels and VCs, and cooperates with the local "Venture Investor Club" (angel network) to general leads to promising companies. A particular strength of MEC has been in naming, promoting and branding their programs in this way.

For example, MEC's Dry Run™ teaches CEOs how to make a pitch for funding. The executive's presentation is heard initially by internal staff, and after, by a panel of outside advisors similar to those assembled by the Oregon Marketing Business Initiative (OMBI).

MEC finds money from: Federal, county, fee for service (mentoring program), and state and university matching funds. MEC's funding dictates that they must service small and minority businesses. But as community leaders agree that high-growth potential businesses are usually technology-based, MEC finds it can bend/leverage all its funded programs to encourage high tech entrepreneurship. MEC does mentor/ incubate direct competitors, but at such early stages that "it doesn't matter."

University involvement is not a critical success factor for MEC, according to Dr Stough, but is good for the university, especially due to student involvement in community relations and fund raising. MEC's network provides leverage for research contracts that come into the university having to do with measuring specific aspects of the local and state economies.

MEC is linked with academic programs in entrepreneurship throughout the university (business school, engineering, public administration, art/multimedia) leading to university-wide minor. GMU doesn't have a full-time MBA program, so MEC fielded a campus-wide "entrepreneur profile" questionnaire to find students with experience starting businesses. These students will be MEC mentors and interns.

Dr Stough is also a faculty member at GMU's The Institute for Public Policy (TIPP). MEC depends on TIPP's fund raising skill, but is kept arms-length from TIPP to avoid intra-university jealousies.

There are cultural as well as budget tensions within university because in MEC speed, not consensus, is of the essence. The university is better for coaching launch of non-Internet companies, Stough says, because it can take the time that is customary for university activities. One MEC success was the launch of a heritage-based travel service. But even this company leverages the net for, e.g., real-time itinerary changes.

AOL and other northern Virginia companies have created 4,000 millionaires and several billionaires. MEC leverages these for a 400-strong "knowledge network," drawing on these executives for advice on fast turnaround/short window dotcom opportunities. The Internet enhances communication among these advisors – especially if they have worked together before.

MEC hired a retired Peat Marwick executive as Executive in Residence (at $90,000/year) to leverage his network for the benefit of MEC companies. The executive mentors companies and mentors incubator managers. This works well; Roger may hire another such executive.

Pieces of MEC have been evolving since 1986. Not a planned from scratch effort, in fact, according to Dr Stough, it is "something of a mess." MEC's total budget is $7 million/year. MEC worked with 1,600 companies last year in one way or another, and helped companies get money from $50 k to $10 m.[9]

While MEC continues to manage incubators on contract for the county and the military, it is moving away from in-house, physical incubators. Roger advises not building bricks-and-mortar incubator unless a big region doesn't have a private one. Only do bricks-and-mortars in rural areas if the state provides funding specifically for that purpose, he says. Otherwise, just do traditional SBDC activities in rural areas. But other arms of MEC can buy the time of SBDC staff to help with urban incubators. The University's contribution, then, is to manage incubators for private parties with low-cost student labor.

Why may we count Washington, D.C., as a technopolis but not another large city like Chicago that also hosts many technology firms? Washington's beltway, where most of the city's tech firms locate, facilitates the cluster criterion of "maximum one hour travel time among cluster members."

The life cycle of technology entrepreneurship initiatives

Sölvell *et al.* (2004) surveyed 239 industry cluster initiatives around the world. (Cluster initiatives are a good proxy for RITEs, because they often utilize the same kind of decentralized public–private networking.)

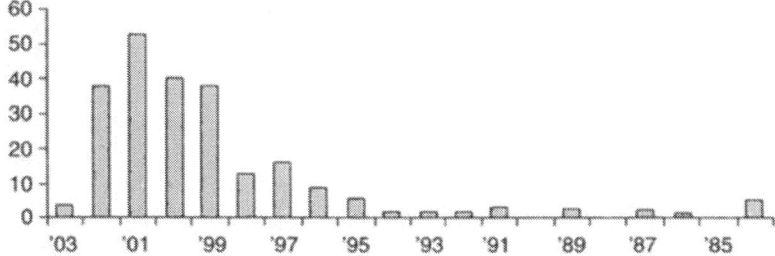

Figure 17.1 Launch year of cluster initiatives surveyed by Sölvell, Lindqvist *et al.* (2003, p. 31)

Though a very few responding initiatives were as much as 25 years old, 195 of the 239 had been launched within the six years ending in 2002 (Figure 17.1). That is, most older initiatives had failed, run out of funding, disbanded for some other reason (possibly including success), or did not respond to the term "cluster initiative" simply because they were launched before the term "cluster" became current in the 1990s. Presumably, the newest initiatives did not yet feel confident to report on their activities.

Cluster and RITE initiatives should have a good start, effective follow-up, and sustaining activity. The term "sustaining" in no way implies coasting, or a relaxation of vigilant scanning for crises and opportunities. These three phases, in addition to the data in Figure 17.1, define the "life cycle" of RITEs.

A "good start" is a hopeful one that shows an understanding of globalization, the modern transformation of competitive advantage, and the changing role of cities. No region has a natural transportation cost advantage with regard to information. Rather, regions build competitive information advantage via investment in education, telecommunications infrastructure and software. To the extent that people have lived in or traveled to cities for proximity to information, cities are obsolete. Future cities will exist to emphasize the creative spark, the person-to-person skills transfer, and the human satisfaction that comes from proximity to other people. Innovative regions build on these sparks to attract talent and companies that, because of their knowledge- and skill-intensive nature, will attract still more talent and enterprises.

These are the facts that lead regions to believe the Silicon Valley phenomenon can be replicated elsewhere. They are the facts that justify substantial economic development investments in small geographic areas, and they are the facts that ensure small investments will be wasted.

Technology entrepreneurship-based economic development depends on attention to these things in the early stages:

Political organization. A RITE must organize to gain the support of governors, presidents, and representatives to national and supranational legislatures, so as to benefit from all possible grants and appropriations for technology development.

Mental set. All elements of the community must have an accepting, or at least tolerant, attitude toward change and innovation, toward entrepreneurship, and toward other sectors, agencies and community elements.

Strategic Positioning: choosing a pony to ride. With limited resources, a community must leverage its natural advantages to produce a profitable fit with a very focused investment in technology. Examples include Austin (software and semiconductors), North Carolina (biotechnology), Tsukuba, Japan (government laboratories), and Kansai City, Japan (private companies' research laboratories). An examination of other regions' success factors and failures aids the positioning exercise.

Making it Work: riding that pony. The positioning choice is followed by an effective balance of attracting relocating companies in the chosen industry; retaining and nurturing indigenous companies; starting new companies; and building innovative institutions to support the latter three activities (for example, the Austin Technology Council and Austin's Technology Advisors' Group).

The role of universities. Universities should produce not just graduates, but a steady flow of new ideas, devices and spin-out enterprises that can be commercialized for the region's economic benefit. Universities in technology growth-pole regions are partners in economic development with governments and companies.

Tourism, music and the arts. Technology entrepreneurs and engineers are of course educated people who appreciate a fine quality of life in their communities – preferably coupled with a low cost of living. They are attracted by many of the same amenities that attract tourists. A thriving artistic community and a healthy tourist trade can quickly find common interest with the promoters of environmentalism and clean, modern technology industry.

Marketing the region. An art/tourism/high-tech alliance is an attractive product. Nonetheless it takes sophisticated public relations, advertising and media executions to ensure a steady flow of attention, visitors and funds.

Role of innovation parks and incubators. Innovation parks spur the region's growth by providing an attractive setting where an atmosphere of creativity can flourish, and where a critical mass of technologists, scientists and thinkers can build on one another's ideas. The park serves as a showcase for industry and a magnet for students.

Building the community: the role of the visionary. In every case I've studied, one influential individual has translated all the above elements into meaningful objectives for his or her region. This person has formulated a vision, evangelized it, and marshaled the political, popular, and financial support needed to make it real. This visionary individual has inspired others in the region to translate the objectives into programs and execute the programs. These others may become absorbed in the particulars of the programs they are implementing. But they are always able to rely on the "godfather" to maintain the integrity of the vision. I cannot overemphasize that this visionary godfather or godmother must be a very extraordinary individual, combining technological knowledge with planning acumen, personal charisma, and political savvy.

Orchestrating the technopolis – overture. The first step in formulating a regional strategy is to gather global examples. What have other regions done? Can these examples be translated into local success? Answering this question is an opportunity to kill three birds with a single stone. An initial regional conference or workshop gathers expert opinion on the region's potential strategies and outlook for success. It also draws local people who can implement programs into the orbit of the visionary. As a public relations event, it draws early, perhaps nationwide, attention to the region and tests the waters regarding public opinion and potential support for moving forward.

Orchestrating the technopolis – first movement. The support of professional and community organizations must be obtained, and new organizations started where necessary. A comprehensive plan should be drawn. The plan should be ambitious but flexible, and is not necessarily written down. Fast success of the entire plan should not be expected. But seed money should be obtained while early momentum exists, and must be used to achieve and display small early successes.

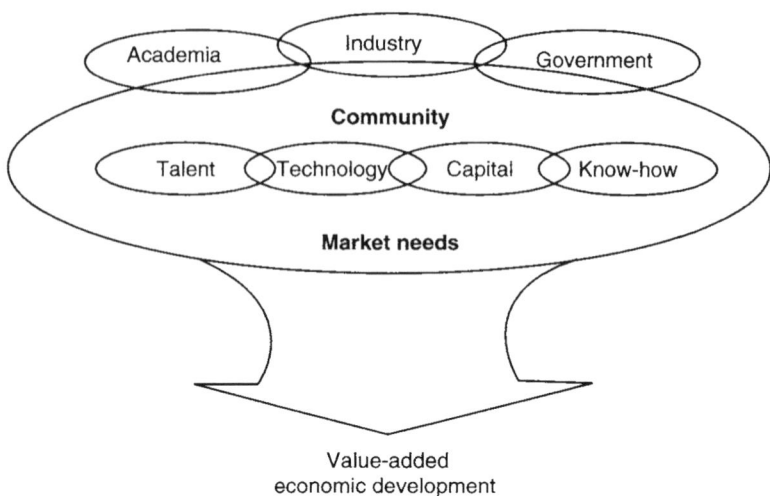

Figure 17.2   The IC² model of value-added economic development
Source: IC² Institute.

The picture of the IC² Institute's model of value-added economic development, Figure 17.2, implies foremost that the initiative for economic development comes from the local community. In an age of rapid technological change, only the local region can identify its own best opportunities in a timely way. The picture shows that success depends on the cooperation of the government, academic and business sectors. These sectors collaborate, perhaps in new ways, to bring together entrepreneurial talent, capital, technology, and business management expertise that will identify and satisfy new market needs.

Critical success factors for sustainable initiatives

It is now clear that a more comprehensive list of initiative critical success factors (Table 17.4) looks quite different from the technopolis CSFs of Table 17.1. All initiative CSFs, however, are oriented toward facilitating technopolis CSFs. Needless to say, if the RITE objectives become overly focused on preservation of the initiative, rather than on desired results for the region, the initiative will lose the support of its constituents.

Many of Table 17.4's bullet items are self-explanatory or have been explored earlier in this paper. Others require further comment, and this follows.

Table 17.4 Success factors for regional technology entrepreneurship initiatives

---

Financial
- Continuity of funding.
- Diversification of funding.
- Encouraging businesses and individuals to reinvest locally.

Leadership and planning
- Continuity of vision and commitment.
- Continuity of leadership, ideally by "godfather/godmother."
- Lead by spotting the parade and jumping in front of it.
- BHAGs rather than timid goals.
- Fuzzy objectives rather than quantified, timed objectives.

Management and communication
- Self-reliance rather than use of outside consultants for solutions. (It is all right to hire consultants to help the RITE learn to network.)
- Respect for participants' time.
- Successful cultural change.
- Networking effectiveness.
- External/international orientation.[a]
- Well-considered design and use of space.
- Scandal-free transparency.

Organization and public relations
- Vigorous public relations.
- Design long term programs that show early visible success.
- Flexibility to capitalize on unexpected events, crises, and early successes.
- Ability to quickly give up on something that isn't working.
- Cross-sectoral rather than business-centric or government-centric.

Pragmatism and balance
- Balance of infrastructure, recruitment, and workforce development efforts.
- Balance of entrepreneur-pull over technology-push.
- Balance of consensus, initiative, and government acquiescence or support.
- Pragmatic.
- Careful, realistic identification of technological strengths.

---

[a] Putnam (2003) distinguishes "bonding" social capital from "bridging" social capital. The former is inward-looking and conservative; the latter, outward-looking and open to wider communication.

How can a RITE leverage some bits of its region's history, overcome other bits, and establish and maintain social capital? One important answer is a *godfather*. The godfather (who could be a godmother, of course) is the keeper of the vision. A visionary himself, he is steadfast and persistent, and has excellent local and external networks of acquaintances. He may profit from economic development activities, but is not in it primarily for personal monetary or status rewards. Indeed he is usually financially comfortable already, which enables him to hang in there, sustaining the vision for decades if need be. He is a longtime member of the community, trusted by varied community groups. In Austin, this was George Kozmetsky; in Curitiba, former Mayor Jaime Lerner; in Oita, Prefectural Governor Morihiko Hiramatsu, and in Hyderabad, Chandra Babu Naidu (Biswas 2004), who persuaded Microsoft's Bill Gates and Steve Ballmer to dub the city "Cyberabad."

The godfather's politics are non-partisan, and he is careful not to cause irreparable rifts in the community. His imprimatur on a project attracts people to it; they know he will not support it if it is a cover for graft or hidden agendas. Like mathematicians flaunting their Erdös numbers, members of the community gain status by their closeness to the godfather. Silly? Perhaps, but very effective for economic transformation. Often the godfather can be more effective if he is *not* an elected official.

The godfather does not create technology trends, but rather brings attention to, and lends mentorship to, promising initiative-takers. Austin has mastered this tactic; to note two examples of many, George Kozmetsky mentored Michael Dell, and Willie Nelson moved from Nashville to lead – and benefit from – Austin's vibrant music scene. Both pursued BHAGs (an Americanism, "big, hairy, audacious goals"), recognizing their inspirational quality and their practical necessity in an economy driven by positive feedback and "tipping points" (Putnam 2003).

External networking is the key to accelerating take-off when (as is usually true) a single region lacks all the ingredients for quick success. It is also key for established regional economies that continue to look for the best suppliers, customers, expansion locations, and technologies in the world. Networking is a learned skill. Consultants can help RITEs and other community elements learn both internal and external networking. Austin, for example, was advised by the pioneering scholar of innovation diffusion, Everett Rogers (Gibson and Rogers 1994).

After sitting through his nth cluster meeting, the director of the Portland Development Commission stated, "I've got roads to build; I'm not coming to any more meetings," thus pointing up the need for RITEs to respect participants' time. Austin's Technology Incubator (ATI) was designed to minimize demands on tenant entrepreneurs' time, e.g., by bringing educational events and professional society meetings to the incubator. Taiwan's Science-Based Industrial Park at Hsin Chu was designed considering the total life requirements of its workers (according to Dr Alvin Tong, SBIP's first Deputy Director-General; see Phillips, Roberts *et al.* 1999). This consideration was notably absent in the celebrated design of the Tsukuba Science City in Japan (Eto 2005).

Many RITEs and their communities consider the design and use of space and land, and how these factors affect company location. ATI's atrium and common rooms encouraged constructive encounters among tenants. Mallorca launched its RITE with an architectural competition. Portland's renovated Ecotrust building is an effective lure and showcase for environmental companies. Curitiba, Brazil, has demonstrated the positive impact of its newer public spaces on civic pride. Where Portland attempts to wean companies away from large suburban campuses toward inner-city, high-density locations, outlying Hillsboro and Portland work together to provide the right real estate for the firms that are and are not quite ready to embrace that transition. Other cities including Austin work in coordination with private Chambers of Commerce and commercial realtors to plan re-tenanting and re-design of vacant corporate campuses.

"Quickly give up on something that isn't working" is a principle that Portland, with its quixotic and under-funded quest for biotech, might well consider. NASA's Ames (California) laboratories found its well-entrenched internal incentives led it to favor other government programs for tech transfer rather than the incubator that the IC^2 Institute had helped NASA-Ames develop. Despite some early successes – the incubator had, in fact, demonstrated that a large number of aspiring entrepreneurs demanding access to government technology was more critical to success than a simple excess of licensable technology – NASA and IC^2 gave it up without regret. RITEs and godfathers/godmothers should not, however, interpret this rule to mean they should give up the RITE if fast results are not achieved; the rule applies to the individual programs a RITE might intiate.

The City Club of Portland (Doctor *et al.* 2005) found the Portland Development Commission was raising economic development funds via off-the-books limited liability companies, in a way reminiscent of Enron Corporation's tactics. Though no allegations of illegality were leveled, PDC was criticized for lack of transparency, and Tom Potter, the new Mayor of Portland, has launched an investigation into the LLCs.[10] A subsequent flurry of (arguably undeserved) protests of PDC actions has slowed Portland's development efforts.

An Austin CEO said, "Even though I'd find lower taxes elsewhere, I brought my company to Austin because it's the only place where I heard the same story from the mayor, the chamber, and the university. It gave me confidence in Austin." Consensus on the message is vital; consensus on every RITE objective and timetable is not. RITEs must balance consensus-building, individual initiative (network-based, not centrally controlled), and government support (or at least government acquiescence) in a pragmatic way.

There is no substitute for real achievements in technology transfer and commercialization. However, a total orientation to public relations is another critical success factor for the RITE. (The appearance of Lady Bird Johnson and Luci Johnson, the widow and daughter of the American president, at an ATI graduation ceremony, was unforgettable, and a powerful statement of the importance of the incubator to the community.) As we try to effect a shift toward entrepreneurial culture in our communities, we must tell new stories about ourselves, and these must connect to the old stories. The story each of us wants to tell about our community is part economic vision and part creation/renewal myth. At its heart, it is more anthropological than economic.

Notes

1. These two leaders were, respectively, Pike Powers and Jim Ronay. I gladly acknowledge their superior judgment in this matter.
2. According to Hall (1998, p. 26), the Athenians "argued that *arete*, those qualities which caused human beings to excel, came not from the gods, but were part of human nature, and could be enhanced by teaching; even 'breeding' could be taught."
3. This is not a matter of benefiting from the misfortune of others, but rather of finding a way to benefit everyone.
4. Michael Porter's (1998) influential paper "Clusters and the New Economics of Competition" mentions, in passing, "the social glue that binds clusters together." He notes that Israel's "strong desire" for food self-sufficiency gave rise to its agri-tech cluster, and that clusters succeed "especially when local institutions are supportive." He does not follow up on these ideas. The Council on Competitiveness' report "Regional Foundations of US Competitiveness" (downloadable at www.oregoneconomy.org) is similarly heavy on economics and light on social culture. In only one place does it mention "leadership committed to a shared vision." Cluster theory is thus mechanical ("put this firm here and that company there") and ahistoric.

    Contrast this to Fukuyama's (1995) assertion, noted in this book's introduction, that "Cultural differences will become the chief determinant of ... success in the global struggle for economic predominance ... . Social capital will be as important as physical capital."

    This accurate yet maddeningly vague list of high-tech industry's location decision factors, offered by Deloitte & Touche Fantus (Chen 2000), suggests why initiative leaders become frustrated with consultants: "Access to a skilled and educated workforce. Proximity to world-class research institutions. An attractive quality of life. Access to venture capital. Reasonable cost of doing business. An established technology presence. Available bandwidth and adequate infrastructure. Favorable business climate and regulatory environment. Presence of suppliers and partners. Availability of community incentives."

5. See http://www.generalinformatics.com/technopolistimes.html for information and links on many more RITEs and technopoleis worldwide.

6. See www.portlandedcluster.com

7. Adapted from Phillips (1995).

8. Growing numbers of divorced parents also drive a trend toward "weekend getaways" rather than traditional longer vacations, due to single-parent holidays and the complex logistics of gathering for vacation the children from multiple marriages. Still further trends include, most significantly for Mallorca, the work holiday and the special-interest or segmented market tourism strategy.

9. MEC's website is http://www.gmu.edu/departments/tipp/center/center.htm

10. In July, 2005, the investigators reported that no illegalities had been found.

18
WTO vs. WTA? Exploring the World Trade Organization's Impact on Technopolis

Fred Phillips

For the past twenty years, localities interested in capitalizing on the presence of technology firms have pursued a "technopolis strategy" for sustaining economic development. Dozens of these metropolitan areas from several countries have formed the World Technopolis Association (WTA). In a parallel but very separate development, NAFTA, Mercosur, GATT, WTO, and other free trade efforts worldwide have attempted to regularize trade rules among nations. Are these trends in harmony or in conflict? On their face, WTO's efforts to treat with nation-states rather than regional "citistates" look quaintly old-fashioned, and its discussions of prohibiting differential tax treatment of companies would eliminate exactly the incentives that successful citistates have used to build viable industrial clusters. On the other hand, local technology clusters have benefited from the freer movement of people and material made possible by free trade agreements.

Is it a case of WTO vs. WTA?[1] The chapter assembles arguments and evidence on this matter.

Theoretically, according to Michael Porter of Harvard, "companies' ability to source capital, goods, information, and technology from around the world ... should diminish the role of location in competition." Competitive advantage, Porter says, does not rest any longer on driving down input costs, but rather on making more productive use of inputs, which requires continual innovation. He notes the role of location *is* important, then, as geographical clusters of industries, especially technology-intensive industries, offer conditions conducive to innovation. Market, technical, and competitive information builds up within a cluster, and local firms have preferred access to it. Clusters arise and can flourish because of the special nature of the local population, terrain, or infrastructure.

Porter's argument is correct as far as it goes, but the new free trade agreements (FTAs) dictate the availability of inputs, the disposability of outputs, and even the viability of industrial clusters. Under the now-quiescent negotiations toward a Multilateral Agreement on Investments (MAI),[2] no quid pro quo (corporate performance requirements) would be allowed in exchange for tax incentives, reducing the ability of localities to encourage cluster growth. Public-private partnerships like enterprise zones and many university incubators would be eliminated. Tax incentives that have built competitive local industry clusters would be outlawed by MAI.

Indeed, metropolitan areas, "citistates," and multi-city regions – not nations and provinces – have been the prime loci of recent economic creativity and progress. Much literature reinforces the notion that local culture and local distinctions are a source of economic advantage. FTAs generally oppose any government "distortion" of market allocation of capital, and tax incentives are seen as distortions. MAI would allow no exceptions for health, safety, or environmental standards, or local cultural content. The 1999 Seattle WTO Ministerial, despite President Clinton's urging, did not move toward including environmental or labor considerations in its trade rules.

Ironically, free trade is touted as a spur to innovation, because international price pressures on inefficient industries can force them to re-invent themselves. But in today's world of Silicon Valley style entrepreneurship, innovation is the core culture of the small, fast-growing firms that are adding most of the United States new jobs. The innovation culture is driven by technological fusion, not by price pressure. In an additional irony, the rules-intensive WTO environment creates a bureaucratic structure that could easily stifle, rather than encourage, innovation. In other words, the Seattle WTO Ministerial may easily have been a lot of sound and fury about something that, at bottom, doesn't make business sense for many firms.

The Seattle Ministerial ended with WTO Director Michael Moore conceding that WTO "must be reformed." The following chain of facts and logic may help reform WTO in a direction that is more congenial to technopolis formation:

- The past decade has seen unprecedented expansion in many of the world's economies, including that of the United States.
- WTO wishes to formulate multilateral trade rules that facilitate further growth.
- Yet the greatest part of the recent explosion in new wealth, new jobs, and new companies has occurred in metropolitan regions, the

boundaries of which (with a few exceptions, like Singapore) do not coincide with state, province, or national boundaries.

- Much of this regional growth has been due to innovative companies, sited in proximity and leveraging novel combinations of new technologies. This is the technopolis phenomenon.
- City, county, and regional coalition governments have created inducements for such companies to locate within their boundaries. Often these inducements include tax incentives that are not available to companies outside the targeted industries. It is presumed, though arguable, that such inducements have accelerated innovation and economic growth.
- WTO rules regard such differential taxation as "market distortions," and prohibit them.
- Under current international conventions, only nation-states can conduct foreign policy and make treaties. Thus, WTO is a conference of nations, even though the economic action it addresses takes place primarily in metropolitan regions. While warnings of the decline of the nation-state may be exaggerated, obvious questions result about whether WTO is truly a representative body, and whether it is forward-looking or old-fashioned in its structure and function.
- It is therefore questionable at this point whether WTO rules will increase the world's net economic product, or, by sabotaging regions' technopolis strategies, actually decrease economic growth.
- Peter Drucker wrote that the three great trends of the next decades are globalization, regionalization, and localization. WTO rules deal only with globalization, though imperfectly, and not at all with regionalization or localization.

Foreign policy is the prerogative of nations. Nonetheless, states and cities have the authority to take initiatives on foreign trade. States and provinces, for example, host foreign trade delegations, sponsor trade fairs, and open trade offices in foreign cities. Obviously, they do this selectively, favoring some potential partners over others.

Some localities have declared themselves "MAI-free zones" or declared other questionably legal intentions to opt out of the WTO process.

The state of Massachusetts is now in WTO court over its refusal, motivated by human rights considerations, to buy from companies that do business in Myanmar. Japanese companies with operations in Myanmar have brought the suit. While not a technology or tax issue, the Massachusetts case illustrates the potential of local initiatives to run afoul of WTO rules. Opponents of Massachusetts' action claims that it is de facto foreign policy; supporters say it is a legitimate state trade decision supported by the voters of the commonwealth. As of this date, amicus curiae filings are tallying 300–75 in support of the state.

Another case bearing on this chapter's thesis is WTO's February, 2004, decision against US "foreign trade corporations." This is a tax matter, though these corporations constituted a national, rather than local, tax incentive for US companies engaging in exports.

A third illustrative example comes from a WTO (1997) report on Malaysia titled "Open Trade and Investment Lead to Growth in Malaysia: Some Measures Hamper Efficient Use of Capital":

A central feature of Malaysia's industrial policy is discouragement of labour-intensive activities and the promotion of capital-intensive processes such as the automation of low-skill industries and the development and acquisition of advanced technologies. Foreign direct investment in such activities is actively encouraged.

An array of tax and non-tax incentives exists; some are granted to all sectors, while others are aimed at specific firms or industries . . . The granting of such incentives is administered by the Malaysian Industrial Development Authority (MIDA), the Government's principal "one-stop" agency for the promotion and co-ordination of industrial development. Incentives are, with one notable exception concerning reduced sales taxes on "national" cars, granted on a non-discriminatory basis to domestically- and foreign-owned enterprises. As a consequence, foreign-owned firms accounted for more than two thirds of the value of investment qualifying for Pioneer Status and the Investment Tax Allowance during the period 1992–1996.

While the Malaysian authorities appeared (prior to the 1998 Budget) to be reviewing the use of incentives with a view to making them more selective, the overall utility of investment incentives may be questioned. These measures may have an adverse effect not just on resource allocation, and thus total factor productivity, but also on the fiscal balance, thereby reducing national savings, widening the savings-investment gap, and exacerbating the current account deficit. Estimates of the annual costs of tax incentives in terms of revenue forgone are not available. However, judging from information provided by the Malaysian authorities, such costs may be substantial; for example, the Reinvestment Allowance alone cost roughly RM 1 billion annually in forgone income tax revenues during 1995–96. Such incentives may also contribute to a "beggar-thy-neighbour" situation in which other countries react by offering incentives of their own, just as the Malaysian Government may have responded to other countries' incentives.

The Malaysia report reveals an ideological bias, substituting words like "may" for actual evidence of market distortion or excessive social cost. It may be argued, too, that the competition among governments, remarked upon negatively at the end of the excerpt, will give rise to creative programs that will enhance industrial innovation.

It is beyond the scope of this chapter to settle the question of whether WTO will result in a net increase or net decrease of world growth, or whether it will encourage the right kind of growth. Nor can we predict the specifics of future WTO rules. Through literature search, however, we can ascertain the general tone and approach of WTO documents as they address technopolis-related issues; monitor WTO's effect on specific regional issues that become newsworthy trade disputes; and collect numerical evidence that will flesh out (or argue against) the logic presented before.

WTO takes the view that nations must cooperate for economic growth and more widespread prosperity. Most jobs are created in metropolitan regions where new, knowledge-intensive industries aggregate. As a treaty between nation-states, WTO may fairly be called old-fashioned and irrelevant. WTO must be reformed in a way that recognizes the greater need for complexity, diversity, and freedom in regional innovation strategies.

Notes

1. Phillips (2004a) deals with this topic in greater detail.
2. MAI has been called "NAFTA on steroids." MAI negotiations are currently stalled, having been separated from OECD and not yet embraced by WTO.

19
Why Do Universities Transfer Technology?

Fred Phillips

Your desktop computer can tell a laser to harden selected portions of a tank of photosensitive chemicals. This "3-dimensional printing" produces rapid prototypes of parts for manufacture.

Your next automobile will have voice-operated web browsing. You will be able to ask directions, book flights, reserve rooms, and get traffic reports by talking to your car. And your car will talk back.

The polymerase chain reaction (PCR) makes gene mapping, including gene therapies and criminal DNA identification, easier and commercially feasible.

Did private companies invent the PCR, voice web, and 3-D printing? Or was it NASA? The military? No, America's universities originated these useful innovations and many others. The roads they traveled from university lab to commercial marketplace are strewn with potholes and controversies. Should universities commercialize technologies? How should they be paid for doing this? Doesn't commercialization work against the university's role in advancing the common good?

Many stakeholders see conflicts between university tech transfer activities and the traditional, "proper" role of the university. But these conflicts can be transformed into opportunities, making the new and the old roles of the academy well-balanced and mutually reinforcing. Partnered with education and research, university technology transfer can advance the standard of living and the quality of life in the communities surrounding the academy.

Publish or patent?

The Bayh-Dole Act of 1980 allows universities to keep rights to intellectual property ("i.p.") developed at the university under federal grants. The Act also requires the universities to acquire formal rights (e.g., file patent applications) for some technical advances that may advance the common good, even if the expensive filing process is not expected to bring a financial return. Under Bayh-Dole, universities are allowed to make money on i.p., are sometimes required to lose money on it, and will be able to do neither unless university researchers agree sometimes to forgo the publication of their work in learned journals.

Journal publications advance the researcher's academic career, and make knowledge widely available so that it can be matched with other researchers' knowledge to advance science and technology still further. But publication puts knowledge in the public domain, foreclosing the possibility of a patent (if more than a year passes between the journal publication and the patent application). If no company or other organization can gain the protected monopoly that a patent provides, they have no incentive to bring a product to market. Consumers lose the benefit the product might provide, and the common good is, ironically, ill-served.

The university's incentives are thus mixed and complex, even more so because the university is not a monolithic organization. Individual researchers, students, departments, schools, centers, and administrative support offices within the university – not to mention legislators and other external stakeholders – have different and possibly conflicting agendas. Ideally, incentives are designed to harmonize with the university's missions, but organizational complexity makes this a hard task.

The university's mission

Universities have pursued three traditional missions: research, teaching, and public service. Private universities, notably Stanford and MIT, have embraced a fourth mission, namely, taking a role in local and regional economic development. In the mid-1990s, then-President Robert Berdahl of the University of Texas at Austin announced that UT-Austin, a public university, would also adopt this fourth mission. Other public universities have followed suit, opening new business incubators and expanding their technology transfer offices.

Few have drilled down through their strategic planning processes to make incentives line up with mission. Most universities have used a "fire, ready, aim" sequence – first trying to maximize tech transfer revenue, then declaring economic development to be a mission, and finally, if at all, incentivizing faculty and staff. Not surprisingly, something goes wrong, and the effort is abandoned or gets so wrapped up in rules and arguments that it cannot become effective. And these are just the internal difficulties; social and political forces also act to inhibit technology transfer. Getting past these troubles requires understanding the purpose of technology transfer, and emplacing a strategy-making process that lines up the university's mission with internal and external incentives.

The political economy of university tech transfer

Technology transfer is not an end in itself, but a means to an end. This end is economic development. Why economic development? Not many localities want more traffic and more strip malls. But local initiatives for economic development are a pre-requisite for political self-determination. Home-grown development also ensures there will be good local jobs for the children of local families. When the economy of a region produces little value-added, its labor force must emigrate. If outside investors appear, they may bring only low-paying jobs, siphon profits out of the region, and control local development decisions. The wide-spread American desire for local political control and for family togetherness can only be served by wise economic development. Universities help this happen, by bringing home licensing fees and by spinning off locally-headquartered companies.

Seeking economic development, Anytown, USA, will use three classic strategies: (1) persuade distant companies to open operations in Anytown, (2) help new companies start in Anytown , and (3) help existing local companies to grow. But Collegeville, USA, and its university can focus their strategies more sharply:

- When feasible, the university can preferentially license its technologies to local companies. This creates local jobs and tax revenues, and keeps promising intellectual capital close to home.
- The lure of access to intellectual property may persuade distant companies to relocate their headquarters to Collegeville. The presence of a company's headquarters, as opposed to simple local investment, can make the difference between commitment to the community and exploitation of the community.
- The university can foster spin-off companies that utilize university technology. Companies that originate in Collegeville have reasons to stay in Collegeville as they grow.
- When the commercialization of certain university innovations would not fit local land use patterns or industry clusters, these may be licensed

to distant companies. The university can use the royalty income to support students or for other local purposes.

All these measures balance the university's other sources of income (endowment, tuition, grants, legislative appropriations), giving the academy flexibility as they increase the community's financial and human capital and its control of its destiny.

Opposing forces

Perhaps not having had occasion to become informed about the new tech transfer function of the university, parents who pay high college costs naturally want university professors to spend their time in the classroom. Parents want faculty to educate their kids, not start companies. Responsive to voters' desires, legislators treat the university commercialization function with skepticism. State legislatures may prefer to fund programs that have equal impact in every part of the state, rather than fund tech transfer efforts in the university towns that are often already the most economically privileged regions of the state. In turn, the university may not set high goals for technology licensing income, fearing excessive royalty receipts may lead to reduced legislative appropriations for traditional university activities.

It should be clear that university licensing and spin-off efforts create local jobs for bachelor's and master's grads, and an alternative career path for Ph.D. grads when the market for academic positions is uncertain. The chance to enjoy royalty income and entrepreneurial opportunities helps the university recruit highly accomplished faculty, who will do an even better job of educating young people.

An active university tech transfer function complements academic courses on entrepreneurship, giving students real-world projects to work on. Because patents, rather than publications, are important marks of professional recognition for engineers working in industry, professors can better serve their students by teaching, and having personal experience with, the patent process. Then too, universities are learning that successful entrepreneurs, impressed with the university's entrepreneurship programs, can be most generous donors.

Faculty, too, can oppose tech transfer and commercialization activities when they consider these activities opposed to the university's more traditional roles, to the career interests of faculty, or to a department's ability to gain scholarly stature by traditional metrics. What do faculty want? Most professors want to teach. They want to do excellent research that will be acclaimed by peers, attract grant funding, and help society. They want money. They want to see their graduating students gainfully employed. They want to see their laboratory advances and inventions helping people, in clinics, in safer and cleaner products, and in better industrial processes. They know this doesn't happen as fast or at all if the advances are published in journals. The argument that publication and commercialization should be balanced is an appealing one.

The way forward: balancing short and long term

Where private investment funds ventures – including some applied university laboratories – that are expected to pay off in the short term, tax funds and private donations support university research that may not produce a social or commercial return for ten, twenty, or thirty years. The latter research, usually published in journals, lays the foundation for future prosperity. Short-term research and development also adds to knowledge, and can result in consumer benefits, current profits, and tax revenues, all of which are alternative sources of support for the university.

Gibson and Dearing (1993) remark that spillovers from university research – that is, informal leakage of knowledge for which intellectual property protection has not been sought – benefit the surrounding technopolis. They cite:

- Cambridge University's "benign, supportive and noninterventionist" policy toward faculty-developed IP.
- Yamaguchi University, which leaves "profs and grad students free to pursue research outside university constraints."
- Beijing Institute of Information and Control, "benefiting from encouraging a policy of openness."

Gibson and Dearing quote IC^2 Fellow Jim Botkin: "It takes a long time to build an infrastructure of money and brains." Just as Internet sites grew faster by offering attractive freebies, universities can accelerate local technopolis growth by refraining from extreme tight-fistedness with their intellectual property.

Often, unexpected technical or market developments suddenly make traditional university research the object of investor attention. Organic chemists, for example, were doubtless surprised when their work became pertinent to the design of flat panel displays. A researcher does not know in advance that his or her work will be commercially "hot," and so we cannot simplistically urge universities to concentrate only on "long-term" research.

Instead, we must ensure the university provides career paths, and a culture of peer-acceptance, for researchers who choose the commercialization route for some of their projects. Entrepreneurial leave, university incubators, and entrepreneurship education programs can help faculty make choices that most benefit them and the university. Universities must include commercialization activities in their strategic and budget planning. Finally, every research university should help legislators and the electorate understand that university tech transfer can constructively contribute to the community's quality of life and economic prosperity.

20
Universities and Incubators

Fred Phillips

> "I have been affiliated with our local incubator since its beginning. Since then, I have been on the board of directors to manage the facility. Although we are not affiliated with a university, I can see many benefits of such a relationship. For example, market assessments, prototype development, testing, surveys, etc., can be done by students when available. I believe an incubator in a community is a valuable asset, independent of the form of its organization."
>
> — *Marv Clement, Battelle-Pacific Northwest Laboratories*

This chapter investigates university-connected incubator strategies for growing new businesses. University incubator initiatives should benefit higher education and produce sustainable, equitable economic development.

Because the environment for incubation changed early in this decade due to a growing number of privately owned incubators and due to the Internet revolution, this chapter's survey-based and literature-based investigation of role model incubators was augmented by expert opinion concerning the implications of privatization and the Internet.

The resulting set of conclusions suggest that incubators and universities can offer much to each other, monetarily and otherwise. Moreover, universities should play to their strengths, in order to complement the kinds of services being offered by investor-owned incubators.

In general, according to these recommendations, universities should exercise great caution in building and owning physical (as opposed to virtual) incubators. Exceptions will exist for certain locales, and for cases where the culture and organization of the university can adapt, to thoroughly integrate all applicable university missions, programs and rules with the incubator's imperative to nurture fast-growth companies.

Project background

The purpose of the project described in this chapter was to recommend an incubation strategy for Oregon universities. It was to draw on key success factors from the past and anticipated key success factors for the new environment of the future. This new environment included the proliferation of private incubators (now much less of a force, following the bursting of the dotcom bubble) and the rapidly growing and still evolving impact of the Internet.

Different regions and localities in Oregon want and need to pursue one or more of the following goals:

- Create companies;
- Create jobs;
- Create and preserve high-wage jobs;
- Increase the number of locally headquartered companies;
- Build a mass of local suppliers for large companies located in the area;
- Increase university spin-out companies and technology transfer;
- Leverage and increase the technological vitality of the region;
- Increase exports from the local region;
- Increase international trade;
- Make the region an inviting environment for entrepreneurship;

and to do these things in a way that preserves environmental quality and provides opportunities for minority, immigrant, and women entrepreneurs.

The conclusions in this chapter draw on incubator surveys, interviews and visits, and literature search to point the way to a university incubator strategy that can meet these goals.

Data sources

A questionnaire was administered to a number of incubators throughout the United States, Asia and Europe. Nine incubators, most university-connected, returned the questionnaire. I visited three incubators and two technology transfer-intensive university research centers. In addition, I used extensive notes from incubator visits made prior to this project, and interviewed a small number of incubator directors by phone and in person.

The research plan called for interviews with three experts who are not incubator directors. All three of these interviews have been completed: with

Laura Kilcrease, first director of the Austin Technology Incubator and now a venture capital professional; and with Portland investor/ entrepreneurs Dwight Sangrey and Al Pruesh, both of whom have investigated a number of incubation options for Portland.

How universities and incubators interact and add value to each other

Incubator activities

Incubators generally engage in one or all of the following activities: business assistance to tenants; networking activities; educational activities; public relations activities; infrastructure and services; and interactions with the university. The university can add value to all of these. The following activity descriptions are based mainly on the experience of the Austin Technology Incubator.

Business assistance to tenants. Professional incubator staff and/or MBA students may (under suitable non-disclosure arrangements) review monthly financials with tenant companies; provide access to a "know-how network" of service providers; or introduce the companies to experienced mentors or foreign markets and sources of supply. The incubator hosts venture fairs at which tenant companies may present to VCs and angels their brief pitches for funding.

Networking activities. The incubator introduces the tenant companies' executives to the local business "power structure" and to representatives of other technology regions and companies. This activity includes receptions and social events.

Educational activities. Tenant execs may sit in on university classes. The incubator is the site of brown-bag lectures, workshops, and seminars on a variety of entrepreneurial skills, benefiting students as well as incubator tenants.

Public relations activities. The incubator issues pamphlets, press releases and other literature promoting the tenant companies jointly. The incubator itself is newsworthy as a sign of the community's commitment to supporting entrepreneurship. The incubator helps members of the know-how network publicize their connections with incubator companies.

Infrastructure and services. Needless to say, the incubator maintains attractive space, shared conference rooms, refreshment rooms, and reception area. Services may include shared office machines, receptionist, central switchboard, and security. High-quality wiring and fast Internet access is a minimum requirement.

Interactions with the university. The university and the incubator provide each other with opportunities for interns, spin-off companies, exploitation of intellectual property, and educational enrichment. More about this given later.

Interactions with the university

Indeed, university-incubator interaction enhances almost all the incubator activities mentioned before. In particular:

- *The incubator can host business school classes.* In one such instance, engineering and business students teamed for a robotics venture laboratory, combining technical design and business planning for special purpose robots, with an eye toward launching a new venture. This writer has taught a high technology marketing laboratory for MBA students, using incubator tenants as living cases. Another possibility is the "incubator operations laboratory," preparing students to run incubators and related entrepreneurship-facilitating organizations.
- *The incubator provides internship opportunities for science, engineering, and business students.* In these arrangements, interns learn the reality of entrepreneurship. Interns become employable, as the real-world experience on their resumes demonstrably increases the number of job offers they receive. Internships benefit the incubating companies also; tenants are exposed to the latest academic knowledge, and enjoy intelligent, inexpensive labor.
- *Incubator entrepreneurs are valuable guest speakers in academic classes.* These guest appearances add value to students' academic experience, and give the entrepreneurs a chance to field critical questions.
- *Tenants provide "living cases" and student projects.*Living cases are more interactive than, for example, written Harvard cases, giving students recourse to further information and the chance to actually have an impact on the operations and success of the subject company. Of course, these also can lead to student employment.
- *The incubator provides beta sites for students new venture competition teams.* The prospect of space in the incubator is an added incentive and reward for students competing in university-sponsored business plan contests.

- *The incubator is a link to BBA/MBA concentrations in entrepreneurship.* The presence of a living laboratory for entrepreneurship is a marketing plus for the university.
- *The incubator is a link to university-wide associations and student organizations.* Student entrepreneurship clubs, technology management interest groups, and the like are enriched by the presence of the incubator. Connections to the alumni association are valuable as well.
- *The incubator is a fund-raising attraction.* Alumni may be delighted to see that the university is taking practical steps to encourage entrepreneurship. Many of a university's wealthiest alumni are entrepreneurs.

A 1995 Coopers and Lybrand (C&L) study, quoted in Hayhow (1996), showed that companies availing themselves of university resources "had productivity rates 59 percent higher than peers without such relationships" but that only 40 percent of companies surveyed actually used university resources. "Forging ties with a university is beneficial," C&L conclude, "yet most companies apparently need a push in this direction." Incubators can provide this push; according to Glenn Doell, formerly director of Rensselaer's incubator, "Incubators should consider developing a strong partnership with their local institution of higher learning."

The Milken Institute reports that "Research centers and institutions are indisputedly the most important factor in incubating high-tech industries." Universities attract federal funds and donations from wealthy alumni interested in entrepreneurship. Universities provide a flow of new knowledge, ready access to existing knowledge, able contract research, enthusiastic students, and ambitious, knowledgeable graduates who have a global outlook but also an emotional attachment to their college town. There could be no better ingredient in a recipe for technology entrepreneurship and economic development.

Issues and obstacles in university-connected incubation

The various incubator-related conflicts of interest and intra-university conflicts are summed up by the following, admittedly extreme, scenario.

A professor at a public university, working on a federal grant, discloses a laboratory innovation to the university, which patents it and licenses it back to the professor. The professor starts a company and brings it into the university-owned incubator. The incubator receives equity in the company. Further R&D is performed within the company, and part of it is done in the professor's university lab under a grant from the company to the university.

Objections to these activities start as a trickle and end as a flood. Parents complain that the professor should be in the classroom teaching their offspring, not using university time to start companies. The professor's dean wonders whether the professor is in violation of the university's conflict of interest policy. The university president's office complains that the portion of the company R&D done at the company, that is, inside the university-owned incubator, does not generate overhead cost recovery funds for the university. The university president herself, asked by a local investor whether the company is a viable investment, fears she cannot give a frank assessment of a firm in which the university owns stock. The president, used to dealing with large corporations that are university donors, doesn't know how to interact with small, entrepreneurial concerns. Her clumsy communications lead the company's employees to tell the press that the university president is threatening them.

The campus finance VP is accustomed to viewing only land, equipment, and buildings as university assets (all securities investment activity is handled "downtown" at the university system level). Because the incubator generates stock equity and eats cash, the VP threatens to shut down the incubator. The System Chancellor fears that if the incubator too successfully creates economic development in the local area, state legislators from distant counties will accuse the system of geographic favoritism and veto the Chancellor's bid for increased state funding for the university next year.

Documents that the company views as proprietary (but were generated during a meeting with incubator managers) are released to the public under the state's open records act. The company sues to recover the documents, charging breach of trust and malicious negligence, but fears that either way, the federal Freedom of Information Act may cause them to lose control of their intellectual property because the original research – and the closely related ongoing research under a new NSF grant in the professor's lab – was federally funded.

The professor's need for interns at the company is urgent, but the university's business school has not added entrepreneurship courses, and teaches a curriculum geared only for future employees of large companies. As a result, no qualified interns are available to incubator companies. The professor complains further that the university urged him to commercialize his invention and provided an incubator, but did not counsel him on the problems that would arise, nor warn him that the university would later appear to be working against him.

The provost and the university comptroller call the professor and the incubator director daily, reciting the list of disasters that will occur if any current federal money pays for university equipment or personnel that are used for the private benefit of the company.

Some universities (including University of Alabama; see Hayhow, 1996) avoid some of these difficulties by setting up a private foundation to administer an incubator, with the foundation chartered to benefit the university without being subject to university rules. Other universities set up a for-profit company to hold equity in incubated companies (see Kalis 1997). "The key is to manage conflict of interest situations, not avoid them completely," says Glenn Doell, former director of Rensselaer's incubator (Hayhow 1996), "If you try to completely avoid conflict of interest situations, you lose much of the potential benefit of the [university-incubator] relationship and you won't have any faculty-founded companies." Doell advocates warning all parties (the university IP and research administration offices, plus deans, department heads, and incubator staff) when a potential conflict arises, and urging all to document actions and precautions taken.

One respondent to Bienkowski's (2000) email survey said, "We want to encourage entrepreneurship and faculty startups, but want these enterprises to be separated cleanly from university activities." This is a wish that cannot be completely fulfilled.

Private incubator trends

In the 1980s and '90s, most of the incubators in the United States were what we (at the Austin incubator) dismissively called "real estate operations." This meant that universities were not involved and that tenants received no business assistance other than a shared receptionist and photocopier. James E. Burke, Ph.D., President of Burke Information Technology Services, described[1] the trend toward more responsible, higher-involvement private incubators:

Many of the original incubators were established by corporations first as an effort to commercialize some of their technology and later to allow employees with ideas to develop them with company backing.

These incubators had some success but then the corporations became more flexible about where the startups could locate and got away from maintaining a building site.

A recent development in incubators is the rush to create web-based companies in order to reap the rewards of "dot.com" valuations. These are usually set up, managed and financed by venture capitalists and other sources of financing. Once the management team is in place, the venture capital management oversight function comes to the fore, and its convenient to have all of the companies in one place.

Here is the fate of thirteen private net-incubators identified by Burke and the present author in 2000 (Table 20.1).

Kahney (2000) noted other new (non-incubator) private models for speeding dotcoms along the innovation arrow: "Late last year saw the launch of a slew of new intellectual property marketplaces, including yet2.com <http://www.yet2.com>, which concentrates on selling technology developed by corporations; TechEx <http://www.techex.com>, which focuses on the life sciences; and the Patent and License Exchange <http://www.pl-x.com/>, a patent auction." UVentures.com attempts to broker university patents to potential licensees via the Internet. Its founder, Craig Zolan, thinks university IP generates insufficient returns for universities because university IP offices rely on "a hopelessly outdated business practice": personal contacts. In my opinion, his venture

Table 20.1 Leading private incubators in 2000 and their status in 2005

Still incubating:

- Intelligent Systems Corp., www.intelsys.com
- Dreamscape Ventures, www.dreamscapeventures.com

Changed to a non-incubator model:

- eCompanies, www.ecompanies.com
- Garage.com, www.garage.com
- Idealab, www.idealab.com
- I-Hatch Venture, www.i-hatch.com
- Internet Capital Group, www.icge.com

No web presence in 2005:

- Campsix Inc. (formerly Net2Future), www.campsix.com
- CMG Inc, www.cgmi.com
- Divine InterVentures, www.divineinterventures.com
- eHatchery, ehatchery.com
- Interactive Minds, www.interactiveminds.com
- Venture Frogs, www.venturefrogs.com

(and the similar Knowledge Express in Berwyn, PA) may generate some licenses, but violates the wisdom that "technology transfer is a body-contact sport." Personal contacts will remain important, and thus local incubation will remain an important tool.

It now appears the big accounting/consulting firms have got into the act:

> Note that in chatting with an exec from Deloitte and Touche at a Corp. Investment conference last week, D&T is also planning similar investment/incubation activities and thus, I'd assume PWC and others will follow suit. Wonder if we can count on them to offer not only financial services, but access to ERP, MRP, and/or CRM expertise and capabilities.[2]

I have to note my disagreement with Jim Burke's further assertion:

> A recent development that may turn the web-based incubator approach into an entirely new kind of economic development engine is the creation of wealth through the interactions of the startup companies within an incubator. The image is that of the Japanese keiretsu where all of the startup companies and their partnering (and sometimes funding) corporations have special business relationships with each other.

The Japanese keiretsu have been weakened by their extensive foreign operations, which dilute their cohesive culture. Incubator companies must be networked globally to take advantage of the global markets made accessible by the Internet. The keiretsu is not a viable model, especially when it focuses companies excessively on alliances with other physically proximate companies at a similar life cycle stage.

The Internet

It is now commonly said that "The Internet changes everything." Here is what is meant by that. The Internet provides

- Streamlined inventory and distribution, making otherwise low-margin businesses feasible.
- Fast distribution and customer feedback.
- Global distribution, even to special-interest markets.
- Many new business opportunities for networking the citizens of the world.

While it shifts power to consumers, the Net revolutionizes relationship marketing. Producers, while losing price leverage, gain information leverage.

For software businesses, the Net makes version control easy, and for this and other reasons, empowers small developers.

The Internet allows many kinds of resources to be pooled over larger geographical reaches, indeed globally, and this is the rationale for the recent growth of online incubators and online intellectual property auctions.

The explosive growth of the Internet itself provides business opportunities for companies building net tools, that is, the software that underlies e-commerce, and the hardware (servers, routers, and so on) that carry messages across the net. This is knowledge-intensive work, and naturally its manpower and much of its intellectual property will be supplied by universities.

The Internet is a new communications medium that offers desktop videoconferencing, telephony, synchronous text chat, publishing, broadcasting, virtual reality, and asynchronous bulletin boards. These multiple channels of communication increase the chances that ideas can be conveyed accurately and relationships cemented without travel – although almost all experts agree that in a customer or alliance relationship, face to face ("FTF" in net-speak) contact is needed sooner or later.

If Andrew Grove is correct that "soon all businesses will be e-businesses," then indeed the Internet changes everything.

Summary of survey/interview data

This study used expert interviews and a mail survey as well as incubator visits and literature search to form its recommendations.[3] The expert interview questionnaire consisted of only three questions:

1. How has the Internet changed new business incubation?
2. How has the trend to privatization of incubators, especially under the ownership of investor groups, affected the university's role in incubation?
3. How can universities best interact with incubators in the '00s?

Expert responses

The experts' answers were (in paraphrase):

> Universities need not spend capital at this time to build or run incubators. Nowadays, incubators should pay universities to

participate ... Even back in the 1970s, RPI (Rensselaer Polytechnic Institute, in Troy, New York) recognized privatization was the way to go; all RPI incubators are in partnerships, except its on-campus one. Universities should be paid for the things they are good at (facilitators, nursemaids, incubator managers, educators, technology transferors, supporters of entrepreneurship, and carriers of a collegial culture) – not for things they don't do well, like being landlords ... Private incubators are likely to be boutiques, with a narrow industry interest and focus ... The Internet helps close funding deals after just one FTF. (Dwight Sangrey, April 7, 2000)

Portland senior executives would like to participate [in incubators] as mentors ... With other executives, I have approached a number of private incubators asking them to establish a branch in Portland ... This would facilitate my merchant banking activities, bringing together management teams and investors ... The Internet is great for communicating, exchanging ideas, and proving business ideas in a short time. (Al Preush, April 3, 2000)

Privatization of incubators is driven by the Internet sector and VCs. VCs want fast companies, like Internet plays. Privatization is driven also by the real estate shortage in high growth areas, and by the growth of the stock market. Because all these things can change rapidly, the continuation of private incubation cannot be relied upon. Before the World Wide Web, private incubators tended to last a maximum of two years. Now, with the Net, [the private incubator arm of] Softbank only lets companies stay in for six months! This is not really enough time to lend significant business assistance ... Net companies have intensive supplier/customer networks and have to locate close to similar companies and to sources of labor; with luck, their economic impact will trickle down to outlying regions ... so not all incubator activities will serve all state economic development goals. (Laura Kilcrease, April 4, 2000)

Incubator responses

The following summarizes the most notable patterns in the incubator director survey responses.

1. *Square footage.* Respondents indicated incubator sizes ranging from 1,800 to 40,000 and more rentable square feet. Nearly all, regardless of the size of their incubator, believe their square footage is insufficient to serve market demand and/or achieve economies of scale.

2. *Quality of physical plant.* While undergraduates may find charm in lecture halls that have not been renovated in seventy-five years, incubators do no favor to tenants if the incubation facility is not suitable for entertaining customers and suppliers, or not convenient to airports and major highways. Most incubators surveyed occupy Class-A space, but some of these cite inconvenient location. In addition, while most claim to be breaking even financially, deferred maintenance of physical plant is often cited as a concern, indicating the incubators are not making money on a fully cost-loaded basis.

3. *Tenancy and services.* Most respondents indicated their incubators offer the full range of services prompted by the questionnaire, though most seem to review tenants' financials rather infrequently. Most allowed direct competitors to occupy incubator space at the same time, though this will necessarily cut down on the social interaction that is a prime benefit of physical incubators. Number of tenants housed ranged from 4 to 30, with a mean of 19. Many discount market rents by as much as 50 percent, though experts argue that such discounting is a needless crutch for truly competitive companies and is an unfair return to the incubator considering the services offered (very few respondents take equity in tenant companies to offset rent reductions).

4. *University involvement.* Answers ranged from none/informal university connections to full university-owned incubators. Even the latter seemed to integrate university activities (academics, seminars, internships, and tech transfer) piecemeal or incompletely. All agreed university involvement is good for incubator entrepreneurs, most agreed such involvement is good for the university as a whole, and fewer that university involvement in incubation is essential for either the incubator or for university MBA/BBA programs.

5. *Staffing and finances.* Tenure of directors varied considerably, though most had been on the job a short time. (Incubator directors may use the job as a steppingstone to positions with investment firms or with startup companies, so there is much turnover among incubator directors.) Most incubators claimed "breakeven or better" financial performance. However, most derived funding from a variety of government, philanthropic, and university sources (only one claimed breakeven on rents alone) in addition to tenant rents – so "breakeven" may be a result of university subsidies, rather than net of such subsidies.

6. *Networking.* Most incubators surveyed are members of the National Business Incubator Association (NBIA), and maintain relationships

with at least one incubator in a distant location. All agree the Internet has benefited incubators and incubator tenant companies as a communication tool. The most often-cited benefits were "More dotcom startups are applying to our incubator" and "We are better able to find suppliers and customers for our tenant companies." Close behind were "Our tenant companies can more easily work with other off-site service providers" and "Our tenant companies can more easily work with companies in our allied regions."

Case Studies[4]

Case Study #1: Rensselaer Polytechnic Institute

> "Alums who have ignored RPI for many years have gotten excited again due to RPI's entrepreneurship focus."
>
> — *Mike Wacholder, RPI*

All four campus organizations involved in these areas (see Figure 20.1) are tightly coordinated, even though one is under control of the management dean and the others report to RPI president. It must be said that this tight

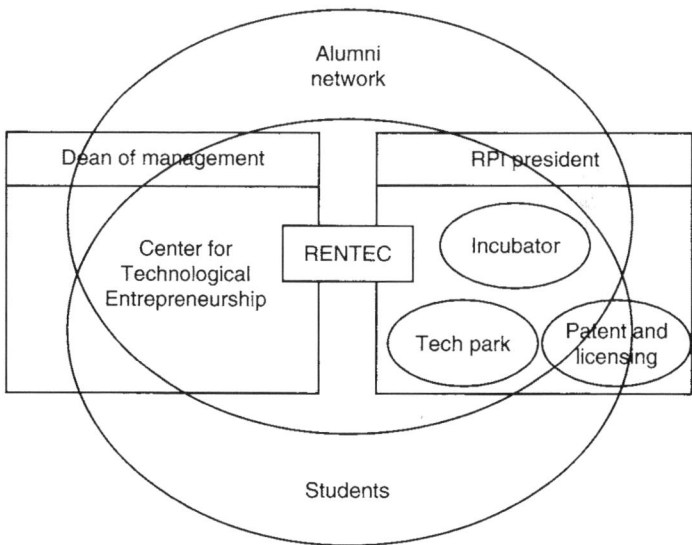

Figure 20.1 Incubation and technology transfer organization at Rensselaer Polytechnic Institute

coordination depends on the goodwill of the four area directors. The four together are called RENTEC. The campus licensing/patenting office is now called Office of Technology Commercialization, and is located in the incubator building.

RPI is known as an entrepreneur-friendly school. Students and faculty come to RPI because they can "bring their companies with them."

RPI files 6–8 patents/year, selective by commercialization potential. As at other universities, very few patents pay off their costs. One answer is being more selective (difficult if faculty with a lot of clout want to file many patents); another is to have similar schools pool efforts.

Bill Stett, a retired entrepreneur who is now Director of the Center for Technological Entrepreneurship at RPI, teaches alliances and acquisitions. Bill confirms that the entrepreneurship center opens new areas of philanthropy. CTE raises as much each year as the Management Dean – but tries not to compete.

RPI's Lally School of Management has a faculty area called "Entrepreneurship & Strategy." This ensures that entrepreneurship is not a stepchild academic area. Stett says indeed entrepreneurship is central at the Lally School. Entrepreneurship faculty can get tenure at Lally. But Lally faculty are not strong in all entrepreneurship skill areas; Stett wishes for a good venture financing course.

Stett recommends getting older entrepreneurs involved first in teaching and mentoring. Donations will then follow.

Case Study #2: Maui Research and Technology Center

This park is currently run by a mixture of state and county agencies. The County of Maui is attempting to buy the park, which was originally a private development. The park is located near the Air Force's astronomical observatory, and houses a major Department of Defense (DoD) supercomputing center, the Maui High Performance Computing Center (MHPCC). While the park houses industry outreach offices of University of Hawaii at Manoa, University of Hawaii at Hilo, and Maui Community College, the universities have no direct role in running the park or its incubator.

The supercomputing center is run by the University of New Mexico (UNM) under contract to DoD (see Table 20.2). The supercomputer center's mission is primarily to analyze signals from the Air Force telescopes – mostly "space junk" and colliding asteroid studies.

The Park's best success so far is a Japanese company, "Micro-Gaia," that produces gene-engineered algae. Real estate in Maui is still cheaper than Silicon Valley, and offers location appeal to Silicon Valley business people who have built strong ties to Maui through a history of vacations

Table 20.2 UNM's cooperative arrangement with DoD requires community outreach

---

- Allows companies to retain all IP to code used at MHPCC. All companies are charged at same level for using MHPCC.
- If labs agree to give free time to a company, the lab (MHPCC) can option the IP or put it in public domain.
- Undergrad and graduate academic programs.
- Can work with foreign companies if via a "US connection". But all work is subject to US export restrictions.
- A company using MHPCC remotely may decide to keep a small local office at MRTC, especially if cooperating with an Asian company.

Source: Margaret Lewis, MHPCC.

on the island. The number of direct flights and carriers serving Maui–California routes is increasing.

MRTC covers 300 acres, with 48,000 sq.ft. of buildings. State funds were provided for "front end" work on the supercomputer, though most of the startup of the park was privately funded. MRTC houses:

- An incubator (2300 sq.ft. leasable);
- The University of Hawaii's tech transfer office;
- Currently, eight companies and "phase-in" companies (for two years);
- Space for "work teams";
- Interim locations for relocating companies.

The period of incubation is less than five years, but is flexible. Services provided include:

- Low-cost space (on par with other Class-A space, but services are included. $1.90/sq.ft; commercial is $2.20) B space is available on Maui at $1.00/ft.
- Copying, and so on.
- Business advice.
- A Small Business Development Center (SBDC).
- A business research library.

MRTC Director Tak Sugimura is "leveraging resources" to "zap the gap," engineering local lab results in order to lure licensees.

The running of the incubator is the responsibility of the Maui Economic Development Board, a 501c3.[5] Thus, MEDB employees may coach incubator tenants without fear of losing control of data due to open records laws. Through MRTC, MEDB was the first Internet service provider on the island.

MRTC has an underutilized videoconferencing facility, but earns some money by renting it out. There are also distance-learning classrooms that haven't been used yet; MRTC wants to network with many US universities.

MRTC is just blocks from hotels, but is a considerable distance from the Maui airport.

Park buildings are state funded. The land is a private development, but land on which the state buildings stand have been donated to the state by developers. The county is trying to buy it all.

MRTC doesn't pay rent, but does have to cover building operating costs, and does get a management fee from the state. The state currently covers major repairs, but doesn't want to ultimately. MRTC is now self-sustaining, exclusive of major renovations. Leases are month-to-month, with companies admitted by business plan.

There are:

- 100 full-time employees in incubating companies;
- +22 full-time for Mauinet (a graduating company);
- +15 part time;
- Direct competitors are allowed;
- Build-out is tenant responsibility;
- No equity taken in incubated companies.

MRTC tries to focus on "good match" technologies. One of these is MicroGaia's algae food supplement, which has a high markup per ounce and can grow in Hawaiian waters. Another is high-speed photography, adapting astronomy photographic techniques to the photographing of water sports. A third is business website design and hosting, which can build the export potential of Hawaii businesses.

MRTC remains weak in connections to VC and angel capital.

Calvin Nemoto is Executive Assistant to Maui County Mayor James Apana. Mr Nemoto is trying to partner with Sonoma State University to build a private high school and a four-year college in Maui. The county's overriding goal is workforce development.

There are "several hundred" technology companies in Hawaii, but most are 1–2 person. The County believes it is important to let people know that there is room to grow their companies on Maui, and that Maui is entrepreneur-friendly. Like Austin in Texas, Maui has a reputation for going its own way, even when that means not cooperating with State of Hawaii initiatives and the wishes of the Governor. The widespread attitude on the island that "Maui No Ka Oi (Maui is the best)" may turn out to be a central factor in their success.

Case Study #3: University of Washington, Technology Enterprise Institute

This case is summarized from Tice (1999). The institute, funded with $4 million from UW, will utilize the best principles of university-incubator interaction, serving learning and teaching objectives for the university and the community at large. Additional funding will be sought from public and private sources. Bob Miller, UW Director of Technology Transfer, says students from business, law, engineering, and the sciences at UW will be involved in the institute, and the new institute should generate additional faculty positions. Intellectual property issues will provide academic fodder for business and ethics students. Faculty will not be allowed to be officers of incubator companies, nor take grants from incubator companies.

In the past, according to UW business professor Ken Walters, more than 140 companies have been created from UW intellectual property, comprising a total of $10 billion in market capitalization. Ninety percent of these companies remain headquartered in Washington state, or keep significant operations in the state after being bought out by out-of-state concerns.

The Technology Enterprise Institute will occupy a 40,000 square foot facility in West Seattle.

Recommendations for Oregon (and other) universities

Should universities build or own physical incubators?

Only if they can leverage an assured supply of:

- High-quality surplus space (office, laboratory, and/or manufacturing space);
- Qualified student labor; and
- Surplus furniture and lab equipment;

and even then, only if internal university concerns about overhead recovery, the non-commercial mission of the university, equity participation in tenant companies, or commingling of funds (commingling can and must be avoided!) are not likely to paralyze the incubator effort.

Ten years ago, the incubation concept was new. Universities provided "proof of concept" and researched the value and operations of incubators. Private incubators were often just "real estate operations," providing no business mentoring to tenant companies. Today, incubation is a well-accepted notion. Well-funded VC firms, angel investor consortia, technology brokers, and even law firms run their own incubators, and have every incentive to provide comprehensive business advice to tenants. Universities still have valuable contributions to make, but will find it difficult to compete economically running a full-service incubator in-house.

Should universities be involved in incubators in any way?

Yes! University involvement in incubators can benefit the university *and* the business and entrepreneurial public. Benefits flow in all directions.

- The university offers valuable knowledge, social support, technical support, and student labor to entrepreneurs.
- The university offers the incubator a credible profile in the community.
- The incubator offers valuable educational and outreach opportunities for students and faculty.
- A university that shows activism in entrepreneurship can attract increased philanthropic donations.

However, a university incubating strategy must fit within an educational and/or economic development strategy. The larger strategy may involve workforce development, entrepreneurial graduates, or one of many other possible such missions. An incubator can be one of several programs that fulfill the larger strategy. In the best of worlds, the director of the collection of programs must be empowered to announce the strategy to the public and to execute the strategy without being pulled in conflicting directions by the differing objectives of the university and multiple funding agencies.

For public universities, two more conditions are important for an emphatic "yes" answer to the italicized question given before:

- The ability to finesse Freedom of Information (FOI) regulations.[6] A procedural firewall must exist between tenant company meetings and state/university employees. Any university property used in connection with tenant company business – or any notes taken by university employees extending business coaching to incubator tenants – may open the door to FOI requests. The danger of this would discourage high-potential companies from applying for admission to the incubator.

- An explicit policy within the university that incubation is part and parcel of the university's teaching and community service roles. Through operational programs and public relations messages, the university must integrate incubator activities with the missions of the university: Education, research, community service, and state and local economic development.

How can universities demonstrate the success of their incubator efforts?

Universities running incubators should be prepared to use sophisticated methods of branding and targeted selling to recruit companies, capital, and mentors, as well as to market the incubator internally to faculty and students.

An incubator with a three-year exit policy cannot have a large economic impact in the short term. However, politicians, funding agencies, and university administrators who support the incubator will ask for quick results. The incubators should strive for and publicize:

- The number of companies admitted
- The number of companies applying
- The admittees' initial funding levels
- The square footage filled
- Tenant company's subsequent funding
- The frequency and quality of educational and networking events, and size of audience attending
- Employment growth in tenant companies
- Public cost per job created
- The number of professional service providers pledging pro bono hours
- New product launches.

and other measures that, individually or as ratios, indicate a promise of significant economic impact.

Only a sustained, high-intensity effort will bear fruit for a regional strategy. One networking or speaker event per month will not materially help entrepreneurs, nor create economic growth. Trying for a year to build an entrepreneurial environment, then giving up, will do no better. Can universities, investors, service providers, associations, and governments work together to assure two or more educational events per week for five years? Only this level of commitment and performance can build a perceived presence and offer programs that actually reach busy entrepreneurs and executives.

What attracts desirable incubator tenants in the 2000s?

A focus on strategic technologies and business areas. The Maui Tech Park is strong in this regard, emphasizing opportunities for building businesses around ocean farming, natural nutraceuticals, and technologies deriving from the local strengths in astronomy and supercomputing (high-speed photography and "space junk" technologies).

The Internet facilitates low-cost collaboration at a distance – after people have become acquainted face to face. It also provides worldwide markets for local companies. According to Intel founder Andrew Grove, "All businesses will be e-businesses." But this does not diminish the importance of "FTF" (face to face) contact with customers, investors, and suppliers.

Universities can contribute to the e-business success of tenant companies by using their Internet expertise to provide support and new employees to the tenant companies, and by giving the incubator enough autonomy to truly help companies competing "on Internet time." Universities tend to operate on consensus, not on speed. This mode is not acceptable if the university incubator represents that it can help Internet startup companies; any bureaucratic slowdown that stalls an Internet company will be broadcast over the Net at light speed, with sudden and total loss of credibility for the university and the incubator.

Universities can contribute to the face-to-face aspect of globally networked entrepreneurship by leveraging visits of foreign scholars and officials by introducing them to incubator tenants, and by using their downtown centers in major metro areas to host meetings for entrepreneurs and incubator tenants from statewide and beyond.

Low real estate costs are an attractor for new and relocating high-growth-potential companies that are potential incubator tenants, but are not sufficient, if there is not also excellent transportation and communications infrastructure surrounding the incubator. Universities with attractive surplus space are better suited to take equity from companies, as cash flow is not critical to most universities. Therefore, there are opportunities for university-owned incubators in less urbanized areas to attract promising tenants.

What should universities do?

Universities should understand their strengths vis a vis incubation, attract funding to build on those strengths, and play to their strengths and their mission in the marketplace. Public universities serve geographical areas sparse in entrepreneurial infrastructure. They take the long view. They are well connected with local businesses and local problems, but network with far-flung scholars and alumni. They have the loyalty of young people and their families.

Universities may constructively build, own and run incubators

- When the university is located in an area of low-cost real estate.
- To serve companies that are *not* "living on Internet time" and yet have significant growth potential.
- Where a community effort can be sustained without pressure for short-term results.
- If the university can leverage its contacts and its communications/ transportation facilities to connect companies to investors, customers, advisors, and suppliers.

This is, perhaps, a rare situation. But results could range from the creation of a few jobs and companies, to the complete economic transformation of the community. The university can enjoy long-term capital gains from equity in tenant companies.

Universities may partner with investor-owned incubators in more urbanized, high-cost areas, to serve new businesses that face severely limited windows of opportunity.

In either case, universities will incur costs preparing themselves for these roles. Funding can be applied to:

- Expanding academic entrepreneurship programs;
- Educating faculty about the procedures and rewards of university patenting, licensing, and spin-off formation, and helping them decide when to publish and when to "disclose" to the university intellectual property office;
- Joining the National Business Incubation Association;
- Offering outreach programs to immigrant, women, and minority entrepreneurs;
- Setting up internship programs;
- Sending student teams to national and international new venture competitions;
- Engaging more business executives and investors in university classes, organizations, and activities.

Conclusion

Universities have a constructive role to play in new business incubation. Universities should take care that their incubation activities complement rather than duplicate those now provided by private investors;

universities should play to their strengths, and these strengths include the ability to take the long view, to creatively utilize real estate assets, and to create, disseminate, and apply advanced knowledge.

The actions recommended in this chapter should not be taken as immutable; the stock market and investor enthusiasms will inevitably shift, opening new opportunities for universities. But for now, universities should not attempt to "help" dotcom/e-commerce companies with narrow market windows by putting them in incubators that are subject to restrictive rules of university bureaucracy. These companies are better served by private investor incubators, but the university can assist by contracting with the investors, to create the maximum interaction with university programs and resources.

University-owned incubators can best help other kinds of high-growth-potential companies. In rural areas, this might mean plant biotechnologies (like the algae projects in Maui's incubator), or telemarketing/ service center businesses, or multi-level businesses that do not require venture capital to kick-start their growth. University and rural incubators can take heed that "all businesses will be e-businesses," helping local businesses survive and gain efficiency by automating their transactions. University and rural incubators can grow companies that provide the telecommunications or other infrastructure services that facilitate the Internet economy. They can also nurture companies that take the long view of the transformative power of the Internet, looking beyond the quick-hit profits to be made by "attracting eyeballs" to websites and selling groceries over the Net.

Tornatzky *et al.* (1996) provide an admirable comparative view of many university-connected incubators. While those authors, and the case studies above, include many universities in the eastern United States, the individualistic ethos of the west might suggest that Oregon look to other western role models. Two of Tornatzky *et al.*'s summaries are extracted below to conclude this chapter.

UBC Research Enterprises at University of British Columbia is a good example of a positive organizational arrangement. This office deals with all aspects of the university's portfolio of sponsored research with industry, as well as all aspects of intellectual property management, patenting, and licensing. In addition, it takes on the task of functioning as an incubator without walls ... The office is willing to assist faculty inventors as they work through the entrepreneurial process. In contrast with many university technology offices, which tend to focus exclusively on licensing to already established companies, UBC Research Enterprises routinely provides (or brokers) many of the services that traditional incubators offer.

Wichita Technology Corporation is one of three nonprofit "commercialization corporations" established by the Kansas Technology Enterprise Corporation (KTEC), each of which is collocated with a state research university ... the commercialization corporations are independent not-for-profits. However, they are programmatically linked with the university. ... The commercialization center will review technologies emerging from the university and ... identify those that have the potential ... for a significant business. WTC's role ... is ... putting together the business – which might imply pulling in other technologies – identifying other business partners, securing capitalization, and so on. Since the parent organization, KTEC, also invests heavily in university-based research centers of excellence, the commercialization corporation has ready access to university technologies.

See Chapter 22, "Short Takes," for more about incubators.

Notes

1. Via email, March 8, 2000.
2. Via email, from Christopher J. Meyers, Vice President, Corporate Services, Select University Technologies, Inc. (SUTI), Costa Mesa, California. The Deloitte and Touche initiative is still active in 2005; see, for example, http://graduates.deloitte.co.uk/index.cfm?p_id=40.
3. The incubator survey form was rather extensive. A low response rate was the result of over-surveyed incubators in that period of time. However, the project's multiple modes of gathering data (including the expert interviews) mitigated the low incubator survey response rate.
4. The case study on Virginia's Mason Enterprise Center, presented in Chapter 18, is also relevant to this chapter.
5. 501c3 is the paragraph of the US tax code that enables some kinds of non-profit corporations (NGOs).
6. FOI or similarly named regulations in many countries dictate that documents produced with public funding should be open for inspection by the general public.

21
Does Place Matter? Quality of Life and Wandering Alumni

Fred Phillips

Geographers are fond of saying "Everything happens somewhere." To retort "So what?" may be philistine, but is also legitimate. What differentiates one place from another, and do those differences *make a difference* for economic development? Does place matter?

Novelist John Banville (2003), via a character's soliloquy, argues in the negative:

> I find this city [Turin] no more attractive or interesting than any other I have known. Customs, legends, tales of colourful characters and events, such stuff leaves me cold; the picturesque in particular I find revolting. I do not care what battles Emanuele Filiberto won or lost, or where Cavour liked to eat his dinner. History is a hotchpotch of anecdotes, neither true nor false, and what does it matter where it is supposed to have taken place? I ... despise those novelists ... whose scenes were set on thyme-scented islands, or in pine-shaded hilltop villages ... As if place meant something; as if being somewhere vivid and exotic ensured an automatic intensification of living. No: give me an anonymous patch of ground, with asphalt, and an oily bonfire smouldering, and vague factories in the distance, some rank, exhausted non place where I can feel safe, where I can feel at home, if I am ever to feel at home, anywhere.

Neal Peirce (2003) of Citistates Group takes a contrary view:

> A national survey ... shows Americans are now significantly more favorable to cities, willing to spend time or live in them, than in the mid-1990s. People increasingly believe ... that strong cities, with their concentrations of universities, health care providers and critical

industries, generate environments that attract more young qualified workers and are a key to national prosperity. A bottom line here: Even in an Internet age, place matters.

What differentiators, if any, matter? Universities, technology, college graduate in-migrants, or amenities and quality of life? Can one of these, alone, enrich a region? Or does the region need two or more of these factors in combination? If so, must one come before the other? Which is the cart and which is the horse? Which the chicken and which the egg?

I side with Peirce. We can, though, learn from Banville's character, who displays not only some self-hatred, but a rejection of history as well as geography. It is elementary that civic pride drives economic development programs. An implicit local belief that "We don't deserve success" or "We are a second-class place" works against successful development, and every locality should engage in the introspection that can prevent such self-defeat. Certain places are known for attracting people, like Banville's protagonist, who wish to erase their personal histories. In so doing, these places (several are in the American west, midwest, and south) lose their regional history, building physical environments that are bland and undifferentiated, offering little of distinctive value (except raw population growth) for business development.

We can say with certainty that place matters. As for universities, technology, college grads, and amenities, we know a few preliminary answers, and we know the next questions that must be asked.

The CEOs for Cities study (Weissbourd and Berry, 2003; See also Costa and Kahn 2000 and Florida 2000) that Peirce cites makes these claims:

- In the 1990s, "many Sunbelt cities spurted in population but languished in income growth. Only three cities (Austin, Colorado Springs and Charlotte) managed to be leaders in both income and population growth ... The more an area adds college graduates, the greater its prosperity. While better weather attracts population overall, college graduates tend to go to places with worse weather."
- Regions that started the '90s with high incomes now lead in wage growth. "With innovative business networks rising in importance, the luckier regions seem to be 'locking in' paths to success."
- Ten years ago, the envied life involved escape to a "quaint small town, electronically connected" but far from the madding crowd. Americans are now "significantly more favorable" to city life than in the mid-1990s.

Hall (1998, p. 78) notes the "predominantly very young population" of the historic Tuscan cities, "even by medieval standards; and it was continually decimated by plague, so that it needed to recruit anew. Florence was a magnet to young, able and ambitious people from the surrounding countryside ... Most of these immigrants were of some standing, owners of land and small businesses, and semi-professional men such as notaries." Now as then, in the knowledge economy, wealth is built by knowledgeable people, not by uneducated muscle. Overall population growth does not lead to wealth any more. Beyond that simple truth, though, lies a host of complications.

I am a college graduate, and I've spent decades avoiding cities with bad weather. However, I spent one of those decades in the market research industry, where I learned a lesson all economic developers should take to heart: *If everyone were just like me, I would not need market research.* The outdoor life so beloved of the boomers may lack appeal for the Nintendo generation. There are ways to find out, and ambitious regions should engage in the survey research necessary for gauging the attitudes and migratory motivation of young college grads. (It is not, incidentally, a simple matter of there being a lot more cold cities than warm ones. The US Bureau of the Census (2000) list of the hundred most populous US metropolitan statistical areas shows roughly 53 of them in regions with chilly weather.)

While many cities are losing young college grads, Portland, Oregon is known for attracting a large net influx of this group. For the most part, they come without jobs, and without families. Thus the thriving music and art scenes in Portland, and the number of small and boutique advertising and P. R. agencies. Portland, with its excess of educated underemployed, would seem to be ripe for the kind of high-tech renaissance that Austin experienced in the 1980s. However, the city is not entrepreneur-friendly, nor even small-business-friendly, and as tech industry recovers it is off-shoring jobs rather than reinstating them in Oregon. The dynamics of this have yet to play out. Portland's young college grads are not enjoying family-wage jobs, and may move away when they are ready to start families.

A recent doctoral thesis at Portland State University (Mayer 2002) argued that the high-tech corporations of Silicon Forest, playing the role that large research universities do in other cities, kept Portland a technological leader despite its lack of a first-tier diversified research university. The CEOs for Cities report suggests there might have been an intervening factor: The companies attracted the educated graduates that created the wealth. Intel alone employs 15,000 in the Portland metro area. The mild climate and the cultural scene – the latter due in part to the under-employed young non-techies – helped the electronics firms attract the tech workforce to the city.

Biotech in Portland is a different story. The city's biggest employer (11,000) is a respected medical research university turning out steady advances in biomedical devices. Its velocity of pharmaceutical innovation, though, is limited by the lack of collaborations with "big pharma" firms. The latter are in places like Chicago, Philadelphia, and New York – the cold cities!

Other locales – take Maui, for example – are just overflowing with quality of life, and can't seem to sell it. Yes, there is revenue from tourists and timeshare owners, but this is not the scalable entrepreneurial growth that leads to long-lasting, family-wage jobs. Venture capitalists are skeptical of business plans coming from the island, suspecting that the company will attract employees who just want to go to the beach. In fact, Maui has benefited from firms whose businesses (e.g., algal nutraceuticals, underwater photography equipment) *require* employees to go to the beach.

Portland and Maui suggest that quality of life alone will not sustain growth, nor will the combination of technology and an influx of new college grads (see also Gottlieb 1994). Both areas are retirement living destinations, drawing retirees with means. The retirees may be interested in supporting medical research. However, they are heavily targeted for philanthropy by their own alma maters. They are often leaders in tax-reform movements, which hurt the local school districts and make the economic development situation worse in the long run. I've seen no evidence that retirees bring desirable jobs to a region, though they can bring valuable expertise and mentorship.

We are left with an ample research agenda: What is the relationship among strong universities, technology, college graduate in-migrants, amenities and quality of life, retirees, and sustainable economic development? How can regions attract and retain young college graduates? What are the roles of a region's unique identity and distinguishing character?

Foer (2003) analyzed the recent evolution of the world soccer industry. As early exemplars of globalization – having traded players, coaches, and sponsors worldwide for decades now – the sport's teams have retained their home cities' distinct character to a remarkable extent. In soccer, at least, a "level playing field" does not lead to homogenization. Is Foer discouraging globalists, saying their best efforts will never produce frictionless markets? Or is he telling anti-globalists not to worry, globalization can't do that much harm anyway?

Either way, it's clear: local cultures persist, for better or worse. Place does matter.

22
Short Takes

Fred Phillips

Editorial: marketing is where it's at

In this issue we criticize the view, apparently held by many cities, that the infrastructural aspects of economic development are far more important than the marketing aspects. Like many of our readers, the *Technopolis Times* staff are (or have been) in business. If we have survived in business, it is not because we believe "if you build a better mousetrap the world will beat a path to your door." No, we understand that a good product is half of business success, and the other half is excellent advertising and marketing.

There is circumstantial evidence that on average, recruitment efforts don't work. So what? It's a business adage that "half my advertising dollars are wasted; I just don't know which half." That is to say, the same thing is true in business: on the average, advertising only half works. Businesses advertise anyway.

In technology companies, engineers want to build bleeding-edge devices, but the marketers want the engineers to build what the customers say they want. If engineers get the upper hand for too long, nothing gets sold; if marketers prevail for too long, the company loses its reputation for technological leadership. Tension between the two is healthy, just as it is for infrastructural and marketing initiatives in economic development.

But, you might say, people are moving to your city anyway, without outward marketing, and you get some company start-ups there.

Fine, but are they the kind of companies you want? At worst, an influx of random companies can have bad environmental impacts, or if headquartered elsewhere, siphon too much money out of the region. At best, randomly arriving companies fail to contribute to cohesive industry clusters.

This journal believes (though we admit we can't prove) that all successful post-Silicon Valley, post-Boston technology clusters, anywhere in the world, have been seeded by the efforts of governments or public–private partnerships. These entities do strategic and tactical marketing. That is, they target the kinds of newcomer companies they want, and then market to them.

The phrase from *Field of Dreams*, "If you build it, they will come," is fantasy. Good movie, bad business strategy. In real life if you build it, either no companies come or the wrong companies come. Barring dumb luck, of course.

But, you might say, if free enterprise is truly efficient, investors will locate in the right place (for them) regardless of a government's incentives, pretty brochures, or official calls on company presidents.

We respectfully disagree, for three reasons. First, as noted above, the right place for the company is not necessarily the right place for the residents of a particular city. Second, free-enterprise market-clearing arguments can be excuses to do nothing. And third, free-market equilibrium logic simply does not apply to cluster formation.

Using the market-clearing reasoning (in an extreme way, admittedly), Calvin Klein need not advertise, because the efficient market will ensure there are plenty of jeans for anyone who wants them. To take that logic even farther, Calvin need not even bother to do business, because the efficient market will see that if there's a need for jeans, it will be filled.

Would that be important? In a way, no: Calvin's smart, he can always find another way to make a living. He has a choice.

Cities don't have that choice! Like it or not, Portland (for example) is "in the Portland business," that is, in the business of being Portland, improving Portland, and selling Portland. And our "product," our only possible product, is ... Portland.

Finally, an economic equilibrium analysis would show – falsely – that all technology firms will locate in Chicago, Los Angeles, or New York, because that's where they will be close to large markets, large talent pools, large universities, and frequent direct flights to everywhere. This kind of analysis cannot explain why Salt Lake City or Austin became vital technopoleis.

There are many smaller population centers with good quality of life, good universities, and low cost of living. After a "critical mass" of companies have located in one such center, setting its industry cluster at the self-sustaining level, the locale can reduce its marketing budget. Until then, it must – using market distortions if necessary – build exceptional infrastructure and stay in the faces of selected relocating firms, shouting, "Look at me!"

But, you might say, mustn't the city council demonstrate to taxpayers that their ED marketing dollars are productive, no matter how difficult that demonstration might be?

Only in the same way that businesses have to demonstrate it to stockholders. And that doesn't stop businesses from advertising and marketing!

*   *   *

Editorial: that guy from the government who says he's here to help? He might be, really

Will neoclassical economics and the theory/practice of economic development go their separate ways? The US, under its current small-government ideology, is seeing its sick go without costly drugs, and its K-12 education system decline. The Scandinavian countries – the most highly taxed and regulated on Earth, and the bane of small-government dogmatists – are highly innovative and entrepreneurial. That Denmark, Finland, Sweden and Norway are innovative, congenial places to live illustrates what this journal has long noted: Economic development is served by having a healthy, educated populace.

To be sure, the numbers show the US growing its economy faster. The OECD figures for 2003 GDP growth are shown in Table 22.1.

The numbers are clouded by the greater number of hours worked per person in the US (Krugman, 2005 shows that GDP per hour worked is *higher* in France than in the US), America's greater number of two-earner families, and Norway's oil wealth. But at this point we can ask some good questions and make some preliminary conclusions. Questions: How long until US growth slows down, due to the entry into the workforce of uneducated, latch-key kids who have never seen a dentist? How many growth points would the average American be willing to give up for

Table 22.1   2003 GDP growth in selected OECD nations

États-Unis	3.7%
Danemark	1.2%
Finlande	2.9%
Norvège	1.4%
Suède	2.6%
Scandinavia average	2.0%
Non-Scandinavia, non-US OECD countries combined	2.2%

Source: OECD.

better education, health and family life? Perhaps the eight basis points that separate the US from Finland?

Conclusions: Again, the philosophy of this journal is that it is not the work habits of the average American or Dane that is the question. Entrepreneurs in each of these countries work much harder than ordinary people can or should. Yes, successful Swedish entrepreneurs become tax refugees – living in Switzerland, *but still doing business in Sweden.* Successful Portland entrepreneurs, too, cross the Columbia to live in Washington State, where capital gains taxes are lower, but they still do business in Oregon where they can find healthy, educated employees. There is more analysis that can be done, taking into account, e.g., regional differences in risk-taking behavior. And governments are not the only sources of education and health care. However, it looks as though the US is risking much of its future productivity, and a load of ease and enjoyment, for a measly eight-point advantage in current growth.

* * *

Editorial: do economic development programs "work"?

So there's this joke in which an engineer spots a dollar bill on the sidewalk. His companion, an economist, denies that there could possibly be cash on the sidewalk. "If there were," he says, "someone would have picked it up."

The joke lampoons the way economists define market-clearing and justify the economic notion of equilibrium. The story sums up the problem we have with economics: Any theory that has to be stated in the pluperfect subjunctive can't possibly stand up to everyday wear and tear.

In fact, it is scientifically impossible to prove or disprove a "would have." And it is a problem all economic developers face: Would that company have located here without the incentive my city provided?

A recent *Brookings Review* article (Ellen and Schwartz 2000) suggests the answer is "yes." This report agrees with several cited previous studies, looking over many years and many locations. They conclude that companies locate where they wish to locate, whether the site offers incentives or not. At best – and this is really "at worst" – an incentive may cause a company to locate in one suburb rather than a neighboring one, making no difference in the regional employment pattern.

Here's what's wrong with that conclusion. Longitudinal econometric studies can only use what is easily measured by economists: tax incentives, training allowances, land gifts, cost savings from relaxed environmental ordinances, and so on. If these are the variables Brookings and the others studied, their result is not surprising.

Chen (2000) and Gibson and Rogers (1994) argue that incentives make a difference, *up to a point*. Incentives are always less important than a firm's cost of attracting and retaining knowledge workers. Self-investment incentives are not always included in the statistics. Heaven help the economist armed with linear regression!

Technopolis Times has always maintained that (1) success can be measured only in metropolitan regions, not in cities; and (2) the important factors in economic development programs are not cash incentives to firms, but rather, external networking, strong civic organizations, strong links among a region's sectors, self-investment in education and infrastructure, a culture that celebrates ethical business success, a strong technological base, and strong institutions for fostering entrepreneurship.

We haven't run the equations, but we've seen this combination make a difference in a great many regions. The Japanese coiners of the term *technopolis* may have known that the original polis meant not just the land within the boundaries of the Greek city-state, but also the society residing there. Our economist colleagues need to understand this too.

The Buddhist scholar D. T. Suzuki once delivered a long speech on the total uselessness of prayer. "But," he concluded with a sheepish smile, "we all do it anyway." So it is with economic development programs. As long as someone thinks it might work in a particular case – or as long as a politician sees P. R. value in visible economic development activity – we're going to do it anyway!

We'll succeed by building social capital and minimizing cash incentives. We'll succeed by keeping our eye on the real situation, and not on the "would haves."

Our friend the engineer, of course, pocketed the dollar.

* * *

Editorial: needless tension, high irony

The Economist reports (December 1, 2003) that Dell (headquartered in Austin) is reversing its shift of telephone support activity to India, due to alleged customer complaints about the quality of service, in favor of increasing phone support jobs in Texas. Red herrings are already flying, as regards the "strange" accents of operators, and Dell's supposed commitment to economic development in Bangalore. If Indians pulled out of the Bay Area, fumed one Bangalore booster, that would be the end of Silicon Valley!

It should be easy to test satisfaction levels with US vs. Indian operators; any high school student could design the experiment. One irony is that *The Economist* reports no such evidence. Another is that globalization was supposed to spread economic activity around the world strictly on the basis of price advantage and acceptable quality. Seems that political bluster beats out the scientific method, and trumps economic theory too.

We suspect there is no reason for all the rancor. The complaints we've heard personally have been "equal opportunity complaints": Customer support for electronics products is just as likely to be unhelpful and delivered in impenetrable accents regardless of where in the world the operators are located. We hope manufacturers will invest in better service training before customers and suppliers revolt at the same time.

* * *

Editorial: do new business incubators work?

Well, I think they do, but instead of arguing the point, I'd like to discuss some "data collection problems" that impede our ability to answer the question.

First, a great many plain vanilla office suites have decided to call themselves incubators, maybe thinking that it sounds better than "office suite." Real estate services and a shared receptionist do not an incubator make! Any study that includes these "real estate operations" in the sample and draws conclusions about tenant company successes will be severely biased. Real incubators provide expert business services aimed specifically to targeted types of entrepreneurs.

Second, before the crash, many VC investors were running their own in-house incubators. None of these efforts now survive, while university incubators and some other public-private partnership incubators are still going strong. It is tempting for investors to indulge in revisionist history under the circumstances, and just say that no incubators worked. (They are wrong, however.)

Third, investigators may survey incubator successes/failures by interviewing "graduated" companies, and another bias comes into play. Incubator graduates have hit their growth phase, and often have hired new CEOs who have no recollection of their own firm's early incubator experience. These executives want to paint the firm's success as due to their own brilliant management – not due to some university that they're not familiar with (and that might, seeing the survey published, turn around and ask the execs for money)! They will naturally reply that the impact of the incubator on the firm's success was small.

VCs still complain about the "crapshoot" that characterizes each of their investments. Mae West, entering a room where W. C. Fields was playing poker, righteously demanded to know if she was witnessing a game of chance. "Not the way I play it," Fields replied. New business incubation is not a horse race where you put your money down and pray; it is a process that can be managed, to minimize ongoing risks and steadily increase probabilities of success.

* * *

Editorial: San Francisco neighborhoods try to bar chain stores

If you have more than eleven retail outlets with a uniform look, forget about locating in SF's Hayes Valley or Cole Valley neighborhoods, says a new SF board of supervisors ordinance. In southern California, the city of Inglewood voted on April 6 on a similar ordinance (really an initiative to grant a variance on ordinary permitting procedures) that seemed specifically aimed against a Wal-Mart super-center. Inglewood citizens defeated the initiative – and Wal-Mart – by a 2–1 margin. In the Netherlands, many cities restrict store-opening hours to eleven per day. This seemingly non-discriminatory policy has the effect of allowing one-person retail businesses to survive under conditions that are not profitable for big-box stores.

Why a discussion of retail strategy in *Technopolis Times?* Banning chains and big-boxes maintains the distinctive culture and flavor of a locality. This distinction may attract educated knowledge workers, and thus may, in an indirect way, tip a technology firm's expansion decision. However, in the context of economic development, retail strategy is interesting in its own right.

In broad terms (I'll note exceptions below), increasing retail square footage and sales only increases local jobs and wealth if it attracts the shopping dollars of tourists and residents of the near hinterlands. Only in this way does local retail become an export ("traded-sector") activity. Tourists are also attracted by distinctive local flavor, and some cities that have it (London, Paris, Tokyo, Milan, New York) are tourist shopping meccas. So-called "destination shopping" also attracts residents on the fringes of a metro area if the development is downtown (with safe, convenient access and parking) or in major regional malls (which may be in suburbs near major highway interchanges).

Neighborhood strip malls merely circulate the same dollars among local residents, allowing the IRS[1] to skim off a healthy percentage each time. Strip malls may reduce the miles customers must drive to find a certain kind of store. However, unless a neighborhood retail outlet produces a very serious reduction in stop-and-go secondary-street automobile traffic (thus reducing the opportunity cost of time and also the money spent for gasoline, car maintenance, and pollution-related health and clean-up costs), it is not a net contributor to local wealth. When a good strip mall restaurant becomes known throughout the city, it can *increase* traffic.

Now what about chain and big-box stores? Yes, they can employ more local youth at or near minimum wage. Is that needed, or just nice? If the alternative for these youth is gang crime, then it's needed. However, neighborhoods where that's the case are not the neighborhoods most chains are looking to locate in. It is family-wage jobs that create community wealth by generating multiplier-effect jobs, and create stable communities by allowing parents to support families. Generally speaking, more minimum-wage jobs without additional family-wage jobs do not constitute economic development.

Chains may increase local wealth in a way, by selling goods cheaper to local residents. Yet, the University of Southern California's Stefan Schumacher notes that "by squeezing suppliers to cut wholesale costs [Wal-Mart] has hastened the flight of US manufacturing jobs overseas." Can you say, "Race to the bottom"?

Yes, the chains have shown us ways to cut costs. We need to know these methods. However, often, large businesses are not reducing costs, but rather externalizing them – making society pay for things that used to be business expense items. Goods may be cheaper in the short run, but a deteriorating social fabric and community economy will cost more in the long run – and fixing them will be a public expense. It has usually been local merchants who temper short term cost considerations with concessions to local social realities. But even Henry Ford knew he would not have a sustainable business if his own employees could not afford his products.

* * *

Editorial: a great loss: IC² Institute Fellow and innovation diffusion pioneer Everett Rogers passes away

Ev Rogers' book *The Diffusion of Innovation* ran to many editions. Its schema of innovators, early adopters, and so on, became basic to most marketing texts and to almost all corporate marketing programs. Without Ev's pioneering contributions, there would be no *Crossing the*

Chasm, and no social networking web sites. Originally a communications scholar interested in news media, Ev Rogers chronicled the communication networks that gave rise to Silicon Valley. With his student Dave Gibson, he did the same for Austin; the two wrote the book (Gibson and Rogers 1994) on the MCC consortium's decision to move to that city, following the story through to the events that led to MCC's demise even as Austin's technological transformation showed huge success. The book was an important part of the IC² Institute's trailblazing work on the technopolis phenomenon. Ev spent his final years at the University of New Mexico. He died in October, 2004, in Albuquerque. He was a good friend and a wise man.

*   *   *

Editorial: this law, that law, and the 5K Nasdaq

One of Phillips' Laws is, "Demographics explains (almost) everything." A corollary is, "Especially the baby boomers." As my generation reaches and passes middle age, and predictably accumulates wealth – and in the aggregate, if not in my own particular case, that's a lot of wealth – where are we going to put it? In mutual funds, of course. The boomers span more than fifteen birth years, roughly 1948–1965, so as those born later start to invest, the market goes up, regardless of the true worth of the companies on the exchanges. A supply-driven market, or so it would seem; not a market that looks sustainable.

But wait. It turns out the demographic pig in the python is not the only new and extraordinary trend in the world. Three other emergent forces bode well for the underlying value of public companies.

First, we are only now realizing the true productivity gains from computers. Stanford economist Paul David likens the introduction of the computer to the introduction of electric power. At first, we used electricity to power tasks we were doing anyway (running the lathe from a motor, rather than from a mule-powered treadmill). It was much later, more than 50 years later in some cases, that we turned electric power to new beneficial activities only electricity could enable (lighting for the night shift, motorized wheelchairs, home appliances; recall Chapter 1's distinction between "modern" and "modernist" uses of technology). In just this way, we first computerized payroll processing and scientific calculation. Only now, 50 years later, are we realizing the World Wide Web, voice-controlled appliances, and virtual reality. Work at the Rocky Mountain Institute suggests that up to 90 per cent of our industrial processes are waste activity – and that information technology will ultimately eliminate as much as 90 per cent of this waste! Indeed, "we ain't seen nothing yet." The widely shared belief that there is a huge amount of money to be made on the Web is thus correct. Most companies have not yet figured out how to do it – but they will. The opportunities for corporate venturing are staggering in their magnitude.

Second, network externalities combined with falling electronics prices mean companies are getting far more value for their information technology dollar. Computers are increasingly used for communication and less for calculation. Metcalf's Law (the "network effect") means the value of a communication device increases as the square of the number of users. After all, you bought the machine to communicate with others, so the more others you can reach and be reached by, the more valuable it is. At the same time, Moore's Law has the functionality-to-price ratio of the device doubling every 18 months. Combine this one-two punch with the new markets and productive applications noted above, and the sky's the limit.

And third, intellectual capital, so important for growth companies, is not reflected in their balance sheets. *Fortune* magazine reports that what companies *know* is worth an estimated three to four times the value of their capital equipment, inventories, and real estate combined. To be sure, some of that knowledge walks when an employee leaves, and more is siphoned away by IP piracy (Choate 2005). But research and management attention directed at turning individual knowledge into organizational knowledge is bearing fruit. "Knowledge management" will turn organizational learning into profits, even if the knowledge is not quantified on the accounting statement.

These three forces weaken Phillips' Law of Demographic Primacy. But they do point to more effective knowledge-based industries making use of cheap, smart machines that talk with each other, to profitably serve large new markets.

This doesn't mean there can't be swings in the market due to Internet hacking, investor fads, or retiring boomers, or that the economy of another of our trading partners can't crash when banks overextend themselves in uncompetitive industries. But there is ample room, and justification, for optimism.

* * *

Editorial: every good idea gets abused. But keep the faith

As we surf the web's technopolis pages this month, we find two dismaying trends.

First, some writers are using "technopolis" to suggest a dehumanized and dehumanizing pocket of high technology. Do you feel invaded by highway traffic cameras in your city, and monitored email in your workplace? By co-workers who email you at all hours? By your own new-found urge to stay up at night doing business email? Blame it on the technopolis! This unfortunate usage, parallel to Fritz Lang's "Metropolis" of eighty years ago, is in complete contrast to the way we use the word here at *Technopolis Times*. To us, technopolis is a strategy by which people can get the quality of life and standard of living they want. As usual, Kevin Kelly says it better than we can: "Technopolis is a good dream. It is a far better vision than the Metropolis nightmare ... In Technopolis the hand and head seem to appreciate the heart."

The second trend we note is Craig Barrett going around anointing technopoleis. News items appear, saying the Intel chief has made a speech in West Jepip or Lower Wannabevia, lauding the local technology business base and predicting they'll be the next Silicon Valley. The sly implication that the chip giant will build an installation there if the West Jepipians just keep up the good work, results in a new civic web site and a press release announcing the Greater West Jepip Technopolis. Only one news story, never any follow-up.

No need to carry this ironic tone any farther; suffice it to say that industry chieftains making such speeches have a certain self-interest, and that technopolis building requires a balanced, long-term commitment – not just a blessing from a traveling medicine man.

*   *   *

Editorial: knowledge vs. roads and bridges?

A member of the Oregon Council for Knowledge and Economic Development complained that the State's desperately ailing budget slashed funds for nurturing the knowledge economy, while at the same time increasing funds for roads and bridges. This complaint is naïve, both from a political perspective and a business perspective. "Knowledge economy" is a squishy phrase; legislators don't know what it means, though it smacks vaguely of high technology. Marketing, a concept that's so hard to get a grip on, demands cleverness and perseverance, and we haven't seen this kind of marketing of the new economy in Oregon.

Roads and bridges get built and maintained in all parts of the state, creating blue-collar jobs everywhere. What could be more appealing to a state legislator? In contrast, technology and knowledge jobs cluster in the more privileged districts of the state. These are few compared to the number of rural and old-economy districts.

History shows the necessity of keeping the roads and bridges open. After the crash of 2001, however, legislators suspect that the knowledge economy is a flash in the pan or another fraud perpetrated by out of work dotcommers.

Smart and sustained effort must be aimed at selling the knowledge economy to political leaders.

* * *

Editorial: the future of Silicon Valley

Despite two decades of imitation by other regions, Silicon Valley remains the world's beacon for entrepreneurs, investors, and students who want the finest technical education. The Valley is inextricably tied to emerging technologies both past and future.

That said, there are provisos:

- This is the century of biology. A larger regional perspective that includes Silicon Valley plus San Francisco and Berkeley (and their strengths in biological and biomedical research and education) would be constructive.
- The Valley's venture capital industry will emerge from its crisis, probably sooner than the VC industry elsewhere. But it *is* in crisis, and delays can be expected as VCs clear their pipelines, adjust their business models, downsize their partnerships, and recover the confidence that was shaken by the dotcom crash. Even then, digital convergence and technology fusion imply a short-to-mid-term future in which new products arise from combinations of familiar technologies. VCs will be slow to respond, because sometimes these combinations are not patentable, and because fusion gives rise to few of the "big ideas" so beloved by VCs.
- The law of unintended consequences applies to globalization as to all other things, and technology-based economic development in the globalized world is vulnerable to politics. As Dell Computer reverses its earlier shift of telephone support activity to India, intemperate charges fly concerning Dell's commitment to Bangalore. Dell's action must be seen in the context of current US foreign policy, people's high emotion about globalization, and the general difficulties of

doing business across cultural boundaries. Misunderstandings and tensions will continue.

- Startups are entrepreneurial kindergartens for employees who head the next generation of startups. This self-sustaining local entrepreneurial culture is endangered by off-shoring knowledge work. VCs who now favor business plans with "high off-shoreability" are not only harming the Valley, they are eating their own seed corn.
- Markets for products based on "appropriate technologies" of the kinds honored by the San Jose Tech Museum Awards will explode worldwide. Often not capital-intensive, these may not interest VCs, nor give rise to fast-growing companies in the Valley. The technologies do involve Valley executives, however, as philanthropists and advisors.
- The open source movement implies decentralized product development, especially in software, and a reduced emphasis on large capital investment. Already Linus Torvalds has abandoned the Valley for Oregon. The Valley will continue to host repackagers of open-source products, like Red Hat and Caldera, but open-source development will have no geographic center. This trend will not materially affect the Valley's growth in the short term, but it is interesting and should be monitored.
- A corridor populated (if I may be allowed an exaggeration) mostly by stock-option millionaires can result in income stratification, traffic congestion, and real-estate distortions that do not bode well for a diverse, sustainable community.

The region can address the above points by networking and outreach, by policy papers, and by leveraging the Valley's formidable brain trust – in conferences, symposia, and task forces – to generate solutions.

Notes

The short pieces in this chapter are adapted from editorials originally published in *Technopolis Times* and *Technological Forecasting & Social Change*.

1. Internal Revenue Service, the US taxing authority.

23
Technology Is the Engine of a New Russian Revolution

David Gibson

There is a world of talent in a troubled land halfway around the globe, and our tech community is tapping into it. In Russia – despite difficult economic conditions, international banking scandals, the Mafia and renewed fighting in Chechnya – there are thousands of talented technicians and programmers who are either under-employed or out of work. Over the past 20 years, scientists and engineers from the former Soviet Union have emigrated to the US, Canada, Israel and other countries.

In Israel alone, 60,000 Russian emigre scientists and engineers have been key to developing that country's state-of-the-art technical capabilities.

"The largest concentration of technical know-how in Russia is within the nuclear complex," said Siegfried Hecker, former director of Los Alamos National Labs.

To cement ties with this untapped pool of talent, the University of Texas' IC^2 Institute joined with Los Alamos to bring 20 of the best and brightest Russian computer and software wizards to Austin recently.

They came to learn about the "Austin Model" for building a technopolis, and to create partnerships with researchers and software programmers at UT and in Austin's private sector. While here, the Russian visitors dropped in on local tech firms and university research facilities.

Oh, and they took in some Austin music and watched the Halloween festivities from the roof of Maggie Mae's on Sixth Street.

The Russian visitors were from the cities of Nizhny Novgorod and Sarov, home of the prestigious All Russian Institute of Experimental Physics and the new Open Computing Center. The experimental physics institute – the largest research center in the former Soviet Union – is hoping to employ about a third, or six thousand, of its 18,000 workers on private sector projects by 2002.

"Our challenge is to restructure for peaceful programs," said Rady Il'kaev, the institute's director. "The next year or two will be critical in finding constructive and profitable work for our highly skilled researchers."

By working together, US firms get a competitive advantage and the Russians get money and business experience.

Plus, the world becomes just a bit safer for all of us.

Already, entrepreneurial US companies such as Motorola, Intel, Sun, and Apple are successfully using Russian computing expertise for research and development. Intel currently employs more than 100 contractors working on software development for its microprocessors in Sarov and Nizhny Novgorod. Motorola has established a research laboratory in St Petersburg. Computer Science Corporation has brought in excess of 20 Russian programmers to Austin to work on Y2K projects.

Small companies are also taking advantage of Russian computing talent. Siberlink, an Austin software development firm, uses the Internet to employ up to 200 Russian subcontractors for advanced multimedia and graphics software development. Siberlink claims that software development savings is approaching 80 percent.

And the uses of Russian talent by Austin-based companies is expected to increase. Les Belady, director of the Austin Software Council, says that the lack of talented programmers is an increasing challenge for Austin's rapidly growing software companies.

Via the Internet, Russia offers a supply of inexpensive and highly trained and capable talent. Average compensation for Russian experts is approximately 10 percent that of comparable US specialists. John Wood, director of e-commerce at KPMG, says his company is planning to train 70 Russians to work on e-commerce projects, and hopes to expand this program into the thousands.

Certainly, there are obstacles. Language barriers, the lack of business training and bureaucratic hurdles on both sides of the world are problems, says Ken Poecek, the manager of Intel's computational software lab. Still, he said he has "never worked with a more motivated and intelligent group of researchers."

As Dr George Kozmetsky said in his welcoming remarks to the workshop participants in Austin last month, both of our countries are changing, and our partnerships need to be about creating prosperity at home and abroad. "It is about seeing the world from a different perspective, where seemingly impossibilities become obvious."

24
Conclusion
Fred Phillips

Earlier chapters suggested a number of themes for effective technology-based regional development. The concluding chapter recapitulates these and expands on their implications, offering recommendations for action in readers' home regions.

Regions are the relevant actors

Regions – whether citistates, cross-border regions, or multi-city regions like Silicon Valley – are the units to consider in technology-driven economic development. Economists such as Paul Krugman (1991), Joe Cortright (2000), and Paul Romer (1998), and business strategists Kenichi Ohmae (1996) and Michael Porter (1998), agree on this point. Cities cannot act without considering hinterland communities, and nation-states (says Ohmae 1996; see also Cortright 2002a) have become "little more than bit-players."

Unfortunately, it is still easy to get economic data for cities and for nations, but not for regions of the types described previously.[1] The obvious but wrong response to this problem is standardization. Cooperative efforts to fix the region's geographic boundaries, conduct its own data collection, and agree with other regions on data definitions won't really help. The fluidity of today's situation, with changing trade rules and changing technology, means it is too early for standards.[2] It is in the interest of innovative regions to keep their geographies ill-defined. It is the function of innovative regions to invent new categories of activities, obsoleting existing data definitions. The mid-term future will see rapid inter-regional communication of constantly changing data dictionaries and free-form databases,[3] representing regions' best efforts to compare themselves with their peers.

This idea foreshadows the next theme: that adaptive networks are key.

Adaptive networks are the basis of regional competition

The institutional economists, Romer and Douglas North (1990, 1995), see the quality of public institutions as the key differentiators of geographic regions. We have seen that public–private partnerships exchange knowledge, skills, and funds with other regions as technology and market needs (and social networks) constantly change. We can agree with Romer and North only by stretching their definition of "public institutions" to include the public functions of flexible networking and entering into public–private partnerships.

These extended institutions must – no easy task – identify the kinds of knowledge with which history and circumstance have uniquely endowed their communities, and find the best complements for it in other regions. With luck, these other regions will constitute good network partners.

Corporations and universities may create knowledge, but the spillovers that create increasing returns to scale are possible only where there are networks to transfer the knowledge. Knowledge may be created by traditional institutions, but it is the new networks that ensure industrial skills are transferred to where they can be put to constructive use. Networks transfer skills and tacit knowledge that diffuse more slowly than formal knowledge (which people in distant regions can learn from books or web sites). For this reason, local networks are a source of extended local competitive differentiation.

In today's techno-regions, informal networks *are* important institutions. They add to the difficulty of measuring technopolis and making a science of it: These shifting networks, the new institutions, are still too nebulous to measure for purposes of economic comparisons. We know something about what networks *can* do, but we are a long way from consistently measuring what they *do* do.

We do find – Finland and South Korea are excellent examples – that network infrastructure, whether social, wired, or wireless, gives rise to creativity, innovation, and quantum leaps in productivity. When your government fails to encourage broadband Internet, when the wireless provider at your favorite coffee bar fails to offer you a sensible rate structure, when a professional networking expert in your community charges you money for introducing you to people (rather than for teaching you networking skills), when your cellular phone provider fails to offer simple, clear contracts – then your community's future is jeopardized. In each case, the "guilty" party may be taking reasonable, fiscally responsible steps, but these steps are not in the common interest. Citizens may take each such instance as an opportunity to open a dialog, showing the "culprits" that responding to demands for better service will be profitable as well as public-spirited. This is how the Austin Software Council persuaded American Airlines to offer a daily non-stop flight to San Jose. Rarely has there been an empty seat on those flights, and the benefits to Austin's industry have been enormous.

Continual self-renewal is the name of the game

Hall (1998) analyzed historic creative cities, showing their heydays lasted, on average, a few dozens of years. North (1990) gives wealth-creating economies a few centuries. It is reasonable to think that today's pace of technological change will narrow these windows. We have noted that each region must choose a technological pony to ride toward economic development. Today those ponies are winded sooner. (If I am stretching this metaphor, it is because the Pony Express' early network in the American west is a compelling analogy for the role of adaptive networks in economic development.) The network is also the *means for finding a fresh pony*.

Every region that builds wealth on an industry cluster must, in a few years, stake its next wealth-building strategy on a new or redefined industry.

Small government is a tempting but simplistic route to innovation and wealth

Cooperation across sectors has been key to the successes of several regions. The roles of governments, corporations, the press, the arts, and educational and religious institutions in innovative regions are varied and evolving. It is too soon to say that any one of the sectors is obsolete.

Moreover, some of the most highly regulated economies are the most successful; see the discussion of the Scandinavian countries in Chapter 22.

It is a knowledge economy. When corporations build their current bottom lines by reducing research and development activity, less knowledge is created. (There has appeared no evidence that corporations use savings from lower tax rates to increase R&D.) The slack must be taken up by government laboratories and (sometimes publicly supported) universities. Governments take on special roles in the technology sphere, including patent and telecommunications policy.

The goals of modern technology companies and localities overlap but are hardly identical. Companies provide jobs, knowledge, and tax revenue, all valuable to the community. However, metro regions want local economic development, while corporations must respond profitably to the pressures of globalization. This often means corporations must try to privatize profits and socialize costs and risks. The technology IPO process is a notorious example of this. A 2005 *Business Week* cover story provided another example, highlighting companies that sell insecure database products, leaving it to the FBI to launch an anti-hacker task force at taxpayer expense. The "privatize profits and socialize costs" tactic can also manifest itself as a company's effort to maximize the location incentives it receives from a city to which the company cannot afford to commit itself for the long term. When an irresistible overseas opportunity arises, the company will expatriate the profits those incentives made possible, leaving the community responsible for the environmental and unemployment-related problems the firm leaves behind.

Businessmen have convinced Oregon that the State's economic future depends on having a "business plan." High-technology businessmen (they are almost all male, in this instance) offered to organize and lead the Oregon Business Plan. Elected officials have let the businessmen take the ball and run with it, unrefereed. Oregonians will see, in a few years, the disastrous result of their abdication of responsibility.

Voters and leaders who hew to less-government-is-better ideology may be admired for their integrity, but not for their realistic approach to the new economy.

Education matters

Places with higher average educational achievement are more wealthy (Cortright 2002a). The London School of Economics found "Britain and the United States have the worst social inequality among a sample of eight rich nations, due in part to failing educational systems ... measured against Germany, Canada, Norway, Denmark, Sweden and Finland, Britain and the United States came joint bottom (Reuters 2005)." Rising salaries for the highly educated exacerbate the skew in income distribution. The LSE study noted reduced social mobility in the United Kingdom and growing numbers of illiterate public school graduates in the United States. It contrasted Britain and the United States to Germany and the Scandinavian nations, where equal educational opportunities are offered to children from families of all income levels.

The chapter (Chapter 4) herein on shared prosperity noted the threat that income inequality poses to social stability, and to lagging regions' potential for catching up. Education matters for technology-based economic development in all regions.

Cross sectoral, disciplinary, technological, social, geographical, and conceptual boundaries

Austin and Bangalore have benefited from alliance between the high-tech and the music sectors; in this book, Pierre Ouellette urged Portland to do the same. Portland has responded to the advanced nations' demographic trends by combining electrical and mechanical engineering expertise with medical research in order to serve the growing need for biomedical engineering products.

Santa Monica, California, speeded its adoption of Internet use through its response to the city's homelessness problem. Face-to-face dialog between property owners and the homeless was rare and difficult, due to discomfort on both sides. The city installed public Internet terminals in libraries and other sites, and set up an electronic bulletin board for discussion of the issues surrounding homelessness in Santa Monica. The varied constituencies began to talk with one another, a "homelessness strategy" was crafted, and the value of the then-new technology of online discussion groups was amply demonstrated.[4]

In stable times, disciplinary and social boundaries can be useful. When technology and societies are changing rapidly, bold boundary-spanning is the best course.

Geographical boundaries are spanned when a technopolis initiative takes a fluid view of the borders of its metropolitan region, in order to encompass a compact but relevant set of economic activities. They are also spanned by the inter-regional sharing of ideas, visiting scholars, and entrepreneurs that this book has called *shared prosperity*. Austin's shared prosperity initiatives directly generated revenue from the companies in correspondent regions that thought it wise to set up branches in Austin, and from money spent by individual visitors from those regions. They also allowed Austin to engage in the responsible behavior appropriate for a leader, that is, to act as mentor and facilitator to other regions.

Craft a regional response to globalization

Earlier chapters have criticized the modern mechanisms of globalization. These mechanisms prevent the purposeful market distortions which are economic developers' stock-in-trade, and will lock less fortunate regions into permanent disadvantage or disruptively cyclical employment. Is this the raving of an eccentric, dogmatic author? On the contrary, I am *more* optimistic about globalization than the now-retired CEO of

Intel, Andy Grove, who said, in Nocera's (2005) paraphrase,

> Although mainstream economic thought holds that America's history of creativity and entrepreneurship will allow it to adapt to the rise of such emerging economies as India and China, Grove sees that as so much wishful thinking. In his view, globalization will not only finish off what's left of American manufacturing, but will turn so-called knowledge workers – supposedly America's competitive advantage – into just another global commodity.
>
> What particularly bugs Grove is that he can't see a way out; he can't see a way that [the US] can find the equivalent of a disruptive technology that will allow it to retain its current place atop the economic heap.

Though he mentions the United States, Grove is clearly implying *no* nation will be able to attain sustainable competitive advantage when knowledge is a commodity and industry continues to move R&D and production from one region to another in pursuit of the lowest-wage knowledge workforce.

However, even declining nations will show regional variation internally. This variation is the grist for regional strategies and promotion. Furthermore, if an advantageous technology does appear on the horizon, who will recognize and exploit it, if not knowledge workers? Finally, national and regional character – and thus the kind of work that is best done in that region – persists. For example, software development managers know that US programmers like to show creativity; Indian programmers, virtuosity; Chinese programmers, adherence to procedure and specifications; and Japanese programmers, completeness and good appearance. Smart managers will channel parts of projects to the regions where they can best take advantage of these traits. The regions, in turn, will learn new methods from the code segments relayed to them from other locales.

Globalization is an enormous danger, but one that is perhaps not as lethal as Andy Grove suggests. This book has noted American responses ranging from state governors' letters to the US President, to protests to the US Trade Representative, to civil disobedience. Your locality must have its own strategy for dealing with globalization and trade agreements.

Respect history, but don't let it defeat you

The critical-mass or lock-in phenomenon in clusters seems unarguable (Arthur 1987; David 1997; Krugman 1991, 1999). To believe in the more general impact of small, random events on a city's history (the "butterfly effect") is plausible and fashionable, but not yet firmly supported by evidence. The important lessons at this juncture are: Build toward critical mass, and avoid the fatalistic attitude that may arise from taking the butterfly effect too literally.

Experienced and creative individuals may spot the potential of one of these small, random events, and build on it where its effects might otherwise be allowed to damp out. The same individuals, who may be the godfathers discussed earlier, may be able purposefully to damp other effects that they see as dangerous. Outstanding individuals play a key role in technopolis (see Cortright 2002a), and may themselves be the influences that lead to positive tipping points.

It seems wise to believe in the ability of management, entrepreneurship, and evangelism to tip potentially chaotic systems, like the historical dynamic of technopolis development, in desired directions. Moreover, there is some factual basis (Phillips and Kim 1996) for such a belief (though it has been demonstrated convincingly only for mechanical systems and not for social systems).

According to Kawasaki (1992), "Evangelism is the process of convincing people to believe in your product or idea as much as you do." Entrepreneurs of innovative products rely on evangelism to create markets sooner than a large firm – with more resources but presumably less passion – could hope to do. Indeed, this may be the very core of the entrepreneurial opportunity; entrepreneurs identify opportunities and evangelize them into markets. This is, in essence, the management of chaos, positive returns, and historical lock-in, as applicable to building technopolis as to building a new company.

Make the most of what you've got

The Introduction noted that "all or most" of the items in Table 17.1 ("Technopolis Success Factors," reproduced here) are needed for

Table 17.1 Technopolis success factors

- Embracing change.
- Social capital, especially with cross-sectoral links.
- Cluster strategies that target specific company groups for collocation.
- Visionary and persistent leadership.
- The will to action.
- Action.
- Constant selling.
- Self-investment in infrastructure.
- Outreach and networking.

technology-based economic development. Making the most of what you've got involves, first, assessing the community's status with regard to these factors, then aggressively putting its best foot forward, and finally selling the region consistently, persistently, and systematically. Using fuzzy objectives increases the probability of being able to announce successes.

Medieval Florence, a banking center, "undoubtedly did ... lead Europe in the direction of full-blown capitalism," according to Hall (1998, p. 83). "It did not need technology [except for the mechanical clock], though it did need advances in commercial organization." The latter included double-entry bookkeeping and the use of Arabic numbers. Florence illustrates not just the use of compensating advantages, but also that the real issue in economic development is *innovation* – whether that innovation happens to be technological, social, financial, or organizational – rather than technology *per se*.

Modern Cambridge, England, has little industry marketing and distribution infrastructure. It does have outstanding academic resources and a culture that endorses commercialization of new technologies. Cambridge representatives tour worldwide, touting the city's capabilities and cementing technology brokerage partnerships.

Bangalore, India, is weak on hard infrastructure (see inset later) but strong in its knowledge workforce and its empowerment of youth culture that increases quality of life (from the perspective, at least, of the young workforce).

Portland has strengths in biomedical devices and in innovative outdoor-living products, offsetting the city's late start in biotech. But Oregon's unfortunate marketing slogan, "Oregon is for Dreamers," seems to suggest that doers ought to go elsewhere.

Regions must sell, sell, and sell some more. All the sophisticated techniques of brand marketing are applicable, but not widely used (or well-used) in economic development circles. The branding of the Mason Enterprise Center's services (Chapter 18), and Austin's "Technaissance" trademark, are positive exceptions.

Then celebrate (and chronicle) your successes. Fete the true contributors. Do not become a community whose citizens simply enjoy throwing award banquets for each other, regardless of actual achievement; make sure there is substantial progress to recognize. If the triumphs are in public relations and positioning, that's substantial, too. As any marketer will affirm, perceptions are as important as reality.

Smart community leaders recognize that some important factors are more mobile than others. Globalization has made investment capital, and even the presence of individual corporations, harder for regions to hold onto for the long term. Artists may migrate to cities with lower rents or more tourists. Community leaders – good networkers – may get better job offers elsewhere. As knowledge and networking skills are the key success factors for the region, governments, universities, and new network-based institutions must take responsibility for maintaining the local knowledge base and networking skills.

Meyer (2003) has shown that large, high-tech corporate presences with thousands of local employees also constitute an immovable knowledge base. As Cortright (2002a) notes and the previous examples illustrate, whether it is public or private investment, "places that invest more in research and development seem generally to be more prosperous."

Persist

Be prepared to devote 20 years or more to your metropolitan area's cultural change. Watch for crises and opportunities, ideally having a technopolis initiative organization in place, ready to take advantage of these events. Find a godfather or godmother who can sustain the regional vision, evangelizing it and inspiring others. Come to early agreement with consultants about what results may be expected over a specific time horizon.

Attend to the principles of Table 17.4: "Success Factors for Regional Technology Entrepreneurship Initiatives." Jettison programs that don't work, but never give up the overall goal. Bide your time when the tides of events, technology, or social culture are not conducive to progress; move quickly when the situation demands speed.

The experience of Bangalore illustrates many of these themes: using an advantage to compensate for a weakness elsewhere, crossing sectoral boundaries, focusing on well-paying jobs in a targeted industry, good public relations, and taking smart advantage of historical accidents.

> Bangalore, which is often referred to as India's Silicon Valley, doesn't have a fraction of Singapore's amenities. Its airport is a mess; roads often exist only to join one pothole with another; water is scarce; only three-fifths of the city's garbage gets cleared; and computer-software companies keep enough fuel handy to run backup generators in case power goes out for a few days.
>
> And yet, Bangalore is buzzing. Between April and December 2004, hotels in the city charged an average $199 a night, more than double

Singapore's average room rate of $71 in the same period and a whopping 80 percent increase from a year earlier.

[...] shopping malls, art galleries, lounge bars and pubs also are booming. Bangalore has displaced the Taj Mahal from the itineraries of some visiting dignitaries. It's also emerging as a hub for popular culture, having served as host for rock stars like Elton John, Sting, Bryan Adams, Mark Knopfler and Roger Waters during the last few years.

It's all being made possible by the thousands of new jobs that are being created every month. Motorola Inc., which last year closed its semiconductor design units in Singapore and Taiwan and moved them to China and India, has 2,000 researchers in Bangalore, a number it wants to boost by a quarter each year. (Mukherjee, 2005)

Table 24.1 gathers the ten themes of this book for convenient use.

"I know that the world is not flat. Don't worry. I know," writes Thomas Friedman (2005) in his book about the inexorable progress of globalization and the "flattening" of the world. "I have engaged in literary license in titling this book *The World is Flat"* – Friedman adds this qualification in recognition of the billions still living in the un-flat world, without access to the networks of opportunity flatworlders take for granted. Electronic networks, and the extended social networks the hardware creates and fosters, zip formal knowledge and digital "grunt work" around the globe instantly. Aside from the half of the human race that remains unconnected, however, there are several more reasons

Table 24.1   Themes for technology-based economic development

1. Regions are the relevant actors.
2. Adaptive networks are the basis of regional competition.
3. Continual self-renewal is the name of the game.
4. Small government is a tempting but simplistic route to innovation and wealth.
5. Education matters.
6. Cross sectoral, disciplinary, technological, social, geographical, and conceptual boundaries.
7. Craft a regional response to globalization.
8. Respect history, but don't let it defeat you.
9. Make the most of what you've got.
10. Persist.

why the world is not flat:

- Skills transfer, as we have seen, is a body contact sport. Despite web sites that purport to teach salsa steps, it remains generally true that we cannot stuff skills into a wire. The slow diffusion of skills slows the flattening of the globe.
- We have made progress on security and authentication of passwords and so on, recognizing that trust is key to making the extended network work. Trust in the integrity of the individual at the other end of the electronic connection is a different matter, however, and this is not yet digitized. We trust the people near us (some of them, anyway), whose behavior we can observe and judge in a variety of contexts.
- Participants in a knowledge economy might take some tips from scientists and professors, who have always lived in a knowledge economy. In their culture, more honor goes to creators of knowledge than to conveyors or users of knowledge that was created elsewhere. "America is always on the edge of the next creative wave," says one of Friedman's Indian informants. While America takes creative honors in the ICT realm, we might ascribe similar ongoing primacy to Italian product design, Brazilian music, or Japanese manufacturing management.
- The dynamics of FTF (face-to-face) networking also slow the flattening of the world. World-class opinion leaders are seen and heard in person more frequently in their hometowns than in far-flung technopoleis. The more nuanced nature of FTF communication results in un-flat knowledge transfer. (This could be taken as more evidence of the positive-feedback/critical-mass effect,[5] but these leaders are mobile and can choose where to make their speeches.)
- As earlier chapters have emphasized, popular culture is inextricably bound to TED. Music, film, and games demand technological advances, are the vehicles for advertising products that flow from these technological advances, and are attractors for the young, educated knowledge workforce. Images from popular culture are reinforced through the social and hardware networks, and the catchphrases of pop culture combine with technical jargon to create "COMDEX patois," the language of deal-pitching in the high-tech world. This language remains peculiar to Americans, the American-educated, and workers in American-owned multinational corporations (though there are some well-developed but less influential British and Chinese variants). The point is that those on the periphery of these

networks hesitate to speak out, because nothing is more embarrassing than to attempt, and bungle, a pop culture reference in front of a hip audience. America is the font of pop culture. Although Americans might offshore routine jobs, they have not offshored the power to shape opinion in the technology world. It is they who speak the patois most confidently, and thereby retain opinion leadership and the economic benefits that flow from it.

- Culture is sticky. Knowledge workers who add high economic value enjoy their families and their local amenities, customs and networks. Except for the few who crave adventure in foreign lands, they, and their productive activities, will stay put. Unemployed knowledge workers are another story, willing to migrate if they can find work. Regions must, via RITEs and the like, endeavor to retain those who show flexibility, initiative, and the propensity to learn – or, as the case of India's expatriates and prodigals proves, to keep in touch with them if they leave.

Moreover, there are forces and incentives that un-flatten even a flat world. Every course in economic geography begins with Hotelling's (1929) linear location game. This game takes place on an imaginary strip of beach, uniformly populated by seekers of sun and fun. An ice cream vendor sets up shop. Knowing that the bathers will not put themselves out overmuch even to get an ice cream, he serves the convenience of the greatest number by locating in the middle of the beach. A second vendor, selling cones at the same price, sets up immediately next to the first vendor, thus capturing an entire half of the market. Families newly arriving at the beach may decide to pitch their umbrellas and towels close to the ice cream stands, further increasing density near the middle of the beach. An innovative third vendor, selling better or cheaper cones, can choose a location away from this center and still attract customers. In this manner, a "flat" beach world becomes un-flat, developing multiple centers of activity and an interesting differentiation that pleases consumers and profits vendors.

Whether microchips, nanomachines, or ice cream, the message is clear: regions that take charge of this process can become new centers of activity for the new century.

Notes

1. The Progressive Policy Institute has attempted to do so in its Metropolitan New Economy Index, http://www.neweconomyindex.org/metro/index.html

2. Theories of technical standards (Libicki 1995) say the optimal time to set an industry standard is when the technology has matured but the market has not yet matured.
3. Maastricht School of Management's worldwide partner network uses a Lotus Notes database for exchange of this semi-structured information.
4. Everett Rogers told this story.
5. Friedman and I also agree that while history is very important and lock-in is real, historical determinism is bunk.

Appendix: A Primer on Technology-Based Economic Development

Part I, Economic foundations: an informal look, with special reference to Portland, Oregon

Economic development discussions always turn to the recruitment of foreign companies and the creation of jobs for a local population. These activities refer to the region's external flows: companies and people flowing in and out. We are concerned about growth inside the region, so why focus on what's outside the region?

We will use a thought-experiment to answer this question. A sealed, closed-loop economy may be possible in principle, with no immigration, emigration, or external trade, and with consumption only of locally produced goods and services. However, even the population of such a utopia will age. If they have not had babies in a steady, reliable fashion, labor shortages will ensue. This disruption to a delicately balanced economy may put it in a fatal tailspin.

What's more likely, of course, is that someone will decide to move (migrate) in or out. Or a local will decide he just can't live without a certain consumer product that's made only in Hong Kong.

How to pay the Hong Kong producer for this item? One answer, often used throughout history, is to export unprocessed natural resources. This has always resulted in the same outcome: makers of "high value-added" manufactured goods always enjoy such pricing power over natural resource producers that the latter end up impoverished, or colonized. In the modern world, economic colonization means foreign ownership of landmark buildings and resorts, and the snapping up of homegrown businesses by outside concerns. (This is why there are no corporate headquarters to speak of in Oregon.)

Closed-loop does not necessarily mean "subsistence." Wealth could increase in a closed-loop economy, as local innovations augment the productivity of local enterprises. In this case, cash or local manufactured goods can be exchanged for manufactured goods from Hong Kong once external trade commences. But Hong Kong and other regions can innovate as rapidly as our utopia, or more so, meaning that the race to innovate has been joined. The more innovative the region, the more its value-added exports are valued by foreigners. More export revenue accrues to the region, thus increasing the region's ability to import attractive goods, support local social services, and develop local infrastructure.

This is why economic development officials emphasize growing jobs in the export sector. (Low labor cost can substitute for innovation, for a while, but not in Portland. The United States is a low-wage country compared to Sweden or

218

Germany, but sky-high in cost compared to China, and Oregon has a higher minimum wage than many other states. Advantage can also be maintained in the short run by having an over-valued currency. Only nations, though, can revalue their currency – not states or municipalities.)

In the modern world of taxation, only very rich closed economies would have even a small chance of maintaining their isolation. They cannot circulate the same dollar indefinitely in the local region. In fact, if the national and state tax rates sum to 33 percent, the dollar can only circulate three times before it's all gone. (That math is not quite right, but it's not far wrong.) Economies close to subsistence (read Nichols' *The Milagro Beanfield War*) can be stable for centuries, but inevitably succumb to colonization when taxed, that is, if the tax dollars do not come back to the region through national/state programs and rebates. Capturing those programs can be an essential part of an economic development program.

Milagro Beanfield War is set in New Mexico. New Mexico has enjoyed local federal expenditure far in excess of the taxes it has sent to Washington. This is because of the huge federal laboratories at Sandia and Los Alamos. The labs, of course, do not employ many former subsistence farmers, but hire highly educated scientists. Wealth "trickles down," but New Mexico has a very skewed income distribution – that is, much income inequality. The state's population is not of a revolutionary temperament.[1] But where similar economic conditions exist in Africa and the Middle East, there is violence in the streets. (New Mexico is similar to Oregon in that it has a tiny population and a huge land area, with half the population concentrated in or near a single city. Significantly, though, Oregon has no large federal laboratories or military installations.) It is generally believed that social stability is served by a less-skewed income distribution, and this is why, for example, many politicians have striven to create a Mexican middle class near the US border.

Income inequality can be ameliorated by redistribution, that is, taxing the rich to feed the poor. This does not seem to be popular with Oregonians; we have a Sizemore[2] but no Robin Hood. In any case, redistribution reduces the economic surpluses that are available for investment in innovation. Moreover, additional unemployed individuals are free to move to Oregon, and a new round of redistribution would be needed, and the economy would spiral downward.

Huge income inequality on the one hand, and radical redistribution on the other are both unattractive and unstable. A more palatable path is that of *opportunity:* a socio-economic mobility that gives the less skilled/favored a chance to gather education, training, and wealth. Ideally, the upwardly mobile feel they have a stake in the social order, and in moving up the economic scale, they make room for other ambitious immigrants. Immigrants may come to Portland with or without a job. Unemployed arrivals can either increase Portland's wealth by filling a labor shortage, or decrease it by demanding social services, or both.

Educated in-migrants, of which Portland attracts many, may start their own businesses, resulting in job growth. We must, though, recognize the difference between a small businessperson and a true entrepreneur. Conventional small businesses cut the existing economic pie into smaller pieces, sending that ever-diminishing dollar round and round. Entrepreneurs innovate (products, services, manufacturing methods, or business processes), thus making the whole pie bigger, via increased productivity and via increased exports. (It is worth noting that a new small business that does not innovate – say, a convenient dry-cleaning outlet – can still enhance the community's productivity by reducing trips and traffic. After a saturation point, however, one more dry cleaner will do little but reduce the income of the others.)

One problem with defining economic development involves the idea of "quality of life." It would be simpler to exclude this notion from the economic development discussion, and focus only on what can be measured by number of jobs and dollars. However, to see the relationship between exports and quality of life, let us consider the maquiladoras on the US–Mexican border. These companies offer mainly low-paying jobs that are attractive only to single people. Young singles migrate from hinterland villages, send most of their wages home, and return home with their savings after they've accumulated enough to get married. None of those wages, except for food and rent, are spent in the border towns, and it shows in the towns' substandard infrastructure. Criminals prey on these youngsters who do not enjoy the close protection of their families.

If the quality of life were better in Laredo and Matamoros, if there were public investment in infrastructure, and private companies offering "family-wage" jobs, families would come to those towns and stay, and in a feedback process, the local economy and society would become ever more attractive. Giving locals a reason to spend locally is good. Reducing outward cash remittances is almost as good as reducing imports, and that is almost as good as increasing exports.

Thus, sustainability is not a new-age notion at all. Exports of value-added goods and services sustain a region. Every region needs its own export strategy. Japan has concentrated on goods, sending us cars and electronics; Switzerland on services, re-insuring our insurance companies, and hosting our numbered bank accounts (well, yours, maybe, not mine). The United States has "exported" higher education, attracting the tuition payments of the foreign students who come to America for the best education.

These are the reasons that bringing in wealth from outside the region is the key to every region's economic development strategy.

* * *

Part II, Economic development defined

In Part I of this Appendix, we looked at the economic foundations of economic development (ED), and made some effort to define ED. We did not, though, mention the role of technology in ED. In 1999, the Milken Institute (DeVol 1999) reported that two thirds of economic growth in the 1990s in US metropolitan regions was due to high technology industry. As a result, today, more and more regions are attempting tech-based economic development initiatives.

A region's public and private technology infrastructure attracts the high-tech companies that create jobs. In turn, these companies contribute still more communications, health, education, transportation, and research infrastructure.

Various regions have made tech-based economic development efforts spanning a spectrum that is roughly described in Table A.1.

In Part II, we will further define economic development in terms of the activities that comprise ED, and then go on in Part III to explore what makes technology-based ED (which we will abbreviate as TED) different from any other kind of ED.

Table A.1 Levels of tech-based ED initiatives

Naïve 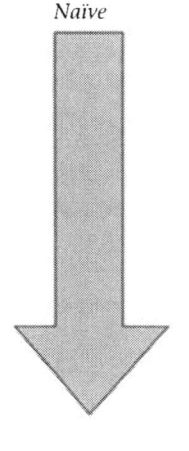 *Sophisticated*	Produce more patents, licenses, and journal articles. Try willy-nilly to attract technology companies. Over-emphasize military-to-civilian tech transfer. Target and pursue companies that might form a viable cluster and enhance a distinctive regional identity. Balance recruitment, retention, and entrepreneurship initiatives regionally. Balance self-investment in hard and soft infrastructure, university and federal-lab tech transfer, and marketing efforts to attract and build companies. "Integrate and partner the academic, business, government, foundation, and not-for-profit sectors ... [to mobilize technology as] a means of attaining economic, social and cultural status for individuals, as well as a way of achieving institutional objectives and ensuring the general welfare of society" (Kozmetsky 2003).

For effective ED, a locality must have a good product – sites, energy and water supply, schools, airports, optical fiber, and "business environment" – and sell it intelligently and energetically. This balance of hard infrastructure, soft infrastructure, and marketing is suggested by Table A.2. Table A.2 also details the assets and activities that comprise each of the three ED thrusts.

Good ED balances all three. However, technology changes with spectacular rapidity. Revolutions in genomics and nanotech closely followed the fantastic developments in computing that transformed industries in the last decade. Marketing follows technology commercialization without significant lag. Because the middle column of Table A.2 involves attitudes, social ("soft") infrastructure is the bottleneck limiting the pace of a region's transition to a technology-driven economy.

Table A.2's "hard infrastructure" column indicates that ED is possible when companies have access to land, mobility, and reliable utilities, and the citizenry is productive by virtue of being fed, housed, healthy, secure, and connected to sources of information and education.

Parts of the Table's second column also have to do with the education, security and health of the populace, or "human capital." Other parts address social capital, that is, people's propensity to form civic, trade, and professional organizations, agitate for change and follow through on it, and communicate with like organizations in other techno-regions for business exchange and data-gathering purposes.

Government planning, zoning, and permit processes are an important part of the business environment that makes a locale attractive to companies. Tourism aids ED by bringing in dollars to local businesses, and by displaying the region's attractions to outsiders (at their expense!) who may later bring more trade or businesses in. "Research" includes creating new knowledge, new technologies, new uses for recent technologies, and new ways to support the transfer, productization, marketing, and use of the technologies.

Table A.2 The three elements of economic development

Hard infrastructure	Social infrastructure	Marketing
Transportation	*Social capital*	*Outward marketing*
Sanitation/H$_2$O	Associations	To companies
Telecomm	Cultural mindset	To individuals and groups
Voice	Demographics	*Inward marketing*
Data	Entrepreneurial	*Targeting*
Wireless	environment	Leading industries
Building/Construction	External networking	Leading companies
Housing	*Education / Training*	• With technology products/
Corporate sites	Pre-K through 12	processes
Buildable lots	Higher education	• Green/sustainable
Public spaces	Workforce development	*Packaging/Positioning*
Architecture	Continuing education	*Incentives*
Hospitals	*Health Care*	To companies
Schools	*Government*	Self-investment
Laboratories	Planning	*Competitive intelligence*
Security/Anti-terrorism	Land Use Policy	*Support to existing businesses*
	Permitting	
	Zoning	
	Tourism	
	Research	
	Law enforcement	
	Taxation	

Target marketing (see column 3 of Table A.2) implies a regional strategy: Local organizations cooperate to identify industries that fit with the region's strengths and aspirations and offer opportunities to capture company startups, relocations, and even headquarters. Targeting also means attracting new residents with desirable demographics, for example, families, retirees, affluent couples, or new college graduates. Competitive intelligence is the process of gathering and analyzing information to assess the fit, the opportunities, and the progress of rival regions.

Outward marketing means proactively reaching out to prospective companies, individuals, and groups. Inward marketing means tracking and responding to incoming inquiries from prospects. Both are done well if they stick to a core message reflecting the "packaging," competitive positioning, and branding of the region.

Competitive intelligence also reveals what other cities are offering in order to attract relocations and entrepreneurs. The region can then calculate the prospects for payback on an incentive package, the "price ceiling" on any given recruitment project, and the wisdom of joining any particular bidding battle. Incentives may be direct payments, variances, or abatements to a company, or may be self-investment in university faculty positions, new university laboratories, new parks or roads, or airport renovations.

Marketing also includes the measures that governments and local organizations take to make startups and existing businesses feel welcome in the region.

Finally, taxation in the region and its component municipalities (and the states in which they are embedded) must, to the extent possible under many conflicting demands, finance all those listed before.

Aligning ED goals: fable of a northwest city

Let us assume that a city council (specifically, the Portland city council) wants a liveable city with a growing tax base, and that residents want convenient jobs and shopping; safe neighborhoods; low taxes; and homes they can afford, with reliable, affordable utilities and good schools. Under these reasonable assumptions, the interests of citizens and city do not make a perfect alignment, and I haven't yet mentioned a third major actor in the Portland ED scene, the Portland Development Commission (PDC).

In the 1950s, the new concept of urban renewal, supported by US federal funds, caused Portland to create PDC as the city's urban renewal agency. Urban renewal upgrades the infrastructure of blighted neighborhoods. In theory, the upgrade attracts residents and businesses, and in the long run, raises the tax base. This is economic development. Indeed, the elements of economic development are:

- Physical infrastructure (including transportation)
- Recruitment of relocating businesses
- Retention and growth of existing businesses
- Incubation of new businesses and encouragement of entrepreneurship
- Work force development
- Innovative organizations and partnerships that make the above activities work better in one city than in another city, and thus make one region more attractive than another for workers, executives, and firms.

Tax-increment financing (TIF) supplemented federal dollars as a way of paying for urban renewal. TIF temporarily freezes the tax base of urban renewal districts (URDs). This can create some discord in the community, as schools and other real community needs fail to see the funding increases they would get were the tax base not frozen. Discord in Portland got worse as federal matching money dried up, leaving TIF as the sole means of financing urban renewal, and thus the sole means of financing PDC – and because of some abuses (ejection of families from long-established neighborhoods) on PDC's part in the agency's early days. The abuses gave rise to questions of transparency, accountability, and public input to PDC decisions.

Picking up on the convenience and cleanliness aspects of "liveability," the city opted for a high-density growth strategy, disdaining environmentally dirty industries. Both were worthy decisions. High density means lots of concrete gets poured per square foot of URD, perhaps bringing a higher payoff for TIF funding than other municipalities experience. However, high density also means there are few large campus development opportunities for companies; urban land is at a premium. Portland's bias against dirty industry shaded into a general anti-business reputation for the city, whose largest employer is a university. This put a damper also on prospects for relocation of corporation headquarters to downtown Portland buildings. Well-known as a planning-oriented city, Portland caused relocating companies to hesitate in ways they would not hesitate, for example, were they considering a move to Houston, a city that is known for free-market based land development and is poles apart from Portland in its approach, philosophy, and (some would say) liveability. Portland's embrace of clean multi-media, software, and creative services companies came curiously late, and though it has been successful in some ways, these companies are not becoming major employers.

Because of this anti-business reputation, and because TIF may only be used for physical infrastructure, the last five elements of economic development have gotten short shrift in Portland.

Several further forces affected the history of PDC and ED in Portland: First, the city never revisited PDC's mission after the agency's initial charter in 1957. The passage of time has rendered some aspects of the original charter irrelevant. Second, the amount of land under URD designation reached the 15 percent (of total municipal area) statutory limit. Third, there is not a strong chamber of commerce working to recruit, retain, grow, and launch businesses. PDC is "the closest thing" to an economic development agency in the city. Fourth, the trend toward regionalism – an approach to economic development that crosses city and county boundaries – in many parts of the United States conflicts with PDC's juris-diction, which ends at city limits. Fifth, much of the land within recent URDs is owned by tax-exempt non-profit entities like Oregon Health and Science University and Portland State University. Urban renewal will not increase the tax base on this land.

For good reasons as well as bad reasons, then, PDC has essayed a course of "mission creep," taking on responsibilities and activities beyond what was origi-nally envisioned. The definition of "blight" became nearly infinitely malleable. This lets additional neighborhoods look like worthy urban renewal projects once existing URDs sunset and free up their portion of the 15 percent. PDC sees its future as an economic development agency, not just as an urban renewal agency. There is, however, no funding mechanism for non-infrastructure ED projects. PDC responds by (1) earning revenues by coordinating some ED activities of outlying cities, (2) winning some state and federal grants, (3) raising independent investments via the "Portland Family of Funds," and (4) concentrating on infrastructure development at the expense of recruitment and business support activities.

PDC has filled a void in regional and city ED. Some say ED should happen outside PDC. This would be the end of PDC as an agency, because urban renewal seems to be going out of fashion. Some facts – for example that PDC is a public agency subject to open records acts,[3] and some business recruitment projects are more successfully done in secret – simply mean that PDC needs private-sector partners who can take on these facets of economic development. PDC may indeed have the expertise to engage in ED, and as ED becomes more urgent (under globalization and a prolonged recession), PDC is the only major-league ED game in town.

The issue then becomes one of accountability and oversight. I view accounta-bility as having these dimensions:

- *Transparency.* Taxpayers need to be able easily to find out what PDC is doing and how it is being paid for.
- *Sharing cost and risk.* PDC projects should not be seen as give-aways to private developers. PDC, and thus the city and the taxpayers, should share in the

potential economic upsides of development projects in URDs (or wherever PDC's future jurisdictions take the agency) as well as the downsides. Realized upsides will help fund economic development.

- *Public input.* PDC must continue to hold regular public hearings, town halls, and similar events.
- *City–PDC relationship.* PDC must respond to the council's wishes, as the agency is a creation of the council, and *show* that it is responding to those wishes.
- *Business opportunities for small/new/minority developers.* Accountability and transparency demand that opportunities for development profits on URDs not be confined to a small, exclusive club.
- *Simple, clear rules.* Because Byzantine rules, customs, and procedures amount to barriers to entry for new developers, another element of accountability is simplicity.

* * *

Part III, What is technology-based economic development?

This brings us to Table A.3. It shows that every element of Table A.2, without exception, may either be supported by technology or spur technological innovation. A region that mobilizes technology in most of the ways shown in Table A.3 is a technology-based economy ("technopolis").

I have mentioned the possibility that a region's strategy may, admirably, target green and sustainable economic activities. This may lead to low-tech objectives, like more commuter miles traveled by bicycle rather than automobile, or it may lead to high-tech objectives like the manufacture of hybrid vehicles. The bicycle strategy is easily copied by other regions, and results in no comparative economic advantage, regardless of the real, absolute benefits of reduced pollution and a healthier population. Specializing in the innovative manufacture of a clean vehicle, on the other hand, yields a distinctive competence that is a sustainable advantage.

The indented items in Table A.3 reinforce the view of economic development as the collection of efforts a region makes to cultivate a healthy economy. This is a general view of ED, but useful because it helps us avoid the tunnel-vision perspectives that ED is just recruiting or that ED is just infrastructure development. Again, a healthy economy requires a healthy, productive work force with access to information and education – the items in Table A.3's first column support this – as well as export-sector companies that are attracted by success in all three columns and in turn finance the three columns' activities via taxes, payrolls, and donations.

The meaning and significance of most of the indented items are self-evident, especially in the first column of Table A.3. Some in the other columns, however, want further explanation. Let us start with social capital. In Austin, a law firm maintains a pro bono web site listing all meetings of the city's technology-related organizations each month. This facilitates encounters between people who need to touch base with each other, and allows them to augment their project teams by meeting others with needed skills and interests. In Portland, project teams of Oregon RAINS (Regional Alliance for Infrastructure and Network Security) meet

Table A.3 Technology-based economic development (TED)

Hard infrastructure	Social infrastructure	Marketing
Transportation Intelligent Vehicle/Highway Systems	*Social capital* Social networking online	*Outward/Inward marketing* CRM systems
Maglev, TGV, other advanced public transportation	Online meeting spaces, master schedules	Technology-oriented conferences, conventions
Modern international airport	Smart physical meeting spaces	
Sanitation/H$_2$O Water treatment, wastewater treatment, sewer system, pest control, water supply	*Education/Training* Targeted retraining programs	*Target companies having ...* Leading basic technologies
Telecomm	Enrichment programs, science fairs, science and tech museums	Green/sustainable technologies
Proximity to trunks, switches	Distance learning	Health care technologies
Last-mile infrastructure	New academic programs	Technology products and creative/support services for export to emerging world markets
Public access to Internet at libraries, kiosks, public wireless sites	University-connected new business incubators	
Building/Construction Advanced/appropriate construction methods, tools, software, materials	*Health Care* Telemedicine, home health maintenance	*Packaging/Positioning* QOL, amenities for creative knowledge workers
Recently updated building codes	Teaching hospitals	Mathematical models for marketing analysis
Security/Anti-terrorism Monitors, screening devices/procedures, reporting, 911 response Search and rescue	*Government* Digital government. Intercity technology development alliances Public-private technology partnerships	*Competitive intelligence* Knowledge Management
Vaccine supply Computer security expertise	*Tourism* Reservation systems; multi-media tourist information	*Incentives* Data mining tools for pricing and effectiveness analysis
	Research Advanced researchers Online collaborative research technologies	*Support to existing businesses* Electronic clearinghouses

in a virtual meeting space called eRoom. This software records all proceedings automatically, reduces highway traffic, and makes meeting attendance easier for members of this alliance for building Portland's computer security cluster. When FTF ("face-to-face") meetings are needed, the cities' smart meeting spaces, with videoconferencing, decision groupware, multiple projection systems, microphones and workstations at every seat, and other electronics make it easy to communicate complex ideas quickly. These spaces also make the city attractive for advanced research conferences and technology conventions that bring world knowledge leaders to the region.

Education is enriched by science fairs, student inventor and student entrepreneur competitions at the primary, secondary, and collegiate levels. Guest speakers brought in via teleconferencing also enhance the learning experience, as do facilities for online experimentation at remote laboratories and online research collaboration. The benefits of university-connected technology business incubators are detailed elsewhere in this volume.

Teaching hospitals make a city known for the most advanced treatment modalities and surgical techniques. These hospitals tend to be in large cities, so a regional TED strategy will include telemedicine to bring the benefits of advanced medicine to outlying areas. As populations age, the medical monitoring and home health maintenance industries will boom, and pioneers in these products will gain competitive advantage.

"Digital government" is an umbrella term for the ways government agencies facilitate communication, compliance, security, and other functions of governance using information technology. (Useful sources on this subject include the newsletter dgOnline, published for the National Science Foundation by the Digital Government Research Center at the University of Southern California, http://www.dgrc.org. View dgOnline online at http://digitalgovernment. org/news/stories/dgonline_latest.jsp.) Networking among techno-regions is essential for finding suppliers, customers, alliance partners, advice, companies that want to locate in a region like yours, and expansion sites for homegrown technology companies. This kind of networking is done through non-profit organizations like the Association of University Technology Managers, the World Technopolis Association, the National Business Incubator Association, and the Technopolicy Network. Governments also do this directly, viz., the "technology alliance" between the cities of Austin, Texas, and Curitiba, Brazil.

S&T museums draw tourists and conventioneers as well as students. Information services directing tourists to attractions and bargains advance the double-win: Tourists bring their own dollars to be exposed to life in your city. In what other industry do customers pay producers to watch their ads? Tourism applications are also a great way for the region's technology and arts communities to work together.

Distinguished, leading-edge academic researchers are likely to draw the best graduate students, generate patents and attract licensees, and create (perhaps via their students) spin-off companies. When they publish in short-cycle online journals, use the latest electronics for collecting data and sharing lab notebooks, conduct experiments at distant laboratories via remote-control waldos, and allow distant researchers to do the same with their own advanced equipment, this further increases the velocity of innovation.

In some ways, localities are farthest behind on the technologies listed in Table A.3's third column, because public and not-for-profit entities have been slow to adopt the sophisticated marketing techniques of the private sector. CRM systems track the progress of prospects through the sales funnel, do contact management, and generate automated messages and reminders. They enable database marketing by preserving data on customer/prospect preferences and responses.

These databases can be linked to competitive intelligence and market research reports, and statistically analyzed to optimize marketing programs.

Regions want to attract companies that produce a steady stream of innovative products that are important to large, fast-growing, industries. Ideally, these products should be not only environmentally friendly and export-oriented, but should enhance the region's TED goals by enhancing the health, wealth, and happiness of the region's population. Electronic markets, electronic auctions, and electronic data interchange can connect to local small businesses, allowing them to be successful suppliers to larger companies.

This explains the individual elements of TED. The possibilities for creatively and super-additively combining these elements seem almost endless. We will close with just four examples of these synergies:

1. Inter-sectoral cooperation lets these technological facilities be used most effectively and in a way such that everyone need not, for example build his own smart auditorium. Sharing does not always amount to charity and need not be seen as a cost item. On the contrary, sharing allows people with different talents and similar goals to meet each other and get things done more efficiently. A regional development plan should anticipate and account for such synergies. (Without implying that it is a good example or a bad one, I refer the reader to http://www.oregonbusinessplan.org.)

2. Citizens and government officials who are knowledgeable about technology, active users of technology, and creative about applying technology in new ways to enhance their lives and their neighbors' lives, are important to this recipe. Examples include the legendary technopolis godfathers Mayor Jaime Lerner of Curitiba and Governor Morihiko Hiramatsu of Oita, and former Austin Mayor Kirk Watson and former Austin City Manager Camille Barnett.

3. In the high-tech region, government agencies and businesses (even small businesses) stay in touch with constituents through a variety of electronic means. See (Phillips, Donoho *et al.* 1997) for a detailed treatment of multimedia e-commerce.

4. In this era of globalization, technology executives' daily focus is well beyond city limits, and it is difficult to get them to make commitments to local community-building. The few who are committed locally, and who say (as one of my Austin friends does), "When I wake up in the morning I ask 'What can I do today to make Austin the very best place in the world to live?' " are a terrifically valuable resource.

Different regions will use this TED recipe in very different ways. However, the items detailed in these tables are the basic ingredients of technology-based economic development.

* * *

Part IV, A taxonomy of technology-based economic development initiatives[4]

Regions grow their technology-based employment by the means shown in Table A.4.

As it is now widely known that a critical mass of complementary talent and technology is needed to firmly establish a knowledge-intensive industry in a region (Porter 1998), new local institutions often take the form of "cluster initiatives." Other regional initiatives also focus on just one or more of the bullet items of Table A.4, without attempting complete integration of all of them. These varied initiatives, listed in Table A.5, are the objects of this study.

These several kinds of initiatives can be distinguished by their focus on one or more of the elements of Table A.4: Their degree of central direction vs. decentralization, their inward-looking vs. outward-looking orientation, their degree and kind of internal and external networking, and so on. These are the dimensions on which this appendix examines each type of regional technology development initiative. Our aim is to clarify terms, and to help economic development (ED) practitioners make wise choices when designing new programs under limited budgets.

While few existing initiatives attempt a total integration of all the activities of Table A.4, it is also true that few find benefit in pursuing only one item to the exclusion of all others. For example, large companies can provide the technologies, management talent, financing, and ambitious entrepreneurs that are the essential ingredients for a vibrant new venture community. Large and medium

Table A.4 Strategies for increasing technology-based employment

* Attracting new companies;
* Nurturing existing indigenous firms;
* Encouraging entrepreneurial start-ups;
* Providing a supportive educational, social, tax, quality-of-life, physical-infrastructure, and cultural context for research, technology entrepreneurship, and business;
* Networking with other regions worldwide; and
* Starting new kinds of institutions that integrate and/or support the five activities listed before.

Table A.5 Types of technology development initiatives

* Entrepreneurship initiatives
* Cluster initiatives
* Technopolis initiatives
* Shared prosperity initiatives
* National systems of innovation
* Regional systems of innovation
* Investment promotion agencies

companies are often the natural customers of start-ups. For these reasons, a regional strategy focusing solely on high-technology start-ups would have little chance of success; a balanced strategy is needed, reaching out to start-ups, SMEs and large companies alike.

This appendix will discuss each of the initiative types of Table A.5, offering examples and evaluative remarks when possible. A discussion section will note overlaps and exceptions to our definitions and those in the literature. A summary will bring together the salient features of the various initiative types.

Entrepreneurship initiatives

Often energized by university centers or trade associations, these initiatives (called RITEs in Phillips (2005a), for Regional Initiatives for Technology Entrepreneurship) seek to foster technology entrepreneurship and intrapreneurship in the region. They do this via educational programs, incubators, competitions, student internships, mentoring programs, and networking/speaker events. Some, like the University of Oregon and the University of Texas, via their student entrepreneurship competitions, network local entrepreneurs with entrepreneurs outside the local regions, in order to expand the entrepreneurs' contacts and their sources of suppliers and alliances.

Most entrepreneurship initiatives now follow the largely successful model pioneered by the IC^2 Institute of University of Texas at Austin, in which the university, government, and corporate sectors work together to:

- Assemble the capital, entrepreneurs, technologies, and managerial experience needed to make a new company thrive, and
- Ensure the social, educational, and cultural climate are supportive for entrepreneurs and entrepreneurship.

University entrepreneurship initiatives may ally with varied and rich sources of technology. These connect entrepreneurs with sources of ideas for improved products and processes. Washington State University's program is connected with Battelle-Pacific Northwest National Laboratories, University of New Mexico's with Sandia and Los Alamos, and University of Texas at Austin's with NASA. These connections help the national laboratories also, as, with decreasing budgets, it is in the labs' interest to help their talented scientists and engineers find entrepreneurial career alternatives.

Entrepreneurship initiatives suffer from several limitations, especially if the initiatives are not integrated into the context of a larger economic development program:

- As mentioned in this section's introduction, there may be insufficient connection with large companies. This robs the initiative of valuable potential entrepreneurs, technologies, management talent, and capital.
- Though it tolerates the entrepreneurship center, the university knows its major donations come from large corporations and not from startup entrepreneurs. The center finds it difficult to get the attention of the university president when it is needed.
- Small and family businesses – those that slice the existing economic pie into smaller slices – are far more numerous than innovative entrepreneurs who

make the pie larger. Eventually the initiative finds it more profitable to serve the small-business market, which is willing to pay for good business advice.

- Contrariwise, it is difficult to find funding for initiatives to support high-growth entrepreneurship. Venture capitalists' rigid business model does not allow much in the way of promotional expenditures, and by the same token, VCs frown on university incubators' desire to take a small percentage of equity in assisted start-ups. Soon after these startups "graduate" from the incubator, they may experience changes in their top management; new managers with no memory of the incubator's contributions to their firm's early success hesitate to offer financial support to the incubator.

- It is widely acknowledged that no viable funding mechanism supports technology startups through the "Valley of Death," the period between proof-of-concept and prototype development. Though it is reasonable to suppose a public-private entrepreneurship initiative might solve this problem, none has yet done so in the United States. Other nations taking less laissez-faire approaches to the matter have conducted companies across the valley of death, but there is debate about the efficiency of these approaches.

- The initiative may take too narrow a view of high technology, for example, looking only at IT or semiconductor sectors. Austin, Texas has successfully extended its entrepreneurship-facilitating efforts to the music and computer gaming industries.

Technopolis initiatives

These are the most heterogeneous of the initiatives discussed herein. Early Japanese efforts (Tatsuno, 1986) were centrally directed, locally focused and concerned exclusively with large government and corporate laboratories. Modern technopolis efforts (Biswas, 2004; Araki, 2000; Gibson, Kozmetsky *et al.* 1993) are well-balanced in terms of industry sectors, company segments, decentralized planning processes and worldwide networking.

Technopolis efforts are also, among the initiatives examined here, the most comprehensive and ambitious in scope, with regard to a local/regional economy. Technopolis initiatives may in fact venture into city planning. (This was certainly the case with the first Japanese technopolis, Tsukuba, at which site a city was built from a greenfield, and also with Curitiba, Brazil.) Despite their local character, these initiatives were global "before globalization was cool," perhaps because of researchers' propensity to interact with colleagues worldwide.

While Tsukuba was almost exclusively research-oriented, modern technopoleis (e.g., Daeduk in Korea, where the World Technopolis Association is now head-quartered) take pains to balance the value chain, collocating research institutes, manufacturers, suppliers, and distributors.

Because of their comprehensive, regional-growth orientation, technopoleis are unlikely to focus on a single industry segment or cluster. Rather, they include several industries while remaining selective about the use of limited resources.

Technopolis growth requires cooperation among broad swaths of local interest groups. For this reason, these exciting initiatives are practical only where the hand of government is strong, where extraordinary public-private collaboration is possible, or where a charismatic "godfather" evangelizes a vision for the region (Phillips 2005a).

Cluster initiatives

Cluster initiatives build on the understanding (Porter 1998) that in the high-tech economy, companies and their suppliers jointly benefit from the exchange of informal knowledge that is made possible by proximity, and moreover that, after a critical mass of companies and employees is achieved, a "lock-in" effect ensures the further growth (or at least continued presence) of the industry in the region.

There is nothing unsound about the idea, and indeed cluster theory describes exactly (if not completely) many of the happenings in the last decades in Silicon Valley and elsewhere. However, perhaps because of the powerful Harvard (Porter's employer) marketing machine, economic developers have seized on this well-publicized concept without giving due regard to other options, or have attempted to create clusters where conditions did not justify it (see, e.g., Phillips 2005).

A few other features and limitations of cluster initiatives, in principle or in practice, are:

- Clusters may not involve advanced technology at all; the cluster concept is equally (or perhaps even more) applicable in low-tech industries where the transfer of tacit knowledge is a paramount consideration. Hence the furniture cluster of North Carolina.
- Cluster initiatives may focus exclusively on large firms to the exclusion of entrepreneurial startups.
- Cluster theory's focus on collocation and lock-in is mechanical and does not encompass the social and multi-dimensional characteristics considered by other types of initiatives.
- A focus on a single cluster industry precludes the cross-sectoral cooperation that other initiatives may value, for example, the connection of high-tech with local arts and tourism industries.

Shared prosperity initiatives

Shared prosperity (Kozmetsky and Williams 2003; Kozmetsky *et al.* 2001; Marshall 1999; Phillips 2005) is an idea as closely related to political economy as it is to economic development. It has to do with sharing knowledge with neighboring and distant regions for purposes of accelerated development of both advanced and emerging regions. For these reasons, shared prosperity initiatives (compared to the other kinds of initiatives discussed here) place more emphasis on external networking.

Under entrepreneurship or cluster initiatives, resources are concentrated in order to build companies or the critical-mass presence of certain industries; the subsequent sharing of wealth outside the target group is implicitly left to passive "trickle-down" mechanisms. In contrast, shared prosperity initiatives adopt equity as an explicit goal. Shared prosperity is not about giving a larger share of fixed resources to the less well-off. It is about pooling knowledge and innovation in order to make the economic pie bigger for everyone.

Shared prosperity, then, implies promotion of social/political stability and avoidance of armed conflict, via increased interaction among regions and reduced income inequality. Shared prosperity initiatives recognize that modern development depends as much on exchanges of knowledge and "the sense of possibilities" as it does on transfers of funds. High technology enters the shared prosperity equation because technology industries are visibly knowledge-driven, making them industries in which knowledge and empowerment are truly more important than money. This is because innovation, driven by knowledge and empowerment, should attract investment in the free market, making traditional government aid transfers unnecessary.

Excellent examples of shared prosperity initiatives are the projects of the IC² Institute (University of Texas at Austin) in Belize (Gibson, Cotrofeld *et al.* 2004) and on the Texas-Mexico border (Gibson, Rhi-Perez *et al.* 2002).

Obstacles to shared prosperity initiatives are:

- The new awareness of the power of networking for policy-making is diffusing slowly among political decision makers. (Notwithstanding that networking for individuals' professional benefit is a well-accepted principle!) Because network-based initiatives tend to be decentralized, it is not yet clear to governments how such initiatives may be "directed."
- Similarly, governments and corporations are accustomed to controlling project via their purse strings. The idea that shared prosperity depends on knowledge exchange and transfer of empowerment even more than it depends on funding is one that most institutions have not yet assimilated.

Systems of innovation

In contrast to neoclassical economists' focus on profit-maximization and market variables, the Systems of Innovation (SI) approach comprehends the interplay of economic development agents in a more dynamic way, highlighting the role played by the demand side in the innovation process (Lundvall 2002; Nelson 1993). SI shifts attention to the interaction of the system's actors: knowledge producers (e.g., universities), users of knowledge (e.g., industry), producers of basic research (e.g., R&D departments or centers), and, users of applied research (e.g., firms).

Literature on SI as a framework for analyzing technical or technological change has grown rapidly since the early 1980s. While there is no single, universally accepted definition of the SI concept, there is a consensus that its relevance lies in highlighting the interactive linkages among the components of the system, and the linkages' effects on the innovative activity of economic agents in the geographic or sectoral area of interest.

"Systems" are sets of interconnected elements ("building-blocks") standing in interaction within an environment, exhibiting their own internal dynamics. Innovation systems have three main characteristics. They are *open* to other systems; *evolving* constantly, as they are exposed to transformative pressures from the outside and to institutional learning from inside; and, they are *social* systems, shaped by and shaping human action. Innovation systems are open and evolving but their characteristics and ways of operation have deep historical roots. Examples include the Swedish Iron Cannons Company's systematic innovations in casting techniques from 1630 through 1670 (Davistown Museum undated), or Danish Agro (Christensen *et al.* 2005).

There is a certain level of agreement among scholars that innovative performance depends on the nature of the linkages and relationships among the components of the system (OECD 1997). However, there is no consensus on what constitutes the innovation system's building blocks, their relevance, or their roles in innovative activity. The main actors recognized in the SI literature are knowledge-performing sectors (i.e., universities, research institutes, and technological centers), firms and governments. Due to the different roles that these actors play in different environments, and their unequal importance in various historical times and contexts, there is ongoing debate on the nomenclature for defining the components of the system and the roles they play in innovation.

Broadly speaking, a system of innovation s made up of components, relationships, and attributes. *Components* are the operating parts of the system, consisting of individual actors, organizations, physical or technological artifacts, and institutions. Inter-organizational networks or linkages constitute the system *relationships*, and interactive learning processes give shape to the *attributes* of the system.

SI has been conceptualized both in narrow and broad terms. In the narrow sense, SI includes the organizations and institutions, such as knowledge centers, directly related to searching out and exploring technological innovations. Authors defining SI in broad terms address all habits, routines, practices, rules, norms, and laws which regulate the behavior and interaction of the system's agents, and all interrelated institutional actors that create, diffuse, and exploit innovations. In both contexts, the SI concept rests on the premise that "understanding the web of interaction among the agents involved in innovation is essential to improving technology performance and national competitiveness (OECD 1997; Lundvall 1988, 1992; Johnson 1992)."

As a framework of analysis, the SI concept offers a new approach for understanding innovation in a more dynamic way (Mytelka 2000). It recognizes the importance of knowledge in the economic development of a country, as well as the nature of institutions involved in its generation, and the relevance of the use of the systems approach (OECD 1997).

The study of SI involves formal economic theories, such as division of labor, evolutionary theory, and economic growth. It is an integrative theory, making use of knowledge from innovation and industrial dynamics, economic development, and economic geography. Innovation systems are also a tool for historical analysis (e.g., Freeman's 1997 and Nelson's 1993 studies on Japan and the US), and a tool for policy makers in re-aligning sector policies. It is an analytical framework micro-founded in the user-producer interaction as well as inter-organizational learning and work-interactions including diverse modes of organization and intra-organizational learning. Learning is fundamental in SI, as it underlies social capital and economic development, which in turn are crucial for the valorization of intellectual capital.[5]

The systems of innovation framework embraces all important determinants of the innovation process and helps trace the relationships among its components (governments, industries, firms, academia, institutions) in the development of science and technology (OECD 1997). In tracing these networks, SI authors have found different levels and/or channels of interaction between the building blocks of the system of innovation.

The first and most basic level is the interaction between firms (ECLAC 2002). Firms in the business sector play a fundamental role in economic and technological development (Galli and Teubal 1997). In particular and most strikingly, firms improve their innovative performance through cooperation (OECD 1997).

The ways firms interact, compete, and innovate have evolved, and in the new competitive world, require more complex articulation than in the past. Informal linkages and contracts, alliances, competitive pressures, and movement of personnel and personal exchanges are some of the informal channels through which knowledge flows among institutions. Closer links between customers and suppliers are also essential for the innovative activity of firms (OECD 1997). The user-producer interaction is another critical parameter for innovative success (Lundvall 1992; OECD 1997). The newer, more expansive view of this interaction allows firms to learn from their clients and suppliers, and fosters technology transfer at the consumption and production level.[6]

Other important channels for knowledge flows in innovative processes are the interaction between departments and functions within the firm in "search and problem solving" activities (Freeman 1997; Gjerding 1992), as well as in-house and contractual R&D activities (Teece 1988). Technical collaboration between firms (e.g. R&D collaborations and strategic technical alliances), equipment procurement, joint ventures, cross-patenting, and mergers and acquisitions are also important channels for knowledge transmission between enterprises. These kinds of interactions induce technology transfer at the research and development level (Muller 1999); in diffusing knowledge and technology between firms; and in improving their organizational routines, products and process innovations and diversification, vertical integration and horizontal diversification (Teece 1988; OECD 1997; Oyeyinka 2002).

In order to achieve the benefits of interaction, and to be able to produce new forms of knowledge and achieve higher levels of innovation-related skills, a firm requires certain knowledge bases or learning capability (Ernst *et al.* 1998; Mytelka 2000; Oyeyinka 2002). According to Dosi (1988), this cumulative knowledge capability of the firm defines the technological paradigms[7] that the firm is able to follow in order to achieve further innovations. The codified and/or tacit knowledge that the firm has "stockpiled" will allow it to continue on a certain trajectory of technological innovation (Dosi 1988; Mytelka 2000; Oyeyinka 2002).

However, these interactions among firms (or industries) are not a sufficient condition for innovation to occur. There are other agents in the system (e.g., universities, research institutes, financial organizations, and governments) that contribute to the way interactions take place. When these components of the system are added, a second level of interaction is reached. These other agents constitute important parts of the environment in which the agents perform. This wider network of interaction among the SI actors plays a fundamental role in the innovative activity of the economy, increasing or decreasing the firms' opportunities to improve their technological capabilities (OECD 1997; ECLAC 2002).

Linkages among the business sector, research institutes and universities promote knowledge generation by diffusing and linking the different kinds of knowledge generated in them. Each actor in the R&D-performing sector performs a specific function in knowledge generation. Universities generate basic and generic knowledge; R&D institutes are mission-oriented knowledge producers, and finally applied research and technology development is the competence of the business sector (Galli and Teubal 1997; OECD 1997).

This interaction among the system's actors occurs through diverse channels. The most common channels for formal interaction among knowledge user-producers are, *inter alia:* joint-technology projects, joint-research activities, specific research contracts, market transactions, unilateral flows of funds, skills and knowledge, and financing of staff and researchers (Galli and Teubal 1997; OECD 1997). Informal channels such as contracts or social relationships are also important in knowledge flows and access to technical networks.

Interaction among agents with different orientations, purposes, and natures brings more complexities to the system. In addition, the macroeconomic environment in which the SI is settled has important effects on the performance of the innovation process.

All the macroeconomic features, social interactions, rules and policy restrictions, and formal and informal institutions shape the system, have an influence on the way agents interact, and, as a consequence, shape the innovative activity of the economy. This is what ECLAC (2002) considers the third level of interaction.

Together, these three levels of interaction give shape and character to the "system of innovation" concept.

Innovation systems have been defined at different levels according to the units of analysis, levels of interaction, and scope considered in the analysis. Thus, in the SI literature we can find diverse approaches, such as:[8]

- Transnational innovation systems (Cantwell 1989),
- National Innovation Systems (Freeman 1997; Lundvall 1988, 1992)
- Regional Innovation Systems (Cooke 1998)
- Local Innovation Systems, or Industrial Clusters (Porter 1998)
- Sectoral Innovation Systems (Malerba 2004)
- Corporate Innovation Systems (Granstrand *et al.* 1992)
- Technological Systems (Carlsson *et al.* 2002)
- Triple Helix (Etzcowich and Leydesdorff 1997)

Although these different conceptualizations of SI differ in scope, they should be seen as complementary rather than as rivals. Among them, perhaps the most widely diffused has been the sectoral and national perspectives. The sectoral system of innovation is another widespread SI-approach. It is based on the idea that different sectors or industries operate under different technological regimes which are characterized by particular combinations of opportunity and appropriability conditions, different degrees of cumulativeness of technological knowledge, and different characteristics of the relevant knowledge base (Carlsson *et al.* 2002, p. 236).

A National System of Innovation (NSI) is seen as a system that creates and uses innovation and competences. An NSI analysis addresses not only industries and firms, but also other actors and organizations, primarily in S&T, including governments' roles in technology policy. The analysis is carried out within national boundaries and it fits both with the focus on technological capability and the focus on institutions. Although science communities appear to become global and the national level seems to be losing relevance in this era of globalization, "as long as national states exist as political entities with their own agendas related to innovation, it is useful to work with national systems as analytical objects (Lundvall *et al.* 2002, p. 215)."

When considering SI as a framework for analysis in developing countries, it is important to remember that it is a concept originating in developed economies, based on empirical findings in developed countries. However, countries differ substantially in their organization and characteristics, levels of public and private financing of research institutes, R&D and S&T expenditures as a percent of GDP, and institutional factors, and their innovative and learning capabilities (Niosi *et al.* 1993; OECD 1997; Johnson 1992). As a consequence, the perform-ances of innovation systems are not uniform among countries. The availability of data regarding innovative activities differs substantially among countries, as does comparability of data.

Patents, scientific articles, publications, citations, literature, and firm-surveys are some of the direct indicators used to measure productivity in SI studies. However, such measures are not available in the same degree (or at all) in different countries. Alternative indirect indicators commonly used in measuring innovative vitality in systems of innovation are R&D and S&T expenditures as a percent of GDP, production and trade of high-tech products, and others (Niosi *et al.* 1993; OECD 1997; ECLAC 2002).

Other factors to be considered in measuring the performance of the SI are the ownership nature and size of its units (Gregersen 1992; Lundvall 1992), and the regional distribution of the innovative components of the system, usually measured through network analysis and/or cluster analysis (Mytelka 2000; Oyeyinka 2002).

Different levels of performance among countries and among innovation systems are explained by differences in levels of interaction between the actors of the system; mismatches between basic and applied research in the public and private sector; effectiveness of technology transfer institutions; and information and absorptive differences among the enterprises and other actors of the system (OECD 1997).

It is precisely these differences between countries that make SI a strong analytical approach. SI analyses identify the relationships among the interacting economic participants in the innovation process and highlight interrelationships among policies. SI is a concept that focuses attention on failures or weaknesses in the sys-tem, which affect the innovative performance of the region, industry, sector, or country. It offers new rationales and new approaches for policy-making for enhancing the innovative capability of firms (OECD 1997; Mytelka 2000).

SI brings the proven and powerful tools of system analysis to the study of TED, and valuably establishes this study outside the ivied walls of the economics department. Though the ultimate goal of the SI approach is to enable strategic interventions in the system, it is not clear that this has yet been accomplished. SI has, however, led to some enlightening new comparative views of innovation in different countries, for example Lundvall and Tomlinson (2000).

As with the other initiative types analyzed here, there are some risks attached to the systems of innovation approach. SI is a *reconceptualization*, re-framing ideas from innovation theory and economic geography in systems-theoretic terminology. One risk is that researchers, reveling in the new reconceptualization and busy translating old ideas into new terms, may not actually add new knowledge to our understanding of technology-based regional economic development. A second risk involves the respect of the scientific community. Researchers with a back-ground in systems science, watching organizational behavior scholars' discovery of "systems thinking" in the 1990s (due to the work of Peter Senge), reacted much as the Arawaks might have in 1492, had these Caribbean indegenes seen a news-paper headline announcing "Columbus discovers America." Finally, SI seems more popular in Europe than in the United States, and one hopes methods and terminology will not diverge so far that transatlantic networking of initiatives becomes difficult.

Investment promotion agencies

In order to discuss investment promotion agencies in context, we must make a brief digression into the meaning of foreign direct investment (FDI), its importance, and trends and determinants of its flows.

Foreign direct investment: Definitions and trends

According to the IMF and OECD definitions (Duce 2003), direct investment comprises a lasting interest by a resident entity of one economy (direct investor) in an enterprise that is resident in another economy (the direct investment enterprise). The "lasting interest" implies the existence of a long-term relationship between the direct investor and the direct investment enterprise and a significant degree of influence on the management of the latter. Foreign direct investment gives the investor a controlling interest in a foreign company (Daniels and Radebaugh 2004 p. 11). This control distinguishes direct investment from portfolio investment. When two or more companies share ownership of an FDI, the operation is a joint venture.

FDI includes corporate activities such as plants or subsidiaries in foreign countries, and buying controlling stakes or shares in foreign companies. It does not include short-term capital flows (Progressive Policy Institute, undated). There are two ways companies can invest in a foreign country. They can acquire a controlling or influential interest in an existing operation (acquisition or merger) or construct new facilities (Daniels and Radebaugh 2004, p. 251). The latter is called a greenfield investment.

Foreign direct investment is thought to be more desirable for the invested region than non-controlling investments in the equity of its companies. This is because portfolio investments are so mobile they may be withdrawn as soon as a better opportunity arises elsewhere. FDI is generally patient whether things go well or badly in the short term.[9] By generating employment, raising productivity, transferring advanced managerial skills and technology, and enhancing exports, FDI plays an important role in regional development strategies, particularly contributing to the host region's industrial and technological development.

In recent decades, different factors have helped to bring about an increased growth rate in FDI worldwide. These include rapid increase in technology, liberalization of government policies on cross-border movement of trade and resources, development of institutions that support and facilitate international trade, and increased global competition (Daniels and Radebaugh 2004, p. 7).

Developed countries remain the prime destination of FDI, accounting for more than three-quarters of global inflows and more than 90 percent of outflows. Flows to developing countries rose from $158 billion in 2002 to $172 billion in 2003, but varied by region. Inward FDI to the Asia-Pacific region reached $107 billion, up from $95 billion. Latin America and the Caribbean, however, experienced a fourth consecutive year of decline, although it was marginal, from $51 billion in 2002 to $50 billion.

FDI inflows to Africa totaled $20 billion in 2004, only 3 percent of global FDI inflows (UNCTAD 2004). Africa recorded 28 percent higher inflows in 2003 ($15 billion, up from $12 billion in 2002), driven mainly by natural-resource projects. The structure of FDI in Africa remains skewed towards primary products, although inflows to services are rising.

Quality Foreign Direct Investment

The quality of FDI inflows is connected to the depth of involvement of the investment project in a host country, the participation in technology-intensive projects, or the generation of knowledge spillovers to the host country (Kumar 2002). Quality FDI brings jobs, strategic technology, knowledge, and skills to the host region. It is export-oriented and encourages sustainability of the region's or the country's balance of payments. Quality FDI is also expected to comprise long-term, environmental friendly investments, with sustainable production linkages with local companies.

Determinants of inward FDI growth

This section lists the factors that determine FDI inflows into a given geographical location. Each factor reassures investors that they may expand their sales, acquire needed resources, and minimize business risks. Not all factors are equally important to every investor in every location at all times.

- *Regional trading blocs* (RTBs) are essential determinants of FDI. These represent various forms of economic integration among countries. They are designed to promote cross- or inter-country trade and mobility of factor services from within member countries by fostering a more market-oriented pattern of intra-regional resource allocation.
- *Language and business culture* are also determinants of FDI inflows. In a destination where, for example, English is commonly spoken by the majority of the population, one would expect more FDI inflows from English speaking countries than if the case were otherwise.
- *Tax exemptions, tax holidays, or tax reduction,* for foreign investors, and similar incentives can play a positive role in attracting FDIs into a given destination. Some other types of incentives that may play similar roles include guarantees against arbitrary treatment in case of nationalization.
- *Labor availability* and relatively low labor costs, high skills, and efficiency are important factors determining FDI inflow into a given destination.
- *Economic and structural reforms* in a country are very important in winning foreign investors' confidence to take their investment funds there. Such reforms can be very wide and far-reaching. The reforms involve the relaxation of entry restrictions in various sectors, deregulation in various industries, abolition of price controls, easing of controls over mergers and acquisitions and trade practices, removal of government monopoly, privatization, independence of the Central Bank, elimination of import licensing, removal of foreign-exchange, and exchange rate and interest rate controls.
- *Non-discriminatory treatment* of investors, consistency and predictability in government policies are also among the FDI determinants. Investors need to

be in a position where they can plan their activities efficiently within the policy environment of the government. Those government policies that directly or indirectly affect investments should be reliable, accessible, up to date and widely publicized.

- *Economic growth* in turn determines market prospects. It is more likely that FDI will flow more to destinations with promising economic growth both in the short and long run.
- *A country's membership in a binding multinational investment agreements and institutions* concerning FDI can reduce the perceived risk of investing there. When the risk of investing in a location is reduced, we expect to see an increase in investments there. Such agreements include several bilateral investment treaties and double taxation treaties. Among the organizations that have an impact on the flow of FDI are the World Intellectual Property Organization (WIPO); the convention establishing the Multinational Investment Guarantee Agency (MIGA); the Convention on the recognition and enforcement of foreign arbitral awards; the Convention on the settlement of investment disputes between states and nationals of other states.
- *The presence of investment opportunities and natural resources* in a country, needless to say, is another important FDI determinant.
- *Attractiveness of the host country's market*: A large domestic market implies a greater demand for goods and services and therefore makes the host country more attractive for FDI.
- *Infrastructure development*: Good infrastructure increases the productivity of investments and therefore stimulates FDI flows.

Strategy and organization for investment promotion

Wells and Wint (2001) define investment promotion as "activities that disseminate information about, or attempt to create an image of the investment site and provide investment services for the prospective investors." Promotion includes the granting of incentives to foreign investors, the screening of foreign investment, and negotiation with foreign investors, which is normally conducted by organizations dealing with investment promotion activities.

The national policy context is an integral part of effective investment promotion. An investment promotion agency (IPA) will find it difficult to market and promote its location unless the basic policies to facilitate FDI are in place. As UNCTAD (2004) argues, an FDI-enabling framework is a pre-condition. The enabling framework includes macroeconomic policies, investment policies, and a degree of economic stability. For an effective IPA strategy, it is important that there is clarity of objectives with a strong logic behind them. The size, structure, and priorities of the IPA will be influenced by why a country wants to attract inward investment.

Effective investment promotion is focused on targeting key sectors or industry clusters. Where to focus depends on the country's objective and what the country wants to promote. That is, does it need new greenfield investment, expansions by existing investors, joint ventures, M&As, or other types of strategic partnerships? If the country's objective is to focus on sector size or on sector positioning, then that is where it will target its investment promotion. Singapore

Economic Development Board (SEDB) is an extreme example among IPAs in that it will not support investors unless they are in target sectors or clusters.

Incentives can and do affect investment location decisions (Loewendahl 2001). Some of the incentives that attract FDI include tax reductions, national, regional, or local grants, and other special purpose incentives, employment incentives, recruitment and training assistance, and site or infrastructure improvements. However, emphasis on incentives varies considerably across regions. For example, the Industrial Development Agency (IDA) in Ireland, SEDB and Investment, Trade and Tourism of Portugal (ICEP) are among the few agencies in the world that have control over incentives and can put an "offer on the table" to an investor even before they have committed to invest. At the other extreme, Denmark does not offer any incentives at all for foreign investors. In the middle of this spectrum, the Portland (Oregon) Development Commission is organized to obtain a quick consensus on incentive offers from many constituent agencies and neighboring governments (Doctor, Albers *et al.* 2005).

Main functions of IPAs

Governments compete to attract foreign direct investment into their regions, and establishing an Investment Promotion Agency has become a central part of most countries' development strategies (UNCTAD 2002). Since the early 1990s, governments have been establishing Investment Promotion Agencies (IPAs) with the specific objective of attracting inward direct investment, which brings needed capital and access to international markets. As investors have many good locations to choose from, IPAs must promote the attractiveness of their region by making investors aware of its investment opportunities, by improving the region's image, and by providing an enabling investment environment. According to UNCTAD (2004), today there are over 500 IPAs worldwide, and the number is increasing steadily.

These are institutions established to coordinate investment activities and encourage investment flows into a country. They have a role in communicating and disseminating investment information to investors. IPAs also have a role of coordinating most activities aimed at improving the business environment in the host country. This role can range from providing assistance to potential and existing investors in their daily problems to lobbying for key policy and legal reforms (World Bank 2003). Investment promotion can be divided into four main activities: Strategy and organization, lead generation (targeting and marketing), facilitation (project handling), and investment services (after-care services).

Morisset and Andrews-Johnson (2001) list the major functions of IPAs:

- *Image building* is the function of creating the perception of a country as an attractive site for international investment. Activities commonly associated with image building include focused advertising, public relations events, and the generation of favorable news stories by cultivating journalists and opinion leaders.
- *Investor facilitation and investor servicing* refers to the range of services provided in a host country that can assist an investor in analyzing investment

decisions, establishing a business, and maintaining it in good standing. Activities in this area include information provision, "one-stop shop" service aimed at expediting approval process, and various assistance in obtaining sites, utilities, and so on.

- *Investment Generation* entails targeting specific sectors and companies with a view to creating investment leads. Activities include identification of potential sectors and investors, direct mailing, telephone campaigns, investor forums and seminars, and individual presentations to targeted investors. Investment generation activities can be done at home and overseas.
- *Policy advocacy* consists of the activities through which the agency supports initiatives to improve the quality of the investment climate and identifies the views of the private sector on that matter. Activities include surveys of the private sector, participation in task forces, policy and legal proposals, and lobbying.

Hurdles for the further development of IPAS are:

- In the race for maximizing FDI flows into developing countries, policy makers often tend to overlook the quality of incoming FDI. Investment inflow still tends to be short-term, low-technology and labor-intensive. In order to be more competitive, developing countries need to attract more long-term manufacturing sector projects, involving high technology and capital-intensive methods of production.
- Developed countries have used IPAs effectively in their process of development; it is now the turn of developing countries to use them.
- FDI statistics are published for nations rather than for regions. It is difficult for regions to use public statistics as a policy tool, or generate their own regional statistics.
- IPAs may experience controversy regarding their level of autonomy (Doctor, Albers *et al.* 2005).

Exceptions and hybrid initiatives

Many techno-regions led by "godfathers" – Austin, Curitiba, Oita, and Hyderabad come to mind – have been driven more by the force of their personalities than by the specificity of their goals. It is, therefore, difficult to categorize the initiatives that have taken root in those cities. Especially when they are not elected officials, godfathers find it expedient and constructive to utilize "fuzzy objectives" (Phillips 2005) that blur the taxonomy.

That these initiatives are not readily pigeon-holed does not reduce their effectiveness. The Portland Education Cluster[10] adopted its cluster initiative mission only after its third meeting. To draw people who might have been reluctant to commit to participation in a cluster initiative, the organizers billed the first events as simple social networking for executives in the city's education-oriented companies. A proposition was put forth that if the group were to find common interests that could be advanced by common effort, more meetings would be held. Otherwise, they could enjoy each other's company, go home after a pleasant evening, and no more would be said. The bottom-up energy that spurred working groups and a web site led to the group's coalescing as a cluster project that has kept the initiative thriving since 2003.

Further comparisons and summary

Regional entrepreneurship initiatives and cluster initiatives share an emphasis on internal and external networking, on learning, and on exchange of information and skills.

Though technopoleis may involve many industrial clusters, technopolis initiatives predated our formal understanding of knowledge industries' positive returns to scale, which is the underpinning of high-tech cluster theory. If early technopolis initiatives were effective in building clusters – and it is clear that they were – it was because of historical happenstance and because of the initiative organization's informal, seat-of-the-pants grasp of what is needed to build a modern industry. (And in the case of government-led technopoleis, because of the governments' ability to muster resources outside the market price system.) In addition, technopoleis usually involve public-private partnerships that work to build a local presence in several industries rather than just one cluster.

Sölvell, Lindqvist *et al.* (2003) find that a dedicated facilitator is essential to cluster initiatives. Technopolis and shared prosperity initiatives, in contrast, need a godfather or godmother with much more social status, connectivity and clout than even experienced professional facilitators can bring to bear.

Nonetheless, cluster initiatives and entrepreneurship initiatives have many common concerns and features. Sölvell, Lindqvist *et al.* (2003) show that cluster initiatives are growing common even in technology-follower regions, involve cross-sectoral cooperation, and depend on a regional vision for the future. The latter, in turn, depends on intensive discussion, networking, and consensus-building.

We find systems-of-innovation (SI) approaches to be more scholarly and passive. Like the others, SI zeroes in on networks as the key phenomenon. Rather than *doing* networking, however, SI approaches *study* existing networks. While other initiative types for the most part recognize the primary importance of metropolitan regions, SI researchers study national, transnational, regional, and sectoral innovation systems with equal interest.

Table A.6 summarizes the key features and differentiators of the types of initiatives discussed previously.

There are many kinds of economic development programs other than those seen in Table A.6. These have been excluded from discussion here because, generally speaking, they are of less interest for technology-intensive regions or regions wishing to become technology-driven. We have, for example, excluded tax-free Enterprise Zones and Export Zones (EZs). EZs, because of their location or because access to them is restricted, are unlikely to generate the knowledge spillovers that are the lifeblood of a techno-region. EZs are short-term measures for increasing port activity or for increasing small-business opportunities for low-income people, and are valuable for those purposes. They are unlikely, however, to offer tax revenues, long-term jobs, significant attraction for venture investors, or diverse improvements to urban infrastructure.

The near-universal embrace of technology-related objectives by economic development organizations has given rise to the variety of initiatives discussed in this appendix. The authors hope the "annotated taxonomy" offered earlier will help those involved in economic development to conceptualize and operationalize ED projects more effectively.

Table A.6 Technology-based ED initiatives: Key features compared

	Goals	Geographical focus	Degree of central direction	Orientation and kind of networking	Theoretical basis
Entrepreneurship initiatives	Encourage innovation. Build supplier base. Balance the ED strategy. Enrich Educational offerings.	Metro area. With state universities, may have state-wide mission. There are some national entrepreneurship organizations.	Little.	Mostly within the local entrepreneurial and investor community. Some (like Texas' Moot Corp™) network worldwide.	Finance. psychological and sociological theories of entrepreneurship. Otherwise, experimental and experiential.
Cluster initiatives	Build self-sustaining mass of supplier/manufacturer/customer companies in one or a few industries.	Metro regions.	Little.	Intra-industry.	Information economics (positive returns). Economic geography.
Technopolis Initiatives	Sustainable, diversified technology economy for the metro region and hinterlands.	Metro regions.	Technopoleis in e.g. Japan, Korea, still very much government initiatives. Elsewhere, reliance on public-private partnerships.	Internal (but cross-sector) and external networking. External networking is to link to other cities at similar levels of development.	Strategic technologies. City planning. Social network theory. Mapping of industry flows; input/output analysis. Marketing.

Shared prosperity initiatives	Equity. Stability. Diversify sources of innovation.	Networks of regions.	Little government involvement in early stages. Decentralized initiatives.	Focused on selected neighboring or distant regions. External networking dominates.	Political economy. Development economics.
National systems of innovation	Understand the linkages among all actors in the innovation process, and ultimately enable purposeful intervention.	Nations.	Implied that decisions to intervene in system will be centrally directed. Higher degree of government initiative/direction than other initiatives.	Interactions among local actors and between these actors and a generalized "environment."	Systems theory. Economic geography. Selected parts of economic theory. Theories from diverse other disciplines.
Regional systems of innovation	Understand the Linkages among all actors in the innovation process, and ultimately enable purposeful intervention.	Regions.	Implied that decisions to intervene in system will be centrally directed. Higher degree of government initiative/direction than other initiatives.	Interactions among local actors and between these actors and a generalized "environment."	Systems theory. Economic geography. Selected parts of economic theory. Theories from diverse other disciplines.
Investment promotion agencies	Encourage inward direct investment.	Nations or particular districts within nations.	Government-led in most of the world; occasionally led by private chambers of commerce.	Internal networking for current available facilities; external networking for potential investors.	Marketing. Finance. Labor economics. Logistics. Others.

Notes

1. In fact, the Pueblo people, in a celebrated 1614 revolution, ejected the Spanish from New Mexico. Nichols refuses to admit that his novel and its two sequels were set in New Mexico, but in interviews has added nods and winks to the unmistakable clues in the text.
2. Bill Sizemore is an Oregon small-government and anti-tax crusader.
3. In the United States, laws that make documents and databases accessible by any citizen, if the compilation or publication of the information was paid for by tax monies.
4. Part IV was co-authored by Fred Phillips, Bertha Vallejo, and Patricia Mhondo.
5. See Michael Woolcock's (e.g., 1998) work for more on social capital and economic development.
6. Here Johnson and Segura-Bonilla (2001) cite a 1999 working paper (in Danish) by J. Müller of the University of Aalborg.
7. Defined as "the needs that are meant to be fulfilled, the scientific principles utilized for the task, the material technology to be used ... [They are] a pattern of solution of selected techno-economic problems based on highly selected principles derived from the natural sciences ... a set of exemplars, and a set of heuristics" (Dosi 1988, pp. 224–225).
8. For a more detailed comparison of the various system approaches, see Carlsson *et al.* (2002).
9. http://economics.about.com/library/glossary/bldef-foreign-direct-investment.htm
10. http://www.portlandedcluster.com

Works Cited

Abbott, C. (2002) "This Fair City Fails by Resting on its Laurels." Portland, Oregon: Special to *The Oregonian* 22 September, E1.

Agiplan (1999) *Analysis of Transnational Technology Networking between Existing Clusters of SMEs and One or More Technology Poles.* Mülheim an der Ruhr: European Commission Directorate General Enterprise.

APEC (©2003) "APEC Forum on Shared Prosperity and Harmony." Manila: Asian Development Bank. http://www.adb.org/Documents/Speeches/2000/ ms2000021.asp

Araki, K. (2000) "Technological Innovation, National Urban Policy and Local Development: Policy Implications of the Concept of Technopole and Japan's Technopolis Programme for Developing Countries." London: University College. http://www.ucl.ac.uk/DPU/publications/working%20papers%20pdf/ wp110.pdf

Ariunaa, A. (2000) "Standards for the Prosperity of Society and Peaceful Trade." *ISO Bulletin* October. http://www.iso.ch/iso/en/commcentre/pdf/WSD0010.pdf

Arthur, W. B. (1987) "Competing Technologies, Increasing Returns and Lock-in by Historical Events." *Economic Journal* 99, 116–31.

Banville, J. (2003) *Shroud.* New York: Alfred A. Knopf, p. 32.

Berglund, D. (1999) "University-Industry Partnerships: Examples & Lessons Learned." Westerville, Ohio: State Science & Technology Institute, September.

Bienkowski, R. S. (2000) "Internal Incubators." Great Neck, New York: Office of Technology Transfer, North Shore – Long Island Jewish Health System, 26 January.

Bisoux, T. (2004) "A World of Good." *BizEd* Nov–Dec, 42–5.

Biswas, R. R. (2004) "Making a Technopolis in Hyderabad, India: The Role of Government IT Policy." *Technological Forecasting & Social Change* 71:8, 823–35.

Bixby, P. (1999) "Texas MBAs Hatch Big Ideas at the Austin Technology Incubator." *Texas* Spring, 18–20.

Breamer, D. (1998) "Prospective Tenant Questionnaire." Richland, Washington: Tri-Cities Enterprise Association.

Breschi, S. and F. Malerba (1997) "Sectoral Innovation Systems: Technological Regimes, Schumpeterian Dynamics, and Spatial Boundaries." In C. Edquist, ed., *Systems of Innovation, Technologies, Institutions and Organizations.* London: Pinter.

Caniels, M. C. J. (1996) "Regional Differences in Technology: Theory and Empirics." Maastricht: Maastricht Economic Research Institute on Innovation and Technology (MERIT), May.

Caniels, M. C. J. (1997) "The Geographic Distribution of Patents and Value Added Across European Regions." Maastricht: Maastricht Economic Research Institute on Innovation and Technology (MERIT), August. http://meritbbs.unimaas.nl/ rmpdf/rm98_004.pdf

Cantwell J. (1989) *Technological Innovation and Multinational Corporations.* Oxford: Basil Blackwell.

Carlsson, B., S. Jacobsson, M. Holmén, and A. Rickne (2002) "Innovation Systems: Analytical and Methodological Issues." *Research Policy* 31, 233–45.

Chen, M. Y. (2000) "Let's Make a Deal: In Their Efforts to Lure Companies, Countries Offer All Sorts of Incentives; but There Are Some Things Money Can't Buy." *Wall Street Journal* 25 September, R10.

Choate, P. (2005) *Hot Property: The Stealing of Ideas in an Age of Globalization.* New York: Alfred A. Knopf.

Christensen, J. (2000) "High-Tech Companies Sprout on Former Maui Farm Land." Associated Press, 28 February.

Christensen, J. L., B. Dalum, B. Gregersen, B. Johnson, B.-Å. Lundvall, and M. Tomlinson (2005) "The Danish Innovation System." Department of Business Studies, Aalborg University, Denmark, February.

Coleman, J. S. (1988) "Social Capital in the Creation of Human Capital." *American Journal of Sociology Supplement* 94, S95–S120.

Conceicao, P., D. V. Gibson, M. V. Heitor, and G. Sirilli (1999) "Knowledge for Inclusive Development: The Challenges of Globally Integrated Learning & Implications for Science & Technology Policy." Austin: IC^2 Institute. http://www.ic2.org/main.php?a=3&s=75

Cooke, P. (1998) "Introduction: The Origins of the Concept." In Braczyk, H.-J., P. Cooke, and M. Heidenreich, eds, *Regional Innovation Systems.* London/Bristol PA: University College London Press, pp. 2–25.

Cordero, O. and C. E. Pelaez (2002) "Dynamic Business Intelligence, Automated Decision Making with Fuzzy Cognitive Maps." Poznan, Poland: *Proceedings of BIB 2002.* http://www.bettennanagement.com/library/library. aspx?libraryid=9827&pagenumber=6

Cortright, J. (2002) "The Economic Importance of Being Different: Regional Variations in Tastes, Increasing Returns and the Dynamics of Development." *Economic Development Quarterly* 16:1, 3–16.

Cortright, J. (2002a) "21st Century Economic Strategy: Prospering in a Knowledge-based Economy." Portland, Oregon: Impresa, Inc., February.

Cortright, J. and H. Mayer (2001) "High Tech Specialization: A Comparison of High Technology Centers." Washington, D.C.: Brookings Institution. http://www.brookings.edu/es/urban/cortright/specialization.pdf

Costa, D. L. and M. Kahn (2000) "Power Couples: Changes in the Locational Choice of the College Educated, 1940–1990." *Quarterly Journal of Economics* 115:4, 1287–316.

Culbertson, R. and F. Phillips, eds (1995) *ElectroComm '94: A Conference on Electronic Commerce.* Austin: IC^2 Institute.

Daniels, J. D. and L. H. Radebaugh (2004) *International Business.* Upper Saddle River, NJ: Prentice-Hall, 10th edition.

David, P. A. (1997) "Path Dependence and the Quest for Historical Economics: One More Chorus of the Ballad of QWERTY." Oxford: University of Oxford, November.

Davis, E. (1998) *Techgnosis: Myth, Magic and Mysticism in the Age of Information.* New York: Three Rivers Press.

Davistown Museum (undated) "Hand Tools in History." Liberty, Maine: Center for the Study of Early Tools, Davistown Museum. http://www.davistownmuseum.org/TDMtoolHistory.htm

Department of Foreign Affairs and International Trade (Canada) "Edinburgh Commonwealth Economic Declaration: Promoting Shared Prosperity." http://www.dfait-maeci.gc.ca/foreign_policy/commonwealth/imoc315-en.asp

Desai, C. and F. Phillips, eds (1993) *New Software Technologies*. Austin: IC² Institute.

DeVol, R. C. (1999) *America's High Tech Economy: Growth, Development and Risk for Metropolitan Areas*. Santa Monica, California: Milken Institute.

Doctor, C., M. Albers, A. M. Claire, L. Coward, V. Faatz, P. Fellner, W. Fickler, L.-E. Jenssen, K. Krause, D. Mandell, P. Manson, P. Meyer, F. Phillips and S. Thomas (2005) "The Portland Development Commission: Governance, Structure, and Process." *City Club of Portland Bulletin* 86:34, 1–92.

Dosi, G. (1988) "The Nature of Innovative Process." In G. Dosi, C. Freeman, R. Nelson, G. Silverberg and L. Soete, eds, *Technical Change and Economic Theory*. London: Pinter Publishers.

Drucker, P. and I. Nakauchi (1997) *Drucker on Asia*. Newton, MA: Butterworth-Heinemann.

Druckerman, P. (2000) "The Foreign Invasion: Brazil Once Hoped its Campinas Region Would be a Symbol of Home-grown High-tech Innovation; It Hasn't Turned Out That Way." *Wall Street Journal* 25 September, R21.

Duce, M. (2003) "Definitions of Foreign Direct Investment (FDI): A Methodological Note." http://www.bis.org/publ/cgfs22bde3.pdf

ECLAC, Economic Commission for Latin America & the Caribbean (2002) *Globalization y Desarrollo*. Santiago de Chile: CEPAL (Comisión Económica para América Latina y el Caribe).

Engelking, S. E. (1996) "Austin's Opportunity Economy: A Model for Collaborative Technology Development." New York: New York Academy of Sciences, April.

Ernst, D., T. Ganiatsos, and L. Mytelka, eds (1998) *Technological Capabilities and Export Success in Asia*. UK: Routledge.

Eto, H. (2005) "Obstacles To Emergence of High/New Technology Parks, Ventures and Clusters in Japan." *Technological Forecasting & Social Change* 72:3, 359–73.

Etzkowitz, H. and L. Leydesdorff, eds (1997) *Universities and the Global Knowledge Economy: A Triple Helix of University–Industry–Government Relations*. London: Cassell Academic.

Florida, R. (2000) *Competing in the Age of Talent: Quality of Place and the New Economy*. Pittsburgh: Carnegie Mellon University.

Foer, F. (2003) "Soccer vs. McWorld." *Foreign Policy* Jan–Feb, 32.

Fox, L. (2000) "Hatching New Companies." *UPSIDE* February, 145–52.

Francis, M. (1999) "Garage.Com Shops for Deal among Oregon's Entrepreneurial Elite." *The Oregonian* 29 November, D1.

Freeman, C. (1988) "Japan: A New National System of Innovation?" In G. Dosi, C. Freeman, R. Nelson, G. Silverberg, and L. Soete, eds, *Technical Change and Economic Theory*. London: Pinter.

Freeman, C. (1997) *Technology and Economic Performance: Lessons from Japan*. London: Pinter Publishers.

Friedman, T. L. (2005) *The World is Flat*. New York: Farrar, Straus and Giroux.

Fukuyama, F. (1992) *The End of History and the Last Man*. New York: The Free Press.

Fukuyama, F. (1995) *Trust: The Social Virtues & the Creation of Prosperity*. New York: The Free Press.

Galli, R. and M. Teubal (1997) "Paradigmatic Shifts in National Systems of Innovation." In C. Edquist, ed., *Systems of Innovation. Technologies, Institutions and Organizations*. London: Pinter.

General Informatics LLC (2003–04). *Technopolis Times* (web site). http://www.generalinformatics.com/technopolistimes.html

Gibson, D. V. and P. Conceição (2003) "Incubating and Networking Technology Commercialization Centers among Emerging, Developing, and Mature Technopoleis Worldwide." In Larisa V. Shavinina ed., *International Handbook on Innovation*. Elsevier Science Ltd., pp. 739–49. http://www.ic2.org/main.php?a=3&s=432002-05-15

Gibson, D. V., M. Cotrofeld and IC² Institute staff (2004) *Knowledge-Based Benchmarking for Belize Education, Science & Technology (BEST) Park*. Austin: IC² Institute, The University of Texas at Austin. http://www.ic2.org/publications/best.print.11.18.pdf

Gibson, D. V. and J. W. Dearing (1993) "Technopoleis: Themes and Conclusions." In Gibson D. V., G. Kozmetsky, and R. Smilor, eds, *The Technopolis Phenomenon: Smart Cities, Fast Systems, and Global Networks*. Lanham, MD: Rowman & Littlefield Publishing.

Gibson, D. V., G. Kozmetsky, and R. Smilor, eds (1993) *The Technopolis Phenomenon: Smart Cities, Fast Systems, and Global Networks*. Lanham, MD: Rowman & Littlefield Publishing.

Gibson, D. V., D. P. Rhi-Perez, M. Gipson, M. Cotrofeld, O. De Los Reyes, I. Rodriguez, R. Rodarte, A. Cox, M. Cunningham, and D. Houston (2002) *Cameron County / Matamoros at the Crossroads – Assets & Challenges for Accelerated Regional & Binational Development*. Austin: IC² Institute, University of Texas at Austin.

Gibson, D. V. and E. M. Rogers (1994) *R & D Collaboration on Trial: The Microelectronics and Computer Technology Corporation*. Cambridge, Massachusetts: Harvard Business School Press.

Gibson, D. V. and C. E. Stiles (1996) "Global Networked Entrepreneurship: Linking The World's Technoparks for Shared Prosperity at Home and Abroad." Austin: IC² Institute, University of Texas at Austin.

Gjerding, A. N. (1992) "A Closer Look at National Systems of Innovation." In B.-Å. Lundvall, ed., *National Systems of Innovation: Towards a Theory of Innovation and Interactive Learning*. London: Pinter Publishers.

Gladwell, M. (2000) *The Tipping Point: How Little Things Can Make a Big Difference*. Boston: Little, Brown.

Goldberg, C. (1999) "Across the US, Universities are Fueling High Tech Booms." *New York Times* 8 October, A1.

Goldgar, R., J. Orth, and F. Phillips, eds (1992) *Software Engineering in the 90s: Perspectives for Austin's Growth as a Software Center*. Austin: IC² Institute of The University of Texas at Austin and Austin Software Council, October.

Gottlieb, P. D. (1994) "Amenities as an Economic Development Tool: Is there Enough Evidence?" *Economic Development Quarterly* 8:3, 270–85.

Granstrand, O., L. Hakanson, and S. Sjolander, eds (1992) *Technology Management and International Business: Internationalisation of R&D and Technology*. Hoboken, NJ: John Wiley & Sons.

Gregersen, B. (1992) "The Public Sector as a Pacer in National Systems of Innovation." In B.-Å. Lundvall, ed., *National Systems of Innovation: Toward a Theory of Innovation and Interactive Learning*. London: Pinter Publishers.

Hall, J. (2000) "Presentation for the Meeting with Jim Coonan and Diane Vines." Portland, Oregon: Oregon University System, January.

Hamrin, C. L. (2003) "China's 10th National People's Congress: Promising Shared Prosperity and Good Governance under Party Rule." Washington

D.C.: Institute for Global Engagement, 4 April. http://www.globalengagement. org/issues/2003/04/NPC.htm

Hardison, Jr. O. B. (1989) *Disappearing Through the Skylight: Culture and Technology in the Twentieth Century*. New York: Viking, pp. 129–34; 139–40.

Harrington, P. (2000) "PSU Study: High Tech Here for Long Run." Portland, Oregon: *The Oregonian* Washington County Weekly section.

Hayhow, S., ed. (1996) *A Comprehensive Guide to Business Incubation*. Athens, Ohio: NBIA Publications.

Hernandez, R. (1998) "A Bachelor's Worth Drops a Few Degrees." Portland, Oregon: *The Oregonian* 11 June, p. A1.

Hotelling, H. (1929) "Stability in Competition." *Economic Journal* 39:1, 41–57.

IC^2 Institute (1990 – no author) *The Technopolis Phenomenon*, Austin: University of Texas at Austin.

James, J. (2002) *Technology, Globalization and Poverty*. Cheltenham, UK: Edward Elgar.

Jarret, J. E., M. Bettersworth, M. Gipson, and G. Sirilli (2002) "Accelerating Technology-Based Economic Development in the Concho Valley." Austin: IC^2 Institute. http://www.ic2.org/main.php?a=3&s=432002-05-15

Johnson, B. (1992) "Institutional Learning." In B.-Å. Lundvall, ed., *National Systems of Innovation: Towards a Theory of Innovation and Interactive Learning*. London: Pinter Publishers.

Johnson, B. and O. Segura-Bonilla (2001) "Innovation Systems and Developing Countries: Experiences from the SUDESCA Project" Danish Research Unit for Industrial Dynamics, DRUID Working Paper No. 01-12.

Johnson, S. (2001) *Emergence: The Connected Lives of Ants, Brains, Cities and Software*. New York: Scribner.

Joint Venture Silicon Valley (2002) *Perspectives on the Economy*. http://www. jointventure.org/siliconvalley2010/d2e.htm

Jones, S. D. (1999) "Oregon Makes Headway as Breeder of High-tech." *Wall Street Journal* 15 December, NW1.

Kahney, L. (2000) "A Capital Plan for College Ideas." *Wired.com*, 3 April.

Kalis, N. (©1997) *Equity and Royalty Agreements for Business Assistance Programs*. Athens, Ohio: National Business Incubation Association.

Kameoka, A. (2004) "Next-Generation Innovation Model and New-Type of Technologist 'Technoproducer.' " Tokyo: Graduate School of Knowledge Science, Japan Advanced Institute of Science and Technology (JAIST), 30 July. http://www.nus.edu.sg/nec/reeasia/PDF/REE%20Asia%202004%20% 20Akio%20Kameoka.pdf

Kawasaki, G. (1992) *Selling the Dream*. New York: Collins.

Kelly, J. (1999) "Filling in the Triangle: North Carolina's Tech Center Tries to Come Together." *Upside* December, 229–30.

Kodama, F. (1992) "Technology Fusion and the New R&D." *Harvard Business Review* July–August, 70–78.

Koh, W. T. H. and P. K. Wong (2005) "Competing at the Frontier: The Changing Role of Technology Policy in Singapore's Economic Strategy." *Technological Forecasting and Social Change* 72:3, March, 255–85.

Köhler, H. (2000) "In Search of Stability and Broadly-Shared Prosperity: Reform of the International Monetary System." Brussels: EU Parliamentary Committees. http://www.imf.org/external/np/speeches/2000/110700.htm

Kozmetsky, G. (1996) "Gaining Perspective." (Remarks to the Austin Technology Incubator 1996 graduation ceremony) Austin: IC^2 Institute, University of Texas at Austin, 26 September.

Kozmetsky, G. (1997) "Perspectives on Business and Emerging Trends for the 21st Century." Austin: IC^2 Institute. http://www.ic2.org/main.php?a=3&s=58

Kozmetsky, G., Jackson, M. L., and Boyd, A. M. (2001) "The EnterTech Project: Changing Learning and Lives." Austin: IC^2 Institute. http://www.ic2.org/main.php?a=3&s=432002-05-15

Kozmetsky, G., H. Matsumoto, and R. W. Smilor, eds (1988) *Pacific Cooperation and Development*. New York: Praeger Publishers.

Kozmetsky, G. and F. Williams (2003) *New Wealth: Commercialization of Science and Technology for Business and Economic Development*. New York: Praeger Publishers.

Krugman, P. (1991) "Increasing Returns and Economic Geography." *Journal of Political Economy* 99:31, 483.

Krugman, P. (1999) "Some Chaotic Thoughts on Regional Dynamics." Cambridge, Massachusetts: Massachusetts Institute of Technology, 10 March. http://web.mit.edu/krugman/www/temin.html.

Krugman, P. (2005) "French Family Values." *International Herald Tribune* 30–31 July, 4.

Kumar, Nagesh (2002) *Globalization and the Quality of Foreign Direct Investment*. Oxford: Oxford University Press.

Lee, M. M. (1999) *A Passion for Quality: The First Fifty-Five Years of Electro Scientific Industries, 1944–1999*. Portland, Oregon: Electro Scientific Industries.

Libicki, M. C. (1995) *Standards: The Rough Road to the Common Byte*. Washington, D.C.: Center for Advanced Concepts and Technology, Institute for National Strategic Studies, National Defense University.

Loewendahl, H. B. (2001) *Bargaining with Multinationals: The Investment of Siemens and Nissan in North East England*. London: Palgrave.

Lundvall, B.-Å. (1988) "Innovation as an Interactive Process: From User-Producer Interaction to National System of Innovation." In G. Dosi, C. Freeman, R. Nelson, G. Silverberg, and L. Soete, eds, *Technical Change and Economic Theory*. London: Pinter Publishers.

Lundvall, B.-Å., ed. (1992) *National Systems of Innovation: Towards a Theory of Innovation and Interactive Learning*. London: Pinter Publishers.

Lundvall B.-Å. and M. Tomlinson (2000) "On the convergence and divergence of national systems of innovation." Draft of contribution to special issue of Research Policy, 2 July. http://cc.msnscache.com/cache.aspx?q=2184227456685&lang=en-US&FORM=CVRE4 (last accessed 27 August 2005).

Lundvall, B.-Å., B. Johnson, E. S. Andersen, and B. Dalum (2002) "National Systems of Production, Innovation and Competence Building." *Research Policy* 31, 213–31.

Magnusson, P. (2000) "Burned by the WTO, Corporate America is Scrambling." *Business Week* 20 March, 118.

Magnusson, P. (2005) "States' Rights vs. Free Trade: As Trade Pacts Proliferate, States Start to Howl about Lost Sovereignty." *Business Week* 7 March.

Malecki, E. J. (1997a) "Network Models for Technology-Based Growth: Lessons from Europe and Japan." Austin: IC^2 Institute. http://www.ic2.org/main.php?a=3&s=58

Malecki, E. J. (1997b) *Technology and Economic Development.* Essex: Addison Wesley Longman.

Malerba, F., ed. (2004) *Sectoral Systems of Innovation.* New York: Cambridge University Press.

Malmberg, A., G. Sölvell, and I. Zander (1996) "Spatial Clustering, Local Accumulation of Knowledge and Firm Competitiveness." *Geografiska Annaler* 78B:2.

Mann, C. L. (2002) "Globalization and Shared Opportunities and Challenges for International Dialogue on Globalization and Shared Prosperity." Merida, Mexico, May. http://www.iie.com/publications/papers/mann0502.pdf

Manoa Innovation Center (undated) (Web site.) http://www.htdc.org/mic/mic.html

Marcelli, E., S. Baru, and D. Cohen (2000) "Planning for Shared Prosperity or Growing Inequality? An In-Depth Look at San Diego's Leading Industry Clusters." San Diego: Center on Policy Initiatives. http://www.onlinecpi.org/pdf/planning.pdf

Markusen, A., K. Chapple, G. Schrock, D. Yamamoto, and P. Yu (2001) "High-Tech and I-Tech: How Metros Rank and Specialize." Minneapolis, Minnesota: Project on Regional and Industrial Economics, Humphrey Institute of Public Affairs, University of Minnesota, August.

Marshall, R., (1998) "Back to Shared Prosperity." *Discovery* magazine. Austin: University of Texas at Austin. http://www.utexas.edu/opa/pubs/discovery/disc1998v15n2/disc_prosperity.html

Marshall, R., ed. (1999) *Back to Shared Prosperity: The Growing Inequality of Wealth and Income in America.* Armonk, NY: M. E. Sharpe Publishers.

Maskell, P. and A. Malmberg (1999) "Localized Learning and Industrial Competitiveness." *Cambridge Journal of Economics* 23:2, 167–85.

Mayer, H. (2002) "Evolution of the Silicon Forest." Portland, Oregon: Institute of Portland Metropolitan Studies, Portland State University, March.

Mayer, H. (2003) *Taking Root in the Silicon Forest: The Role of High Technology Firms as Surrogate Universities in Portland, Oregon.* Portland, Oregon: Urban Affairs. Portland State University.

McKinnion, S. and S. Hayhow (1998) *1998 State of the Business Incubation Industry.* Athens, Ohio: NBIA Publications.

McWhinney, W. (1992) *Paths of Change, Strategic Choices for Organizations and Society.* Los Angeles: Sage.

Mitroff, I. and H. A. Linstone (1995) *The Unbounded Mind: Breaking the Chains of Traditional Business Thinking.* New York: Oxford University Press.

Molnar, L., D. Adkins, B. Yolanda, D. Grimes, H. Sherman, and L. Tornatsky (1997) *Business Incubation Works.* Athens, Ohio: NBIA Publications.

Morisset, J. and K. Andrews-Johnson (2003) "The Effectiveness of Promotion Agencies at Attracting Foreign Direct Investment." Washington, D.C.: World Bank Publications, FIAS (Foreign Investment Advisory Service) Occasional papers no. 16, 1 September.

Mukherjee, A. (2005) "Can Singapore Become a Fun City?" Bloomberg News Service, 21 April. http://www.bloomberg.com/apps/news?pid=10000039&sid=aBfOvonc_Yr4&refer=columnist_mukherjee

Mytelka, L. (2000) "Local Systems of Innovation in a Globalized World Economy." *Industry and Innovation* 7:1, 15–32.

National Business Incubation Association (1995) "Industry Facts and Figures." March.

National Business Incubation Association (1996) *NBIA Review*. Athens, Ohio: NBIA, Jan/Feb.

Nelson, R. (1993) *National Systems of Innovation. A Comparative Study*. Oxford: Oxford University Press.

Nichols, J., (1994) *The Milagro Beanfield War*. New York: Henry Holt & Co.

Niosi, J., P. Saviotti, B. Bellon, and M. Crow (1993) "National Systems of Innovation: In Search of a Workable Concept." *Technology in Society* 15, 207–27.

Nishiyama, H. (1999) "Japanese Entrepreneurship and Opportunities for Partnering." Austin: IC² Institute. http://www.ic2.org/main.php?a=3&s=58

Nocera, N. (2005) "Former Intel Chief Boots up Version 2.0 of his Life." *International Herald Tribune* 30–31 July, 14.

North, D. C. (1990) *Institutions, Institutional Change and Economic Performance*. Cambridge: Cambridge University Press.

North, D. C. (1995) "The Adam Smith Address: Economic Theory in a Dynamic Economic World." *Business Economics* 7.

OECD (1997) *National Systems of Innovation*. Paris: OECD.

Ohmae, K. (1996) *The End of the Nation State: The Rise of Regional Economies*. New York: The Free Press.

OregonBusinessPlan.org (2005) "Oregon Business Plan Update: Oregon Business Plan Initiatives Move Forward in Legislature." http://www. Oregon BusinessPlan.org.

Oregonian (2002) Interview with Howard H. Stevenson.

Organization of American States (2002) "FTAA – Committee of Government Representatives on the Participation of Civil Society: Cover Sheet for Open Invitation Contributions." http://:www.sice.oas.org/ftaa/civsoc/Quito/ 50eng.doc

Ormerod, P. (1999) *Butterfly Economics: A New General Theory of Social and Economic Behavior*. New York: Pantheon.

Oyeyinka, B. O. (2002) "Manufacturing Response in a National System of Innovation: Evidence from the Brewing Firms in Nigeria." Maastricht: UNU/INTECH Discussion Paper #2002–3.

Peirce, N. (2003) "For Cities, Population Growth Isn't Enough." Washington, D.C.: Washington Post Writers Group.

Phillips, F., moderator (1990) "The US-Mexico Free Trade Agreement." Austin: IC² Institute Policy Roundtable, University of Texas at Austin, September.

Phillips, F. (1992) "Incubator Activities and the University-Incubator Relationship." Tokyo: Presentation to the Japan Research Institute, June.

Phillips, F. (1995) "ParcBIT and Balearic Economic Development." In A. Font ed., *ParcBIT: Toward New Ways of Living and Working in the 21st Century*. Palma de Mallorca, Spain: Consellería d'Hisenda y Economia, Govern Balear.

Phillips, F. (1997) "A Framework for Distance Learning in a Graduate Management School." Portland, Oregon: Management in Science and Technology Dept., Oregon Graduate Institute of Science and Technology, working paper.

Phillips, F. (1999) "Trade, Corporatism, Clusters, and Japan as Bellwether." Austin: IC² Institute, University of Texas at Austin, February, working paper.

Phillips, F. (2000) "The Battle in Seattle – A View from Tokyo." In F. Phillips, *The Conscious Manager*. Beaverton, Oregon: General Informatics LLC.

Phillips, F. (2001) *Market-Oriented Technology Management: Innovating for Profit in Entrepreneurial Times*. Heidelberg: Springer-Verlag.

Phillips, F. (2004a) "New Directions for Technology-Based Economic Development: Evidence from Austin, Portland, and Beyond." In E. Kaynak and T. Harcar, eds, *Advances in Global Management Development* (Proceedings of the 2004 Congress of the International Management Development Association), pp. 677–84.

Phillips, F. (2004b) "Trading Down: The Intellectual Poverty of the New FTAs." *Technological Forecasting & Social Change* 71:8, October, 865–76.

Phillips, F. (2005a) "Toward an Intellectual and Theoretical Foundation for 'Shared Prosperity.' " Maastricht: Maastricht School of Management. To appear in *Systemic Practice and Action Research*.

Phillips, F. (2005b) "Sustainability of Regional Initiatives for Technology Entrepreneurship." Barcelona: EFMD 35th EISB Conference "Sustaining the Entrepreneurial Spirit over Time," IESE Business School, University of Navarra, 11–14 September.

Phillips, F. and D. Drake, eds (1999) *Navigating Complexity: The Future of Knowledge and Learning in Organizations*. Special Issue, *Technological Forecasting & Social Change* 64:1, May 2000.

Phillips, F. and N. Kim (1996) "Implications of Chaos Research for New Product Forecasting." *Technological Forecasting & Social Change* 53:3, 239–61.

Phillips, F., A. Roberts, and M. Burningham, eds (1999) *Entrepreneurship and Intrapreneurship for Economic Growth and Quality of Life in Oregon and Southern Washington: International Benchmarks*. Beaverton, Oregon: Oregon Graduate Institute of Science & Technology.

Phillips, H. (1998) "Worldwide Standards and Trade: The Players and Their Networks." *APPLIANCE* October, 72–75.

Porter, M. E. (1990) *The Competitive Advantage of Nations*. New York: Free Press.

Porter, M. E. (1998) "Clusters and the New Economics of Competition." *Harvard Business Review* November–December, 77–90.

Prasso, S. (2000) "Can a State Have Its Own Foreign Policy?" *Business Week* 20 March, 130.

Press, E. and J. Washburn (2000) "The Kept University." *Atlantic Monthly* March, 39–54.

Progressive Policy Institute (undated) "Foreign Direct Investment is on the Rise around the World." http://www.neweconomyindex.org/section1_page04.html

Putnam, R. D. (2003) *Better Together: Restoring the American Community*. New York: Simon & Schuster.

Raffalovich, A. (1996) "Austin High-Tech Industry Leader Survey Summary." Austin: Austin Software Council.

Reuters/VNS (2005) "Bad Education Leaves US, Britain with Worst Social Inequality: Study." Ho Chi Minh City: *Viet Nam News* 26 April, 22.

Rivera, D. (2001) "High-tech Pushes Austin's City Limits." Portland, Oregon: *The Oregonian*. 1 April, D1.

Romer, P. M. (1993) "Implementing a National Technology Strategy with Self-Organizing Industry Investment Boards." *Brookings Papers on Economic Activity: Microeconomics* 2, 345.

Romer, P. M. (1998) "Innovation: The New Pump of Growth." *Blueprint: Ideas for a New Century*. Washington, D.C.: Democratic Leadership Council, Winter. http://www.dlc.org

Sachs, J. (1998) "Global Capitalism: Making it work." *The Economist*. http://www2.cid.harvard.edu/hiidpapers/econo912.pdf

Smilor, R., M. Wakelin, and G. Kozmetsky (undated) "The Development of a Bi-National Region: Smart Infrastructures and Economic Development." Austin: IC² Institute. http://www.ic2.org/main.php?a=3&s=432002-05-15

Sölvell, Ö., G. Lindqvist, and C. Ketels (2003) *The Cluster Initiative Greenbook*. Gothenburg, Sweden: Ivory Tower.

Staff and wire reports (2004) "World Trade Organization Rejects Appeal of Offshore Tax Shelter Ban." *The Oregonian* 24 February, 2000, B1.

Tatsuno, S. (1986) *The Technopolis Strategy: Japan, High Technology, and the Control of the Twenty-First Century*. Englewood Cliffs, New Jersey: Prentice-Hall/ Aperture.

Teece, D. J. (1988) "Technological Change and the Nature of the Firm." In G. Dosi, C. Freeman, R. Nelson, G. Silverberg, and L. Soete, eds, *Technical Change and Economic Theory*. London: Pinter Publishers, pp. 256–94.

Thompson, G., and S. Thore (©1992) *Computational Economics: Economic Modeling with Optimization Software*. San Francisco, California: The Scientific Press.

Tice, C. (1999) "UW Incubator to be Learning Center for Students, Faculty." *Puget Sound Business Journal*. http://www.bizjournals.com/seattle/stories/1999/

Tobias, A. J. (1997) MOT is hot; MBA is not. *OEM Magazine* 11 January.

Tornatzky, L. G., Y. Batts, N. McCrea, M. Lewis, and L. Quittman (1996) *The Art & Craft of Technology Business Incubation*. Athens, Ohio: Southern Technology Council and NBIA publications.

UNCTAD (2002) "UNCTAD Workshop on Efficient and Transparent Investment Promotion Practices: The Case of LDCs." Geneva, 6–7 June.

UNCTAD (2004a) "Exchanging Best Practices in Foreign Investment Promotion." Waipa – The World Association of Investment Promotion Agencies – Issues in brief No. 2, UNCTAD/ISS/MISC/2004/2, 26 February. http://www.unctad.org/ Templates/Download.asp?docID=4472&intItemID=2068&lang=1

UNCTAD (2004b) "The Shift toward Services: World Investment Report 2004." www.unctad.org/en/docs/wir2004ch1_en.pdf

US Bureau of the Census (2000) *2000 Census: US Municipalities Over 50,000: Ranked by 2000 Population*. Demographia.com.

Weissbourd, R. and C. Berry (2003) *The Changing Dynamics of Urban America: Executive Preview*. Boston, Massachusetts: CEOs for Cities.

Wells, L. T. and Wint, A. G. (2001) "Marketing a Country: Promotion as a Tool for Attracting Foreign Investment." FIAS Occasional Papers number 1, World Bank Publications.

Western Governors' Association (1998) http://www.westgov.org/wga/publicat/ maiweb.htm, 1998.

Woolcock, M. (1998) "Social Capital and Economic Development: Toward a Theoretical Synthesis and Policy Framework." *Theory and Society* 27, 151–208.

Wong, D. D. (1995) "Comparative Analysis of Hi-tech Entrepreneurship Activity and its Supporting Environment between Portland, Oregon, and Vancouver, British Columbia." Beaverton, Oregon: Oregon Graduate Institute of Science and Technology, December.

World Bank (2003) Foreign Investment Advisory Service (FIAS) Policy Research Working Paper 3028.

World Technopolis Association. http://www.wtanet.org

World Trade Organization (1997) "Open Trade and Investment Lead to Growth in Malaysia: Some Measures Hamper Efficient Use Of Capital." *PRESS/TPRB/67, 1* December. http://www.wto.org/wto/reviews/tprb67.htm

Xirogiannis, G. and M. Glykas (2004) "Fuzzy Cognitive Maps in Business Analysis and Performance-Driven Change." *IEEE Transactions in Engineering Management* August, 51:3, 334–51.

Yim, S.-J. (1998) "Software Firm, School Link Up to Turn Computer into Campus." *The Oregonian* 30 May, E1.

Zachary, G. P. (2000) "Location, Location: A Leading Urbanist Argues That When It Comes to Innovation, Place Really Does Matter." *Wall Street Journal* 25 September, R11.

Zenios, S. (1992) "Parallel Computing." *OR/MS Today* August, 44–9.

Bibliography

Abbott, C. (2000) "The Capital of Good Planning: Metropolitan Portland since 1970." In R. Fishman, ed., *The American Planning Tradition*. Baltimore: Johns Hopkins University Press, pp. 241–61.

Accordino, J. J. (1994) "Evaluating Economic Strategies." *Economic Development Quarterly* 8:2, 220.

Agiplan (1999) *Analysis of Transnational Technology Networking between Existing Clusters of SMEs and One or More Technology Poles*. Mülheim an der Ruhr: European Commission Directorate General Enterprise.

Araki, K. (2000) Technological Innovation, National Urban Policy and Local Development: Policy Implications of the Concept of Technopole and Japan's Technopolis Programme for Developing Countries. London: University College. http://www.ucl.ac.uk/DPU/ publications/working%20papers%20pdf/ wp110.pdf

Arthur, B. (1990) "Silicon Valley Locational Clusters: When Do Increasing Returns Imply Monopoly?" *Mathematical Social Sciences* 19: 235–51.

Audretsch, D. B. (1998) "Agglomeration and the Location of Innovative Activity." *Oxford Review of Economic Policy* 14:2,18–30.

Audretsch, D. B. and M. P. Feldman (1996) "Knowledge Spillovers and the Geography of Innovation and Production." *American Economic Review* 86: 630–40.

Barabasi, A.-L. (2003) *Linked: How Everything Is Connected to Everything Else and What It Means*. New York: Plume.

Baron, S., J. Field, *et al.*, eds (2001) *Social Capital: Critical Perspectives*. Oxford: Oxford University Press.

Biswas, R. R. (2004) "Making a Technopolis in Hyderabad, India: The Role of Government IT Policy." *Technological Forecasting & Social Change* 71:8, 823–35.

Botkin, J. (1988) "Route 128: Its History and Destiny." In R.W., Smilor D. V. Gibson, and G. Kozmetsky, eds, *Creating the Technopolis: Linking Technology Commercialization and Economic Development*. Cambridge, MA: Ballinger.

Braczyk, H. J., P. Cooke, *et al.*, eds (1998) *Regional Innovation Systems: The Role of Governance in a Globalized World*. London: UCL Press Limited.

Bresnahan, T., A. Gambardella, *et al.* (2001) " 'Old Economy' Inputs for 'New Economy' Outcomes: Cluster Formation in the New Silicon Valleys." *Industrial and Corporate Change* 10:4, 835–60.

Bresnahan, T., T. Morant, *et al.* (2001) *Northern Virginia's High-tech Corridor and the Economics of Regional Development*. Stanford, CA: Stanford University, Stanford Institute for Economic Policy Research.

Butler, J. and G. S. Hansen (1991) "Network Evolution, Entrepreneurial Success and Regional Development." *Entrepreneurship and Regional Development* 3, 1–6.

Callon, S. (1995) *Divided Sun: MITI and the Breakdown of Japanese High-Tech Industrial Policy, 1975–1993*. Stanford, CA: Stanford University Press.

Caniels, M. C. J. (1996) "Regional Differences in Technology: Theory and Empirics." Maastricht: Maastricht Economic Research Institute on Innovation and Technology (MERIT), May.

Caniels, M. C. J. (1997) "The Geographic Distribution of Patents and Value Added Across European Regions." Maastricht: Maastricht Economic Research Institute on Innovation and Technology (MERIT), August. http://meritbbs.unimaas. nl/rmpdf/rm98_004.pdf

Capell, K. (2002) "Clouds Over Silicon Glen: Foreigners Who Spawned a Tech Boom Are Pulling Out." *Business Week*. September 2, 49. http://www.business-week.com/magazine/content/02_35/b3797067.htm

Center on Urban and Metropolitan Policy (2001) *Signs of Life: The Growth of Bio Centers in the US*. Washington, D.C.: Brookings Institution.

Cisneros, H. G. (1995) *Urban Entrepreneurialism and National Economic Growth*. Washington, D.C.: US Department of Housing & Urban Development.

Conceicao, P., D. V. Gibson, M. V. Heitor, G. Sirilli, and F. Veloso, eds (2002) *Knowledge for Inclusive Development*. Westport, Connecticut: Quorum.

Cooke, P. and K. Morgan (1998) *The Associational Economy: Firms, Regions, and Innovation*. Oxford: Oxford University Press.

Cortright, J., and H. Mayer (2001) "High Tech Specialization: A Comparison of High Technology Centers." Washington, D.C.: Brookings Institution. http://www.brookings.edu/es/urban/cortright/specialization.pdf

Dasgupta, P. and I. Serageldin, eds (2000) *Social Capital: A Multifaceted Perspective*. Washington, D.C.: World Bank.

De fontenay, C. and E. Cannel (2001) *Israel's Silicon Wadi: The Forces behind Cluster Formation*. Stanford, California: SIEPR, Stanford University.

Devol, R. (2002) "The Economics of Place." *Milken Institute Review: Journal of Economic Policy* Q1 88–93.

DeVol, R. C. (1999) *America's High Tech Economy: Growth, Development and Risk for Metropolitan Areas*. Santa Monica, California: Milken Institute.

Dewar, M. E. (1998) "Why State and Local Economic Development Programs Cause so Little Economic Development." *Economic Development Quarterly* 12:1, 88–93.

Doctor, C., M. Albers, A. M. Claire, L. Coward, V. Faatz, P. Fellner, W. Fickler, L.-E. Jenssen, K. Krause, D. Mandell, P. Manson, P. Meyer, F. Phillips, and S. Thomas (2005) "The Portland Development Commission: Governance, Structure, and Process." *City Club of Portland Bulletin* 86:34, 88–93.

Dodds, G. B. and C. E. Wollner (1990) *The Silicon Forest: High Tech in the Portland Area*. Portland, OR: The Oregon Historical Society.

Dye, R. F. and D. F. Merriman (2000) "The Effects of Tax Increment Financing on Economic Development." *Journal of Urban Economics* 47:2, 306–28.

Ellen, I. G. and A. E. Schwartz (2000) "No Easy Answers: Cautionary Notes for Competitive Cities." *Brookings Review* 18:3, 42–45.

Eto, H. (2005) "Obstacles to Emergence of High/New Technology Parks, Ventures and Clusters in Japan." *Technological Forecasting & Social Change* 72:3, 359–73.

Feldman, M. (1994) "The University and Economic Development: The Case of Johns Hopkins University and Baltimore." *Economic Development Quarterly* 8:1, 67–76.

Fogarty, M. S. and A. K. Sinha (1999) "Why Older Regions Can't Generalize from Route 128 and Silicon Valley: University-Industry Relationships and Regional Innovation Systems." In R. Florida, ed., *Industrializing Knowledge: University-Industry Linkages in Japan and the United States*. Cambridge, MA: MIT Press.

Font, A. (1995) *ParcBIT: toward new ways of living and working in the 21st century*. Palma de Mallorca, Spain: Consellería d'Hisenda y Economia, Govern Balear.

Fountain, J. E. (1998) "Social Capital: Its Relationship to Innovation in Science and Technology." *Sci. Public Policy* 25:3, 103–15.

Fukuyama, F. (1995) *Trust: The Social Virtues & the Creation of Prosperity*. New York: The Free Press.

General Informatics LLC (2003–04). *Technopolis Times* (web site). http://www.generalinformatics.com/technopolistimes.html

Gibson, D. V. and G. D. Brazier (2001) *Assets & Challenges for Accelerated Technology-Based Growth in Hidalgo County*. Austin: IC^2 Institute, University of Texas at Austin.

Gibson, D. V., and P. Conceição (2003) "Incubating and Networking Technology Commercialization Centers among Emerging, Developing, and Mature Technopoleis Worldwide." In Larisa V. Shavinina, ed., *International Handbook on Innovation*. Elsevier Science Ltd., pp 739–49. http://www.ic2.org/main.php?a=3&s=432002-05-15

Gibson, D. V. and G. Gurr (2001) *"Quicklook" Assesment of Greater Adelaide's Assets & Challenges for Accelerated Technology-Based Growth (Part A)*. Austin: IC^2 Institute, University of Texas at Austin.

Gibson, D. V., G. Kozmetsky, *et al.*, eds (1993) *The Technopolis Phenomenon: Smart Cities, Fast Systems, and Global Network*. Savage, Maryland: Rowman & Littlefield Publishing.

Gibson, D. V., D. P. Rhi-Perez, *et al.* (2002) *Cameron County / Matamoros at the Crossroads – Assets & Challenges for Accelerated Regional & Binational Development*. Austin: IC^2 Institute, University of Texas at Austin.

Gibson, D. V. and E. M. Rogers (1994) *R & D Collaboration on Trial: The Microelectronics and Computer Technology Corporation*. Cambridge, MA: Harvard Business School Press.

Gladwell, M. (2000) *The Tipping Point: How Little Things Can Make a Big Difference*. Boston: Little, Brown.

Goldberg, C. (1999) "Across the US, Universities are Fueling High Tech Booms." *New York Times*. October 8, A1.

Goto, K., D. V. Gibson, *et al.*, eds (1998) *The Science City in a Global Context*. Austin: IC^2 Institute, University of Texas at Austin.

Greenstone, M. and E. Moretti (2003) "Bidding for Industrial Plants: Does Winning a Million Dollar Plant Increase Welfare?" Working Paper: Massachusetts Institute of Technology and University of California at Los Angeles.

Grudkova, V. (2001) *The Technology Economy: Why Do Tech Companies Go Where They Go?* Washington, D.C.: EDA National Forum.

Guinnane, T. W., W. A. Sundstrom, *et al.*, eds (2003) *History Matters: Essays on Economic Growth, Technology, and Demographic Change*. Stanford, CA: Stanford University Press.

Hall, P. (1998) *Cities and Civilization*. New York: Pantheon.

Hefner, R. W., ed. (1998) *Market Cultures: Society and Morality in the New Asian Capitalisms*. Boulder: Westview Press.

Hilpert, U., ed. (1991) *Regional Innovation and Decentralization: High Tech Industry and Government Policy*. London: Rutledge.

IC^2 Institute and Angelou Economics (2002) *Accelerating Technology-Based Economic Growth & Entrepreneurship in The Greater Waco Region*. Austin: IC^2 Institute, University of Texas at Austin.

Jaffe, A., M. Trajtenberg, and R. Henderson (1993) "Geographic Localization of Knowledge Spillovers as Evidenced by Patent Citations." *Quarterly Journal of Economics* 108:3, 577–98.

Jarret, J. E., M. Bettersworth, M. Gipson, and G. Sirilli (2002) "Accelerating Technology-Based Economic Development in The Concho Valley." Austin: IC² Institute. http://www.ic2.org/main.php?a=3&s=432002-05-15

Joint Venture: Silicon Valley Network (1995) *The Joint Venture Way: Lessons for Regional Rejuvenation.* San Jose, CA: Joint Venture Silicon Valley.

Joint Venture: Silicon Valley Network (2001) *Next Silicon Valley: Riding the Waves of Innovation.* San Jose, CA: Joint Venture Silicon Valley. www.jointventure.org.

Kassicieh, S. K. (2005) "Statistical Analysis of Variables Affecting Technology-Based Economic Development." *Proceedings of PICMET'05, Portland International Conference on Management of Engineering and Technology,* Portland, OR: Portland State University, July 31–August 4.

Kelly, K. (2003) "Technopolis: Dreaming the Regional Landscape." *Tech Valley Times.* Albany, New York.

Kenney, M., ed. (2000) *Understanding Silicon Valley: The Anatomy of an Entrepreneurial Region.* Stanford, CA: Stanford University Press.

Kimbrough, S. O. and F. H. Murphy (2005) "A Study of the Philadelphia Knowledge Economy." *Interfaces* 35:3, May–June, 248–59.

Kline, M. (1994) "Tiny Business Enclave in Italy Stares down Adversity." *Wall Street Journal.* August 18, B2.

Knack, S. and P. Keefer (1997) "Does Social Capital Have Economic Payoff? A Cross-Country Investigation." *Quarterly Journal of Economics* 112:4, 1251–88.

Koh, W. T. H. and P. K. Wong (2005) "Competing at the Frontier: The Changing Role of Technology Policy in Singapore's Economic Strategy." *Technological Forecasting and Social Change* 72:3, March, 255–85.

Kozmetsky, G. (2003) "Foreword: Perspectives on Creating Value Through Global Knowledge Partnerships." In D. V. Gibson, C. Stolp, P. Conceição, and M. V. Heitor, eds, *Systems and Policies for the Global Learning Economy.* Westport, Connecticut: Praeger, pp. ix–xiii.

Krueger, A. B. (2003) "Economic Scene: A Study Finds Benefits for Localities that Offer Subsidies to Attract Companies." *New York Times.* December 11. http://www.irs.princeton.edu/krueger/EconomicScene.html

Krumme, G. (undated) *Economic Geography Glossary,* Seattle: University of Washington. http://faculty.washington.edu/krumme/gloss/u.html

Kunstler, J. H. (1993) *The Geography of Nowhere.* New York: Simon & Schuster.

Landry, R., N. Amara, *et al.* (2002) "Does Social Capital Determine Innovation? To What Extent?" *Technological Forecasting & Social Change* 69:7, 681–701.

Leach, P. (1998) "Sustaining the Dynamic Growth of Technology-Dependent Communities." *Economic & Technology Development Journal of Canada* (online). http://www.ecdevjournal.com/pubs/1998/art011_98.htm

Leamer, E. and M. Storper (2001) *The Economic Geography of the Internet Age.* Cambridge, MA: National Bureau of Economic Research.

Lee, C.-M., W. F. Miller, *et al.,* eds (2000) *The Silicon Valley Edge: A Habitat for Innovation and Entrepreneurship.* Stanford, CA: Stanford University Press.

Leslie, S. W. and R. H. Kargon (1996) "Selling Silicon Valley: Frederick Terman's Model for Regional Advantage." *Business History Review* 70, 435–72.

Lesser, E. L. (2000) *Knowledge and Social Capital: Foundations and Applications.* Boston: Butterworth-Heinemann.

Lewis, S. (1922) *Babbitt.* Signet Classics Reissue edition.

Lind, M. (2003) *Made in Texas: George W. Bush and the Southern Takeover of American Politics.* New York: Basic Books.

Malecki, E. J. (1997) "Network Models for Technology-Based Growth: Lessons from Europe and Japan." Austin: IC^2 Institute. http://www.ic2.org/main. php?a=3&s=58

Malecki, E. J. (1997) *Technology and Economic Development.* Essex: Addison Wesley Longman.

Malmberg, A., G. Sölvell, *et al.* (1996) "Spatial Clustering, Local Accumulation of Knowledge and Firm Competitiveness." *Geografiska Annaler* 78B:2.

Markusen, A., P. Hall, *et al.* (1991) *The rise of the gunbelt: the military remapping of industrial America.* New York: Oxford University Press.

Marshall, A. (2000) *How Cities Work: Suburbs, Sprawl, and the Road Not Taken.* Austin: University of Texas Press.

Maskell, P. and A. Malmberg (1999) "Localized Learning and Industrial Competitiveness." *Cambridge Journal of Economics* 23:2, 167–85.

Mayer, H. (2003) *Taking Root in the Silicon Forest: The Role of High Technology Firms as Surrogate Universities in Portland, Oregon.* Portland, OR: Urban Affairs. Portland State University.

McKendrick, D. G., R. F. Joner, *et al.* (2000) *From Silicon Valley to Singapore: Location and Competitive Advantage in the Hard Disk Drive Industry.* Stanford: Stanford University Press.

Mukherjee, A. (2005) "Can Singapore Become a Fun City?" Bloomberg News Service, April 21. http://www.bloomberg.com/apps/news?pid=10000039&sid= aBfOvonc_Yr4&refer=columnist_mukherjee

Nichols, J. (1994) *The Milagro Beanfield War.* New York: Henry Holt & Co.

Northern Virginia Institute (1993) *Technology and Regional Economic Development.* Fairfax, VA: George Mason University.

OregonBusinessPlan.org (2005) "Oregon Business Plan Update: Oregon Business Plan Initiatives Move Forward in Legislature." http://www. OregonBusinessPlan.org

Park, P. (1994) "Almost Austin? Knoxville hopes to reach high-tech potential." Knoxville, Tenn.: *The Knoxville News-Sentinel* 7.

Peirce, N. (2003) "For Cities, Population Growth Isn't Enough." Washington, D.C.: Washington Post Writers Group.

Peterson, C., S. Maier, *et al.* (1993) *Learned Helplessness: A Theory for the Age of Personal Control.* New York: Oxford University Press.

Phillips, F. (1995) "ParcBIT and Balearic Economic Development." In A. Font, ed., *ParcBIT: toward new ways of living and working in the 21st century.* Palma de Mallorca, Spain: Consellería d'Hisenda y Economia, Govern Balear.

Phillips, F. (2002) "Oregon's Lack of Investment Means We're Behind." Portland, OR: *Portland Business Journal.* Op Ed page.

Phillips, F. (2003) "Clusters Are Not Enough." (unpublished presentation) Portland International Conference on Management of Engineering and Technology, July.

Phillips, F. (2004) "New Directions for Technology-Based Economic Development: Evidence from Austin, Portland, and Beyond." In E. Kaynak and T. Harcar, eds, *Advances in Global Management Development* (Proceedings of the 2004 Congress of the International Management Development Association), pp. 677–84.

Phillips, F. (2005) "Toward an Intellectual and Theoretical Foundation for 'Shared Prosperity.' " Maastricht: Maastricht School of Management. To appear in *Systemic Practice and Action Research.*

Phillips, F. (2006) *Social Culture & High Tech Economic Development: The Technopolis Columns.* London: Palgrave.

Phillips, F., A. Roberts, and M. Burningham, eds (1999) *Entrepreneurship and Intrapreneurship for Economic Growth and Quality of Life in Oregon and Southern Washington: International Benchmarks.* Beaverton, OR: Oregon Graduate Institute of Science & Technology.

Phillips, F., B. Vallejo, and P. Mhondo (2005) *A Taxonomy of Technology-Based Economic Development Initiatives.* Maastricht: Maastricht School of Management.

Poner, M. E. (undated). *Clusters of Innovation: Regional Foundations of US Competitiveness.* Washington DC: Council on Competitiveness.

Porter, M. E. (1998) "Clusters and the New Economics of Competition." *Harvard Business Review* November–December: 77–90.

Porter, M. (2000) "Location, Competition and Economic Development: Local Clusters in a Global Economy." *Economic Development Quarterly* 14:1, 15–34.

Putnam, R. D. (2003) *Better Together: Restoring the American Community.* New York: Simon & Schuster.

Rabinovitch, J. and J. Leitman (1996) "Urban Planning in Curitiba." *Scientific American*, March, 46–53.

Rogers, E. M. and J. K. Larsen (1984) *Silicon Valley Fever: Growth of High-Tech Culture.* New York: Basic Books.

Rosenberg, N. (1998) "Knowledge and Innovation for Economic Development: Should Universities be Economic Institutions?" Lisbon, Portugal: Second International Conference on Technology Policy and Innovation.

Rout, L., ed. (2000) "Tapping Into Tomorrow." *Wall Street Journal* Special Section, September 26, R1–R26.

Rubin, H. J. (1988) "Shoot Anything that Flies; Claim Anything that Falls: Conversations with Economic Development Practitioners." *Economic Development Quarterly* 2, 236–51.

Ruttan, V. W. (2000) *Technology, Growth, and Development.* New York: Oxford University Press.

Sabel, C. (1992) "Studied Trust: Building New Forms of Cooperation in a Volatile Economy." In F. Pyke and W. Sengenberger, eds, *Industrial Districts and Local Economic Regeneration.* Geneva: International Institute for Labor Studies, pp. 215–50.

Sabel, C. (1994) "Flexible Specialisation and the Re-emergence of Regional Economies." In A. Amin, ed., *Post-Fordism: A Reader.* Oxford: Blackwell Publishers, pp. 101–56.

Sassen, S., ed. (2002) *Global Networks, Linked Cities.* London: New York: Routledge.

Savage, C. (2004) "Swedish Biotech Flourishes with Initiatives & VC." *Genetic Engineering News* 24: 8–14.

Saxenian, A. (1988) "The Cheshire Cat's Grin: Innovation and Regional Development in England." *Technology Review*, February/March: 67–75.

Saxenian, A. (1994) *Regional Advantage: Culture and Competition in Silicon Valley and Route 128.* Cambridge, MA: Harvard University Press.

Saxenian, A. (1994) "Lessons from Silicon Valley." *Technology Review* 97:5, 42–51.

Saxenian, A. (2001) *Taiwan's Hsinchu Region: Imitator and Partner for Silicon Valley.* Stanford California: Stanford Institute for Economic Policy Research (SIEPR), Stanford University.

Scott, A. J. (1993) *Technopolis: High-Technology Industry and Regional Development in Southern California.* Berkeley: University of California Press.

Scott, A. J. (2001) *Global City-Regions: Trends, Theory, Policy.* New York: Oxford University Press.

Shavinina, L. V., ed. (2004) *Silicon Valley North: A High-Tech Cluster of Innovation and Entrepreneurship.* Oxford: Elsevier.

Siebert, H., ed. (1997) *Towards a New Global Framework for High-Technology Competition.* Tubingen: J. C. B. Mohr.

Smilor, R. W., D. V. Gibson, and G. Kozmetsky, eds (1988) *Creating the Technopolis: Linking Technology Commercialization and Economic Development.* Cambridge, Massachusetts: Ballinger.

Smilor, R. W., G. Kozmetsky, *et al.* (1988) "Technology and Economic Development in the Modern Technopolis." *Technology in Society* 10: 433–45.

Smith Jr., D. and R. Gleeson (1997) "Commentary on the Role of Public Universities in Regional Economic Development." In R. Mier, ed., *Dilemmas of Urban Economic Development.* Thousand Oaks, California: Sage Publications.

Sölvell, Ö., G. Lindqvist, *et al.* (2003) *The Cluster Initiative Greenbook.* Stockholm: Ivory Tower AB: 94.

Stough, R. R. (2003) "Strategic Management of Places and Policy." *Annals of Regional Science* 37:2, 179–202.

Sung, T. K., D. V. Gibson, *et al.* (undated) "Characteristics of Technology Transfer in Business Ventures: The Case of Daejon, Korea." Austin: IC^2 Institute working paper, University of Texas at Austin.

Swann, G. M. P., M. Prevezer, *et al.*, eds (1998) *The Dynamics of Industrial Clustering.* Oxford: Oxford University Press.

Tallman, S., M. Jenkins, *et al.* (2004) "Knowledge, Clusters, and Competitive Advantage." *Academy of Management Review* 29:2, 258–71.

Tatsuno, S. (1986) *The Technopolis Strategy: Japan, High Technology, and the Control of the Twenty-First Century.* Englewood Cliffs, New Jersey: Prentice-Hall/Aperture.

Wallstein, S. (2001) *The Role of Government in Regional Technology Development: The Effects of Public Venture Capital and Science Parks.* Stanford, CA: Stanford Institute for Economic Policy.

Walshok, M. L. (1995) *Knowledge without Boundaries: What America's Research Universities Can Do for the Economy, the Workplace, and the Community.* San Franciso: Jossey-Bass.

Walshok, M. L. (1997) "Expanding Roles for Research Universities in Regional Economic Development." *New Directions for Higher Education* 97: 17–26.

Weissbourd, R. and C. Berry (2003) *The Changing Dynamics of Urban America: Executive Preview.* Boston, MA: CEOs for Cities.

The White House (1995) *Technology and Economic Growth: Producing Real Results for the American People.* Washington DC: The White House.

Wolkfoff, M. J. (1985) "Chasing a Dream: The Use of Tax Abatements to Spur Urban Economic Development." *Urban Studies* 22: 305–15.

Worthen, B. (2005) "Why George Bush Needs a Technology Czar." *CIO* Magazine. http://www.cio.com/archive/041505/policy.html

Index

3-dimensional printing, 157
3M Corp., 129

Aalborg University, 81, 246
Aalbu, Jarl, 21
Academic accreditation, 95, 101
Accenture Ltd., 131
Accountability, 56, 223–5
adidas, 113
Advanced Micro Devices, xii
Advantage Austin marketing
 program, 65
Advertising, 6, 145, 188, 190–92,
 215, 241
Affirmative inquiry, 55
Afghanistan, 50
Africa, 22, 33, 41, 59, 239
AIDS, xii, 57, 59, 60, 101, 144, 221
Alaska, 85
Albuquerque, 198
All Russian Institute of Experimental
 Physics, 203
Alliances, 6, 10, 23–4, 32, 35, 40, 46,
 52–3,76, 97, 127, 171, 176, 226,
 230, 235
Almaty, Kazakhstan, 39
Amazon.com, 46
American Airlines, 207
American Electronics Association, 24,
 79, 82
Amman, Jordan, 39
Angel capital, 6, 8, 141, 178, 180
Angelou Economic Advisors, 66
Angelou, Angelos, 18, 21, 129
Ants, 112
Antwerp, 6
Apana, James, 178
APEC, xii, 30, 33
Apple Computer Corp., 204
Applied Materials, 64
Arête, 150
Argentina, 50

Armadillo World Headquarters, 3
Årnedal, Börje, 72
Art, 16, 25, 50, 84, 110, 120–21, 141,
 145, 188, 207, 214
ASEAN, xii, 33, 39
Asia, 22, 37, 41, 81, 91, 92, 107, 164,
 238
Asia Development Bank, 33
Association of University Technology
 Managers, 227
Athens, 26, 46
Auctions, 172, 228
Austin, 3–4, 9–12, 15, 18–20, 22–5,
 34–8, 47–8, 50, 56–9, 61–2, 69–70,
 81–5, 88, 98, 102–04, 107, 114, 125,
 143–6, 151, 160, 164–5, 174, 181,
 185, 194, 203–04, 207, 210, 214,
 219–28, 241–7
Austin Chamber of Commerce, 64
Austin Multimedia Alliance, 20
Austin Software Council, 18–19, 21,
 24, 45, 84, 129, 204, 207
Austin Technology Council, 9, 20, 37,
 64, 128, 129, 135, 144, 165
Austin Technology Incubator, 25, 44,
 57, 84, 144, 145, 151, 181
Australia, 77, 78

Baby boomers, 198
Bachelor's degree education, 92
Baker, Mary Ann, 19
Balearic Islands, 138
Ballmer, Steve, 148
Bandwidth, 58, 151
Bangalore, 107–08, 130–31, 194–5,
 201, 209, 212–14
Bankruptcy, 3, 108
Barnett, Camille, 24, 70
Barrett, Craig, 200
Barnett, William, 46
Bayh-Dole Act, 157, 158
Baylor University, 46

Bechtel, 2, 12
Beijing Institute of Information and Control, 161
Belady, Laszlo, 18
Belgium, 41
Belize, 39, 233
Benda, Miroslav, 46
Berdahl, Robert, 158
Berkeley, 201
Bhimani, Al, 19
Biology, 201
Biomedical Engineering Institute (University of Minnesota), 111
Biotechnology, 46, 57, 71, 73, 96, 105, 136, 144
Bissex, Walter, 19, 129
Blackboard, 99
Bogotá, 81
Bonneville Power Administration, 108
Boreing, Bill, 21
Boston, 19, 62, 113, 126, 191
Boston Computer Society, 19
Botkin, Jim, 161
Bragdon, Peter, 82
Brazil, xvi, 8, 10, 19, 80, 138, 149, 227, 231
Brooklyn Bridge, 16
Broussard, Bill, 121
Browne, Jim, 18
Browne, Lynn, 113
Brubaker, John, 21
Building permits, 212, 237
Bureau of the Census, 188
Burke, James E., 169
Burtzel, Cheryl McManus, 21
Business & Tech. Devel. Strategies Inc., 46
Business Education, v, 46
Business schools, 10, 50–52, 56, 59, 95
Business Week, 89, 129, 208
Butler, John, 46
Butterfly effect, 112, 210–11
Byrnes, Mike, 21

Cairo, Egypt, 39
Caldera, 202
California State University at Northridge, 46
Cambridge University, 161

Cambridge, England, 212
Campanella, T., 61
Campinas, Brazil, 138
Canada, 30, 33, 69, 72–3, 79, 82, 208
Carbonara, Corey, 46
Carey, Drew, 89
Caribbean Basin, 39
Carnegie-Mellon University, 129
Cascade Microtech, 115
Cases, living, 116
Cenquest, Inc., 99
Changsha, 39
Chaotic systems, 211
Charlotte, North Carolina, 187
Chechnya, 203
Cheshire Partnership, 32
Chicago, 142, 189, 191
Chihuahua, Mexico, 50
China, 8, 10, 30, 39, 61, 71, 92, 106, 210, 214, 219
Chu, Xuelin, 46
Clement, Marv, 163
Cleveland, 89
Clinton, President Bill, 129, 153
Cloutier, Madison, 19
Clusters, cluster theory, 2, 130–33, 150, 232, 243
Coahuila, Mexico, 50
Coffee, Joseph, 21
Cold War, 113
Coleman, James, 5
Collaboration technologies, 15, 56, 182, 225
CollegeNet, 137
Collocation, 5, 8, 126, 133, 211, 232
Colorado Springs, 187
Columbia Sportswear, 137
Commercialization of new technologies, 129, 212
Common good, 118–19, 157–8
Communication, xx, 7, 22, 27, 36, 42, 47, 78, 93, 101, 114, 135–6, 147, 172, 175, 198–9, 215, 227
Competitive intelligence, 222, 226, 228
Competitiveness, 38, 46, 105, 111, 150, 234
Complexity, 53, 59, 156, 158

Computational economics, 9, 15, 16, 17
Computer, 16–17, 57, 71, 73, 80, 83, 99, 103, 108, 127, 140, 157, 198, 199, 203, 213, 226
Computer Science Corporation, 204
Conferences, role of, 15, 19, 36, 40, 100–01, 138
Consensus-building, 150
Construction, 46, 64, 85, 101, 106–07, 222, 226
Continuing education, 25, 61, 222
Cooke, Lee, 21
Coopers & Lybrand, 167
Corporate headquarters, location of, 110, 136, 218
Cortright, Joseph, 105
Costa Rica, 39
Council on Competitiveness, 105, 111, 116, 150
Creativity, 4, 22, 49, 61, 63, 110, 138, 145, 206, 210
Crisis, role of in boosting technopolis efforts, 128
Critical mass, 1, 7, 25, 42, 74, 88, 125, 130, 135, 145, 191, 210–11, 215, 229, 232
Cross Border Institute for Regional Development, xii, 37
Crossing the Chasm, 198
Cross-sectoral cooperation, 133, 232
Cuba, 39, 50
Cuban, 50, 78
Culbertson, Robert, 21
Cultural survival technologies, 9, 137
Curitiba, Brazil, xvi, 149, 227
Customer relationship management (CRM), 171, 226, 228
Czech Republic, 54

Daeduk, South Korea, 231
Dale, Al, 21
Dallas, Texas, 36
Data, 5, 15, 16, 29, 41, 43–6, 52, 75, 82, 97, 103–04, 164, 172, 178, 185, 195, 205, 221, 224, 227–8, 242–4
Data Envelopment Analysis, 16
Data mining, 226
David, Paul, 198

Dell Corporation, 128
Dell, Michael, 56, 129, 148
Deloitte & Touche, 156
Democracy, 26, 78
Demographics, 198, 222
Denman, Chuck, 21
Denmark, 81, 192, 208, 241
Denney, Richard, 19
Department of Defense (USA), xii, 176
Development economics, 41
Dhaka, Bangladesh, 39
Diamonds, 5
Digital divide, 81
Digital government, 226–7
Display industry, 103
Distance learning, 92–4, 97–101, 178
Djakarta, Indonesia, 39
DNA, 157
Doell, Glenn, 167, 169
Donoho, Andrew, 21
Dotcom business models, 142, 170, 175, 184
Dresser Industries, 19, 21
Drucker, Peter, 4, 154
Duke University, 46

Economic colonization, 10
Economic Development, xii, xvii, 6–7, 10–12, 15, 23, 37, 46, 50, 52, 58, 60, 61–2, 69–72, 79, 85, 87, 105, 114–16, 129, 137–8, 144–9, 158–9, 167–8, 173, 177, 180–81, 186–9, 190–97, 200, 207, 212, 218–33
Economic development agencies, 60
Economist, The, magazine, 194, 195
Edge cities, 9
Edinburgh Commonwealth Economic Declaration, 31
Education, 2, 3, 7, 23–5, 29–46, 49–60, 61, 64, 66, 69, 72, 77, 79, 80–82, 84, 87, 90, 92–104, 105–11, 117, 118–19, 122, 124, 125–150, 153, 157, 159, 163–81, 193, 194, 197, 208–10, 217, 220–46, 258, 260
Eickmann, Kenneth, 46
Electronic commerce, 20
El Salvador, 89
El-Badry, Samia, 19, 21

Electric power, 198
Electro Scientific Industries, 114, 115
Energy, 35, 49, 51, 58, 82, 89, 91, 108, 127, 221, 242
Engelking, Susan, 129
Engineers and engineering, 58–9, 79, 115, 131
Enron Corporation, 149
Enterprise Europe, 53
Enterprise resource planning (ERP), 187
Entrepreneurship and intrapreneurship, 230
Enterprise Zones, 153, 243
Environment, business and entrepreneurial, 23, 25, 27, 38, 53, 76, 151, 153, 164, 181, 221, 235, 236, 239
Environment, institutional, 74, 94,
Environment, natural, 33, 51, 62, 69, 85, 136,
Environment, social, 82,
Epson Corporation, 106
Equilibrium, 191, 193
Erdös, Paul, 148
Ernst & Young, 24
eRoom, 227
Ethics, 52, 179
Ethiopia, 41
Ethnicity, 56
Eurasia Foundation, 37
European Union, xii
Evangelism, 211
Evolutionary Economics, 46
Expert Application Systems, Inc., 21
Export Zones, 243
Exports, 6, 7, 77, 78, 155, 164, 218, 219, 220, 238

Federal Reserve Bank, 113
Fields, Craig, 76
Fields, W.C., 196
Figel, Ján, 33
Finland, 10, 192–3, 206, 208
Flamm, Kenneth, 46
Florence, Italy, 46, 74, 188, 212
Florida, 31
Ford, Henry, 113, 197

Foreign direct investment, 77, 138, 155, 238–42
Former Soviet Union, 203
Fortune magazine, 199
Free trade, 30, 34–5, 70
Free-trade agreements, 11, 34, 152, 153
Freedom of Information Act, (FOI), 168
Fuel Cell Research Center, British Columbia, Canada, 73
Fukuyama, Francis, 53
Funding and funding agencies, 11, 35, 41–5, 53, 57–8, 73, 78, 99, 132, 135, 138, 140–43, 147, 161, 165, 168, 173–4, 179, 181, 223–4, 231–3
Fund-raising, 36, 57, 91, 97
Furino, Antonio, 46
Fuzzy objectives, 44–7, 135, 147, 212, 242

Games, 215
Gardner, Bruce, 21
Gates, Bill, 148
Gelfand, Norman, 21
General Agreement on Tariffs and Trade (GATT), 152
Genomics, 221
Gentrification, 31
Germany, 41, 131, 208, 219
Gerstner, Lou, 101
Gibson, David, 61, 62, 129, 203–04
Glasco, Darrell, 21
Global positioning system, 58
Globalization, 11, 32, 42, 50–53, 58, 76, 79, 89, 143, 154, 189, 195, 201, 208–14, 228, 231, 236
Globally networked civic entrepreneurship, 76
Godfathers and godmothers, 4, 134, 147, 149
Goldgar, Rick, 18, 19
Goldschmidt, Neil, 138
Gomes, Stephen, 12, 46
Government, 5, 12, 23, 28–9, 33–5, 42, 47, 51–2, 62–5, 70–73, 78, 107, 116–19, 126, 130, 133, 136–7, 139, 144, 146, 149–50, 153, 156, 191–2, 206–07, 213, 222, 227, 233, 239, 241, 243

Government, digital, 226–7
Greater Austin Chamber of
  Commerce, 64
Greenfield investment, 238, 240
Groupware, 16, 227
Grove, Andrew, 172, 182
Gutenberg, Johann, 27

Haikou, China, 39
Hainan, China, 39
Hamilton, Gary, 19
Harvard Business School, 2
Harvey Mudd College, 110
Havel, Vaclav, 54, 55
Health care, 31, 38, 46, 58–9, 186,
  193, 222, 226
Health Care Policy, 46
Hecker, Seigfried, 46, 203
Helsinki, 89
Hewlett-Packard Corporation, xiii
Hibernia Bank, 21
Hicks, Miller, 21
High-speed photography, 178, 182
Hill Country CASE Users Group, 19
Hiramatsu, Morihiko, 148, 228
Hjalmstad, Sweden, 72
Ho Chi Minh City, 39
Hoffman, William, 111–12
Hospitals, 107, 113, 222, 226–7
Houston, 223
Hsinchu Science Based Industrial
  Park, 71
Human capital, 5, 34, 134, 160, 221
Hurd, Jim, 100
Hurley, Laurence, 46
Hyundai Corporation, 84

IBM, 21, 101, 129, 131
IC^2 Institute, 2, 4, 15–16, 18–19, 23–4,
  29, 30, 36–9, 45, 62, 80, 91, 129,
  146, 149, 197–8, 203, 230, 233
IEEE, 15
Il'kaev, Rady, 204
India, 10, 32, 40, 80, 107–08, 131,
  194, 201, 210, 212, 214, 216
Industrial Development Agency
  (Ireland), 241
InFocus Systems, 115
Information technology, 19, 24, 73,
  101, 134, 169, 198, 227

Infosys Technologies Ltd., 131
Infrastructure, 2, 4, 5, 7–8, 27, 29,
  32–4, 62, 75, 81, 89, 107, 115, 126,
  130, 133–4, 140, 143, 147, 152, 161,
  165, 182, 184, 191, 194, 206,
  211–12, 218, 220–26, 240–43
Inglewood, California, 196
Innovation, 7, 9, 16, 22–3, 28, 30, 36,
  41, 43, 58, 61, 63, 70, 75, 79–80, 85,
  98, 106–07, 111–16, 138–40, 144–5,
  148, 152–6, 167, 170, 189, 197,
  206–07, 212, 218–19, 229, 232,
  237, 243, 245
Innovation arrow, xi, 7, 58, 170
Innovation diffusion, 46, 148, 197
Institutions, 10, 30, 34, 35, 40, 81,
  106, 109, 133, 144, 169, 194,
  206–07, 213, 234, 236, 238, 241
Instituto Technológico de Estudios
  Superiores, 38
Integrated Measurement Systems,
  Inc., 115
Intel Corporation, 73, 84, 87,
  108, 115–16, 137–8, 182, 188, 200,
  204, 210
Intellectual capital, 159, 199, 234
Intellectual property, 4, 7, 56, 59–60,
  70, 94, 157, 159, 161, 166, 188, 170,
  172, 179, 183, 240
Internal Revenue Service, 202
International Association of Science
  Parks, 2
International Monetary Fund,
  xiii, 33
International Standards Organization
  (ISO), 30
Internet, 9, 47, 62–3, 70, 80–82, 99,
  102, 127, 138, 140, 142, 161, 163–4,
  166, 170–3, 178, 182–4, 187, 204,
  206, 209, 226
Internships, 40, 97, 110, 116,
  174, 230
Inter-sectoral cooperation,
  2, 228
Investment promotion agencies, 229,
  238–40
Investment, Trade and Tourism of
  Portugal, 241
Israel, 150, 203
Italy, 2, 41

Jakarta, 39
Jamaica, 39
Japan, 1, 8, 61, 72, 87, 106, 144, 149, 220, 234, 244
Jeddah, Saudi Arabia, 39
Jobs, 6, 7, 10, 25, 34–8, 50, 64, 72–3, 92, 102, 106, 111, 128, 136, 150, 153, 156, 159–60, 164, 183, 188–9, 194, 196–7, 200, 207, 213–20, 239, 243
Johannesburg, 6
Johnson, President Lyndon, 23, 38
Johnson, Stephen, 122
Joint ventures, 235, 238, 240

Kaderlin, Norman, 80
Kaiser Aluminum, 108
Kaminsky, Stuart, 78
Kansas Technology Enterprise Corporation, 185
Keiretsu, 171
Kelly, Kevin, 200
Kilcrease, Laura, 165, 173
Knight, Phil, 98, 113
Knowledge economy, 80, 188, 200–01, 207, 215
Knowledge Express, 171
Knowledge spillovers, 239, 243
Knowledge, knowledge creation, knowledge management, knowledge transfer, 2, 43, 74, 199, 215, 264
Kodama, Fumio, 10, 75
Köhler, Horst, 33
Korea, South, 106, 206
Kozmetsky, George, 18–19, 21, 23, 28, 30, 47, 62, 64, 85, 129, 130, 148, 204
KPMG, 204
Krasner, Herb, 21
Krugman, Paul, 113
Krumme, Reiner, 21
Kuala Lumpur, 39
Kuipers, Anton, 72–3
Kyonggi University, 46

Lalalka, Rustam, 46
Lally School of Management, RPI, 176
Land use, 159, 222

Land, Ken, 46
Lang, Fritz, 200
Laredo, 200
Laritz, Charles, 21
Latin America, 41, 50, 80, 238
Lattice Semiconductor Corporation, 115
Laughlin Wilt Company, 115
Law enforcement, 222
Lawson, Harold, 114–15
Learned helplessness, 26
Leatherman Company, 137
Lee, Marshall, 114
Lerner, Jaime, 148, 228
Levine, Ketzel, 85
Lewis, Margaret, 21, 177
Lima, Peru, 39
Linstone, Harold, 43–4, 132
Localization economies, 2, 133
Location incentives, 136
Lock-in, 77, 90, 210–11, 217, 232
Logistics, 59, 151, 245
London School of Economics, 208
Los Alamos National Laboratory, 46, 203
Los Angeles, 191
Louisiana, 2
Low-orbit economic zone, 58
Lundvall, Bengt-Åke, 81
Luxembourg, 41
Lyndon B. Johnson School of Public Affairs, 38

Maastricht, 39, 40–41, 81
Maastricht School of Management, 4, 29, 35, 39–41, 53, 91, 98
Mack, Patricia, 21
Maghreb, 32, 41
Magni Systems Inc., 115
MAKO Computer Corp., 21
Malaysia, 87, 106, 155–6
Malta, 39, 40, 41
Management of technology, 91–2
Manhattan Project, 58
Manufacturing, 1, 3–4, 15, 38, 62, 77–8, 97, 106–07, 115–16, 127, 129, 137–8, 179, 197, 210, 215, 219, 242
Maples, Mike, 20
Market distortions, 154, 156, 191, 200

Market research, 188, 288
Marketing, 1, 8, 16, 20, 25, 37, 49, 52,
  56, 65, 73, 89, 94–7, 101–02, 116,
  126, 134, 166–7, 172, 184, 190–92,
  197, 200, 212, 221–2, 226, 232, 241,
  244
Marshall, Ray, 29
Martin, Paul, 33
Mason Enterprise Center, 140, 212
Massey, Brian, 19, 21
Master's degree education, 92, 95, 96,
  97, 98, 99, 101, 102, 160
Matamoros, Mexico, 220
Materials requirements planning
  (MRP), 171
Mathematical models, 226
Matthews, Kay, 21
Maui, 176–8, 182, 184, 189
Maui Economic Development Board
  (MEDB), 177–8
Maui High Performance Computing
  Center, 176
Mazziotti, Don, 87, 89
MBA, 39, 41, 52, 56, 92, 95–8, 102–04,
  141, 165, 167, 174
MBBNet, 111
McBee, Frank, 129
McCall, Joe, 19, 21
McCombs School of Business, 49–50
McInerney, Charles, 23
McLuhan, Marshall, 53, 55
Medell'n, 81
Mentor Graphics Inc., 115
Mentors and mentorship, 60, 125,
  141, 181, 189, 209
Mercosur, 152
Mergers and acquisitions, 235, 239
Metzner, Wolf, 18–19
Mexico, 19, 33, 37, 50, 85
Meyers, Christopher J., 185
Microelectronics and Computer
  Consortium (later called
  Microelectronics and Computer
  Corporation), 3, 20, 129
Micro-Gaia, 176
Micro-loan programs, 55
Microsoft, 20, 148
Middle East, 41, 50, 80, 219
Milagro Beanfield War, 219

Milan, 196
Milken Institute, 167, 220
Miller, Bob, 179
Ministry of International Trade and
  Industry (Japan), 2
Mitroff, Ian, 43–4, 132
Mitsubishi Electric Laboratories, 20
Mobile services, 9
Mobile telephony, 9
Mohammed VI of Morocco, 32
Montana, 11, 84–5
Monterrey, Mexico, 8, 36
Moore, Michael, 153
Morocco, 32
Moscow Power Engineering Institute,
  46
Motor Industries Co., 131
Motorola, 129, 204, 214
Multilateral Agreement on
  Investments, xiii, 77, 153
Multinational Investment Guarantee
  Agency, 240
Murdock, Jack, 114
Murthy, N.R. Narayana, 131
Music, 3, 23, 27, 50, 84, 107, 120, 144,
  148, 203, 209, 215, 231
Mutual funds, 198
Myanmar, 154

NAFTA, North American Free Trade
  Agreement, 33–4, 77, 152
Naidu, Chandra Babu, 148
National Association of State Venture
  Funds, 22
National Business Incubation
  Association, 174, 183, 227
National Center for Education, 104
National Institute of Standards and
  Technology, 78
National Instruments, 21
National Public Radio, 85
National Science Foundation, 15, 102,
  227
National systems of innovation,
  xiv, 229
Nehru, Jawaharlal, 131
Nelson, Tom, 21
Nelson, Willie, 3, 148
Nemoto, Calvin, 178

Neoclassical economics, 233
Netherlands, the, 3, 39, 81, 196
NETSERV, 21
Networking, 1, 7–8, 15, 19, 22, 24–5, 29, 31–4, 38–42, 45, 47, 56, 72, 76, 79, 81, 98, 103, 111, 125, 133, 136, 148, 165, 171, 174, 181, 194, 198, 202, 206, 213, 215, 222, 227, 230–33, 242–5
New business incubation, 41, 82, 158, 183, 195, 196, 226
New Delhi, 39
New Mexico, 36, 46, 50, 85, 129, 176, 198, 219, 230
New venture competitions, 88, 166, 183
New York, 6, 31, 129, 173, 189, 191, 196
New York Academy of Science, 129
Newsweek magazine, 110
NGOs, non-governmental organizations, 24, 28, 30, 38, 41, 60, 185
Nike, 113–14, 137
Niwa, Kiyoshi, 46
Nizhny Novgorod, 203–04
North Carolina, 2, 69, 144, 232
Northwest College of Art, 110
Norway, 192, 208
Novell, Inc., 21
Nuevo León, 38, 50
Nutraceuticals, 182, 189

Off-shoring, 188, 202
Open Computing Center (Russia), 203
Open records acts, 168, 178, 224
Open-source software, 137, 202
Oregon, 4, 9, 11, 19–20, 69, 73, 79–82, 84–9, 106–19, 137–8, 164, 184, 188, 193, 200, 202, 208, 212, 219
Oregon Business Plan, 137, 208
Oregon Council on Knowledge & Economic Development, 137, 200
Oregon Entrepreneurial Business Initiative (OMBI), 79
Oregon Food Bank, 108, 109
Oregon Graduate Institute of Science and Technology, 4
Oregon Health & Science University, 116, 138, 224
Oregon Innovation Council, 137
Oregon Institute of Technology, 110

Oregon Public Broadcasting, 84
Oregon RAINS, 225
Organization for Economic Cooperation and Development (OECD), 34, 81, 192, 233–7
Organization of American States (OAS), 30
Ormerod, Paul, 111

Pacific Northwest National Laboratory, 72, 230
Pacific Rim, 78, 85
Paige, Satchel, 80
Pakistan, 32
Palma de Mallorca, 131, 138
Panama, 39
Paraná state, Brazil, 80
ParcBIT, 138–40
Paris, 16, 196
Patents, 59, 73, 84, 115, 136, 160, 167, 170, 176, 221, 227, 237
Patrick, Jamin, 20
PCs, 9
Pearl District (Portland), 120
Peat Marwick, 142
Pencom Software, 21
Persistence, 125
Ph.D. and doctoral education, 23, 26, 56, 58, 160
Philadelphia, 31, 189
Philanthropy, 93, 99, 176, 189
Philippines, 106
Phillips, David, 21
Place, sense of, 118
Planar, Inc., 100
Poecek, Ken, 204
Political economy, 29, 43, 47, 51, 159, 232, 245
Political science and international affairs, 46
Politics, 25, 118, 148, 201
Polo de Software, 19
Polymerase chain reaction, xiv, 157
Pontificia Universidade do Paraná, 19
Pony Express, 209
Porter, Michael, 2, 111, 152, 205, 229, 232
Portland, xiv–xxi, 4, 10–11, 69–91, 96–9, 106–10, 114, 120–21, 131,

Portland – *continued*
136–8, 148–9, 165, 173,
188–93, 209, 212, 218–19,
223–5, 241–2
Portland Business Journal, xv, 11, 87,
191
Portland Development Commission,
14, 87, 148–9, 223
Portland Education Cluster, 242
Portland State University, xiv–xv, xx,
82, 84, 91, 110, 188, 224
Positive feedback, 112, 148, 215
Post-conflict planning studies, 55
Powers, Pike, 150
Premji, Azim, 131
Price Waterhouse, 21, 24
Procter & Gamble, 94
Productivity, 6, 7, 57, 111, 116,
155, 167, 193, 198, 206, 218–20,
237–40
Progressive governance, 33
Protocol Systems, 115
Prudential Securities, 21
Pruesh, Al, 165
Public Broadcasting Service, 84
Public relations, 56, 65, 145, 147, 150,
165, 181, 212–13, 241
Public-private partnerships, 107, 133,
153, 191, 195, 206, 243
Pueblo Revolt, 246

Quality foreign direct investment, 239
Quality of life, xv, 3, 7, 23–5, 28, 30,
38, 43–4, 50, 58, 62–3, 71, 74, 82–3,
89, 92, 100, 107–08, 125–6, 144,
150, 157, 160, 162, 166, 173, 178,
186, 189, 191, 200–07, 212, 216,
220, 228–9, 236

Radio, 14, 85, 114–15, 136
RadiSys, 115
Ramaley, Judith, 84
Ramsay, William, 131
Rankin, Lon, Jr., 21
Rapid prototyping, 157
Read, Richard, 82
Real estate, 2, 23, 27, 85, 109, 130,
149, 169, 173, 176, 180, 182–4, 195,
199, 202

Recruitment, 64, 65, 72, 147, 190,
218, 221–4, 241
Red Hat, 202
Reed College, 110
Regional character, 210 *see also* Place,
sense of
Regional Economic Development
Partnership, 89
Regional Initiatives for Technology
Entrepreneurship, xiv, xvi, 128, 230
Regional systems of innovation, 229
Rehn, Olli, 33
Renewal, continual, 207, 214
Rensselaer Polytechnic Institute, xiv,
173, 175–6
Rents, 109, 121, 174, 213
Research and development, 61, 107,
116, 121, 161, 204, 207, 213, 235
Robert Bosch Gmbh, 131
Rocky Mountain Institute, 198
Rogalyev, Nikolay, 46
Rogers, Everett, 46, 129, 148, 197, 217
Ronay, Jim, 19–20, 150
Rostow, Walt and Elspeth, 129
Russia, 8, 12, 46, 203–04

Salisbury, Alan, 21
Salon.com, 112
Salt Lake City, 192
Samsung, 84
San Diego, 22, 30, 32
San Francisco, 2, 85, 107, 196, 201
San Jose, 32, 207
San Jose Tech Museum Awards, 202
San Marcos, Texas, 19
Sangrey, Dwight, 165, 173
Santa Monica, California, 209
São Paulo, 80, 89
Sarov, Russia, 203, 204
Sass, Steven, 113
Scandinavia, 9, 192
Schlumberger, 19, 129
Schutawie, Jay, 21
Schwenk, Mike, 72
Science fairs, 226, 227
Scientific & Engineering Software,
Inc., 18, 21
Select University Technologies,
185

Self-determination, political and economic, 10, 79, 159
Self-investment, 8, 126, 138, 194, 211, 221–2
SEMATECH, 129
Semiconductor industry, 64, 106
Sequent Computer Systems, 115
Shanghai, 8, 39, 89
Shared prosperity, 10, 28–39, 41–7, 208–09, 229, 232–3, 243–5
Shaw, Ralph, 11, 87
Sheffield, England, 113
Shekou, China, 39
Siberlink, 204
Sickinger, Ted, 87
Silicon Forest, 73, 74, 188
Silicon Valley, 3, 9, 25, 30–2, 62–3, 77, 106, 125–30, 136, 143, 153, 176, 191, 195, 198, 200–01, 205, 213, 232
Singapore, 39, 106, 213–14, 240
Singapore Economic Development Board, 240–41
Singh, K.N., 32
Sizemore, Bill, 219
Skunk works, 57, 139
Small and medium-sized enterprises (SMEs), 33, 73, 123, 230
Small Business Development Centers, 141, 177
Soccer, 189
Social capital, 5, 6, 8, 22, 29, 31, 53, 126, 133, 137, 147, 150, 194, 211, 221–2, 225–6, 234
Social entrepreneurship, 38, 55
Social mobility, 46, 264
Sociology, 5, 46, 58
Software, 6, 15, 18–19, 22–3, 26, 35, 45, 73, 84, 96, 99, 102, 108, 112, 127, 129, 131, 136–7, 143, 172, 202–04, 207, 210, 213, 224, 226–7
Software Association of Oregon, xiv, 19, 82, 84
Software Quality Institute, 20, 24
Sonoma State University, 178
Sophia Antipolis, 2
Southeast Asia, 41, 80
Spin-off companies, 166, 227
St. Edward's University, 65

St. Petersburg, Russia, 204
Standard Industrial Classifications, 46
Standards, 30, 31, 33, 78, 95, 119, 153, 188, 205
Stanford University, xx, 130
State legislatures, 135, 160, 168, 201
State of Washington, 179, 193
Stein, Gertrude, 16
Stett, Bill, 176
Stevenson, Howard, 2
Stough, Roger, 140
Strategically chosen industries, 11
Strover, Sharon, 21
Stuart, Kellye, 21
Success factors, 2, 9–11, 22, 24–5, 42, 100, 126, 128, 134, 141, 144, 146–7, 150, 164, 211, 213
Sugimura, Tak, 177
Sullivan, Theresa, 21
Sullivan-Whitney, Jennifer, 21
Sun Microsystems, 204
Sung, Tae Kyung, 46
Supply Chain Management, 46
Sustainable development, 54, 57, 69
Suzuki, D.T., 194
Sweden, 69, 72, 79, 81–2, 192–3, 208, 218
Switzerland, 193, 220
Systems science, 46, 237
Szygenda, Stephen, 129

Taiwan, xiv, 8, 69, 71–2, 79, 82, 106–07, 148, 214
Tamaulipas, Mexico, 38, 50
Taniguchi, Cassio, 80
Tatsuno, Sheridan, 1
Tax rate, 2, 3, 207, 219
Taxes, 24, 88, 149, 155, 193, 219, 223, 225
Tax-increment financing, 223
Taylor, Becky, 21
Taylor, Ed, 18–19, 21
Technaissance, 9, 12, 212
Technical University of Delft, 39
Technological convergence, 201
Technological Forecasting & Social Change, xvi, 202
Technology Advisors Group, 24, 129, 144

Technology fusion, 10, 75–6, 153, 201
Technology licensing, 160
Technology policy, xvi, xx, 46, 80, 236
Technology Resource Alliance, 140–41
Technology transfer, xx, xxii, 7, 29, 33, 37, 42, 76, 116, 150, 157–9, 164, 171, 173, 175, 179, 235, 237
Technology-follower regions, 98, 243
Technopolis, 1–11, 22–4, 39, 49, 61–3, 77, 80–85, 125, 128, 135–8, 145–6, 151,153–4, 198, 200, 206, 209, 211, 213, 225, 227, 231, 243, 244
Technopolis Times, 190, 194, 196, 200, 202
Tektronix, 73, 79, 114–16, 138
Tel Aviv, 6
Telecommunications, 15, 46, 105, 143, 184, 207, 222, 226
Teledyne Corp., 30, 129
Telemedicine, 226–7
Telework, 139–40
Terrorism, 51, 59
Texas, 3, 15
Texas Attorney General, 21, 25, 36–8, 50, 69, 84, 85
Texas Department of Mental Health & Mental Retardation, 21
Texas Department of Health, 21
Texas Information Technology Association, 19
Texas Instruments, 108, 129
The Capital Network (formerly Texas Capital Network), 24, 37, 72, 129
Tipping point, 3, 148, 211
Todd, Bruce, 19
Toffler, Alvin, 30
Tokyo, 46, 196
Tong, Alvin, 71, 148
Toprac, Paul, 19–21
Torvalds, Linus, 202
Tourism, 39, 50, 88–9, 133, 138–9, 144–5, 221–2, 22–7, 232, 241
Tracor Inc., 129
Traded-sector, 196
Transparency, 34, 147, 149, 223–5
Trinidad-Tobago, 39
Triplett, Jan, 21
Tripwire Corp., 88
TriQuint Semiconductor, 115

Truchard, Jim, 21
Tsukuba, 1, 144, 149, 231
Tuninga, Ronald, 53
TUV Rheinland of North America, 21

US Trade Representative, 210
US-Japan Translations, 21
Ulaanbaatar, 39
UNCTAD, xiv, 30, 239–41
United Kingdom, 208
United Nations, 54, 107
United States Forest Service, 114
United States of America, 9, 33, 47, 59, 138, 192, 215–16, 220, 237
Universities, 9, 41, 51–2, 56, 60–61, 64, 70–73, 79, 85, 93, 96–7, 113, 116, 126, 138, 144, 157, 159, 161–91, 206–07, 213, 233–5, 244
Universities, mission of, 179
University of Arizona, 46
University of British Columbia, 184
University of Hawaii, 176–7
University of Massachusetts at Amherst, 110
University of Minnesota, 84, 111
University of New Mexico, xiv, 46, 176, 198, 230
University of Oregon, 113, 230
University of Science & Technology, Hefei, 46
University of Southern California, 197, 227
University of Texas at Austin, xiii, xx–xxi, 15, 28, 30, 36, 38, 47, 130, 158, 230, 233
University of Texas at Brownsville, 38
University of Tokyo, 46
University of Washington, xv–xvi, 179
Urban renewal districts, 223
Urban sprawl, 71
Urbanization economies, 2
US News & World Report, 129
UVentures.com, 170

Vancouver, Canada, 72
Venture capital, 3, 7, 11, 24, 27, 32, 60–61, 72, 80, 83, 88, 90, 106, 128, 144, 150, 165–6, 170, 181, 184, 186, 189, 200–01, 205, 217, 231, 247

Videoconferencing, 103, 140, 172, 178, 227
Virginia, 140, 142, 185
Vision and visionaries, 22, 24, 32–3, 37, 42, 55, 61–2, 119, 145, 147–8, 211, 224, 243
Voice-operated web browsing, 157
Vollum, Howard, 114–15

Wacholder, Mike, 175
Waco, Texas, 19
Wahrhaftig, Ramiro, 19
Wakelin, Mike, 2, 39
Walker, Jerry Jeff, 3
Wall Street Journal, 111
Wal-Mart, 212–13, 196–7
Walters, Ken, 179
Ware, Keren, 21
Washington State University, 72, 83, 230
Washington University, 46, 70
Washington, D.C., 69, 132, 140, 142, 158
Water, 42, 85, 95, 137, 139, 145, 178, 213, 221, 226
Waterloo Records, 27
Watson, Kirk, 80, 228
WebCT courseware, 99
Weber, Max, 27
Wendt, Richard and Nancy, 110
Wessel, Craig, 87, 89
West, Glenn, 19
West, Mae, 196
Weyerhaeuser Corporation, 110
Wichita Technology Corporation, 185
Wilbanks, Martin, 21
Will, George F., 26

Willamette Industries, 110
Willis, William T., 21
Windhoek, Namibia, 39
Winstead, Peter, 21
Winstead, Sechrest & Minick, 21
Winter, Johnny, 3
Wipro Ltd., 131
Wolfensohn, James, 30
Wood, John, 204
Woolf, Ashby M., 21
Workforce, 2–3, 5, 7, 29, 52, 63, 69–70, 87, 89, 147, 150, 178, 180, 189, 192, 210, 212, 215, 222
Working Partnerships USA, 32
World Bank, 30, 33, 37, 241
World Health Organization, 59
World Intellectual Property Organization, 240
World Summit of Young Entrepreneurs, 24
World Technopolis Association, xiv, 152, 227, 231
World Trade Organization, 11, 90, 152, 168
World Wide Web, 173, 198

Y2K problem, 130
Yamaguchi University, 161
Yeh, Raymond, 18
Yemen, 41
Yucatan, Mexico, 39
Yudof, Mark, 84

Zandan, Peter, 18
Zappa, Frank, 120
Zolan, Craig, 170
Zoning, 11, 88, 221–2

Printed in Great Britain
by Amazon

51548145R00172